D1233726

A SINGULAR EDUCATION

A German Bachelor in New York (1964-1974)

by

GUNTER NITSCH

authorHOUSE®

AuthorHouse™ LLC
1663 Liberty Drive
Bloomington, IN 47403
www.authorhouse.com
Phone: 1-800-839-8640

This book is a work of non-fiction. Unless otherwise noted, the author
and the publisher make no explicit guarantees as to the accuracy of
the information contained in this book and, in some cases, names of
people and places have been altered to protect their privacy.

© 2013 Gunter Nitsch. All rights reserved.

No part of this book may be reproduced, stored in a retrieval system, or
transmitted by any means without the written permission of the author.

Published by AuthorHouse 11/20/2013

ISBN: 978-1-4918-3700-9 (sc)
ISBN: 978-1-4918-3699-6 (hc)
ISBN: 978-1-4918-3698-9 (e)

Library of Congress Control Number: 2013921162

Any people depicted in stock imagery provided by Thinkstock are models,
and such images are being used for illustrative purposes only.
Certain stock imagery © Thinkstock.

This book is printed on acid-free paper.

Because of the dynamic nature of the Internet, any web addresses or links contained in
this book may have changed since publication and may no longer be valid. The views
expressed in this work are solely those of the author and do not necessarily reflect the
views of the publisher, and the publisher hereby disclaims any responsibility for them.

Also by Gunter Nitsch:

Weeds Like Us

STRETCH: Coming of Age in Post-War Germany

Eine lange Flucht aus Ostpreussen

DEDICATION

For Mary

ACKNOWLEDGMENTS

With appreciation to everyone who gave my manuscript a critical reading: David A. Aarthun, Mackensey Carter, Annie Desbois, Lane Gutstein, Loring W. Knoblauch, Bonnie Mitchell, James A. A. Pabarue, Simon Silver, Donald J. Townsend, Michael Traynor, and David Vickrey

My special thanks to my wife, Mary, for the editing and re-editing of my many drafts and to our son, Frederick, for his invaluable contributions.

CHAPTER 1

"**S**o what about you, Günter? What brings you to America?"

It was April 1964 and the five other diners with whom I shared a table on the S.S. *France* looked up at me expectantly. I had just heard each of their stories: Walter Licht, a German master jeweler seeking employment; a Dutchman on a business trip; a young banker from Switzerland being transferred to a branch in New York; and a middle-aged French couple on vacation. Now it was my turn.

I could have told them how I had dreamed of coming to the United States ever since I had read *Billy Jenkins* dime novels about the Wild West when I was in my early teens. Or how impressed I had been with the many CARE parcels my mother and I received from a farm family in Pennsylvania while we were living in a refugee camp in West Germany. *How, I had wondered, could farmers afford such generosity?* And then there were all those Hollywood films in which well-dressed middle-class folks drove around in sleek cars roomy enough to seat six. I could also have told them how, after the Berlin Wall went up in 1961, leaving more than half of my relatives trapped in the Soviet Zone, my father had warned me to leave Europe at the first sign that Soviet tanks were rumbling westward across Europe.

Yes, I could have told them all that. But one thing was certain. I couldn't tell them the truth. Unlike them, I wasn't coming for economic reasons or as a tourist or out of fear of a Soviet onslaught. I had left behind a well-paying job in Germany and there was no job waiting for me in America. Other than my clothes, my only worldly possessions were a Green Card, a $99 Continental Trailways bus ticket good for ninety-nine days, $400 in cash, and the address of the Proctor family in California. I had met Bob Proctor when he was working in Germany for a year and his parents had graciously agreed to be my sponsors. If I were honest with myself, I had no prospects in America at all.

In fact, the real reason I was coming to the United States was that, at the age of twenty-six, I was about to put nearly seven thousand miles between me and a beautiful, but emotionally unstable, young woman named Charlotte who desperately wanted to marry me despite my insistence that I was not ready to settle down. When Charlotte had seen me off at the railroad station in Cologne, she had made me promise to return to Germany in a year or two. Since the whole situation did not make sense, even to me, how could I explain it to a group of perfect strangers?

Looking down at my plate to avoid meeting anyone's eyes, I cleared my throat. "I have friends in California," I finally replied.

****

Right after breakfast the next morning I set out to explore the ship. Barely two years since her February 1962 maiden voyage, the S.S. *France* had every conceivable luxury: a swimming pool with a removable glass roof, a huge ballroom, a movie theater, a reading room, and ample space to take walks on deck in the fresh salty air. But

2

my favorite place was the railing at the stern where I could stand for hours watching the waves churning on either side of the ship's wide wake as she sped towards another continent.

Walter Licht, the German master jeweler, came up beside me. From what I had already found out, Walter, who was also in his mid-twenties, had worked in Canada for almost two years and then in New York City for six months. After returning home to Germany for a brief visit, he was now ready to look for a permanent job in the States. Here was someone who could give me some practical advice.

"Mind if I ask you something?" Walter began as he leaned against the railing next to me. "And I hope I'm not prying, but I noticed how you squirmed when people were telling their stories last night. So, tell me, are you really going all the way to California just to visit some friends? Or is there something more to it?" I tried to think of a calm, collected way to respond, but he spoke first. "For instance, it wouldn't surprise me if one of those 'friends' in California happened to be a beautiful lady. What do you say to that?"

"No, it's nothing like that. The Proctor family is sponsoring me, that's all."

"So? Why didn't you just say so?"

"Everyone had such great plans and I had to say *something* last night," I admitted, carefully avoiding any mention of Charlotte. "I didn't want to tell them that I have nothing at all lined up."

"Why not? Lots of people go to the States hoping for a better life. That's what I'm doing. Besides, anyone who has had a practical apprenticeship like mine can do much better there. America desperately needs well-trained craftsmen." Walter paused for a moment and glanced over at me. "You *did* do an apprenticeship in Germany, right?"

"I did mine in the administration of a large chemical company as an *Industrie Kaufmann*. I don't even know how to translate that into English. Office clerk, maybe?"

Walter shook his head. "An office clerk, huh? That unfortunately is quite a different story. They're a dime a dozen in the States. I don't want to discourage you, but are you sure you've thought this whole project through?"

"I'm beginning to wonder the same thing"

"Well, I wish you luck. I really do. It takes guts to do what you're doing. By the way, I also meant to ask you, how long will you be staying in New York before you head out to the West Coast?"

"Just a couple of hours. We dock in the morning and my bus leaves that same evening."

"Great! That should give me some time to show you around the City before you go."

****

On April 29, 1964, after six nights at sea, the S.S. *France* arrived in New York and, along with hundreds of my fellow passengers, I was up at dawn to watch as we sailed past the copper-green Statue of Liberty in the harbor. Looming ahead of us and dwarfing any city I had ever seen before was the towering skyline of lower Manhattan.

Walter and I left the ship together and, as soon as we cleared customs, we took a taxi to the William Sloane House Y.M.C.A., a massive brick building with more than fourteen hundred rooms located at the corner of West 34th Street and Ninth Avenue. While I had a cup of coffee and waited with my luggage in the cafeteria, Walter booked himself a room for the next few weeks and brought his bags upstairs.

He planned to stay there only until he landed a job and could afford a better place.

The Y.M.C.A. was not far from the Port Authority Bus Terminal where I deposited my trunk and my suitcase with Continental Trailways. Then Walter and I set out for Broadway and Times Square. From there, by elbowing our way through the crowds of pedestrians on 42nd Street, we passed the New York Public Library, crossed Fifth Avenue, made a quick detour down a steep ramp into the cavernous great hall of Grand Central Station, and then continued east to explore the grounds of the United Nations Building.

After grabbing a bite to eat in a Horn & Hardart automat (where, to my astonishment, we retrieved our sandwiches by putting coins into a slot to open the doors to little glass compartments) we headed back out to the street. "So," Walter said, "what would you like to see next? We haven't got much time. The Empire State Building? Rockefeller Center?"

"Honestly? What I'd really like to see is Harlem."

"What on earth do you want to go all the way up there for?"

"Because I love jazz and I was hoping to see some famous places where Negroes perform. Maybe even get to hear some amateur musicians playing on a street corner. But, of course, if it's too far out of the way, then we could do something else."

"Well, I doubt you'll see anyone playing music out on 125th Street, but if that's what you want to do . . ." Clearly Walter did not share my enthusiasm, but he was a good sport and soon we were speeding along to 125th Street and St. Nicholas Avenue on the "A" train, which Duke Ellington's orchestra had made famous.

As soon as we emerged from the underground subway station to the street looking like tourists fresh off the boat in our dress pants, white shirts, and blazers, small groups of Negroes dressed in worn-out jeans, baggy suit jackets, and caps with turned up brims loitered on the sidewalk and eyed us with suspicion. Under the watchful gaze of the entire neighborhood we walked past dilapidated buildings and piles of litter, poking our heads into several stores as we went, all to the way over to First Avenue and back. We saw no street musicians along the way. We passed no lively jazz bars. Other than the angry muttering of some of the people who glared at us as we passed by, the only sounds we heard for nearly two hours were the nearby sirens of police patrol cars and fire engines. This was a far cry from the comfortable, middle-class Negro world I had seen depicted in copies of *Ebony* magazine at the *Amerika-Haus* library back in Cologne.

We had just walked back past the Apollo Theater, Blumstein's Department Store, and the Theresa Hotel and, half a block ahead of us, we could see the green railing of the entrance to the IND subway, when an elderly Negro man with a scruffy white beard and wild tufts of gray hair blocked my way. "Hey, Mister, ya got a dime?" he asked.

"Yes, sir," I replied, glancing down at my wristwatch. "It's forty-five minutes after three o'clock."

Instead of the polite "thank you" I had expected, the man raised his fist to my face and screamed, "Why don't you go fuck yourself, motherfucker!"

Walter reached over and put his hand on my shoulder. "C'mon, let's go!"

"But what did I do? What did I say?" I asked as I glanced back at the man who was still shaking his fist at me as we hurried towards the train.

"For heaven's sake, stop turning around and I'll tell you." Walter reached into his pocket and pulled out two coins. "The man asked you for a DIME, not the TIME. Here, look. This silver ten-cent coin is what

Americans call a dime. And this other one, for five-cents, is called a nickel."

"Maybe I should go back and apologize?"

"*Um Gottes willen, nein!*" Walter yelled as he quickly led me down the stairs to the station.

****

Half an hour before my bus was scheduled to leave, Walter and I had just finished a light supper in a restaurant on West 42nd Street, a block away from the Port Authority Bus Terminal. Although it was unlikely that we would ever see each other again, we exchanged our German home addresses, and I also gave Walter the address of the Proctor family in San Anselmo. Then we walked together to the Continental Trailways departure area where the silver bus with the red stripe that would be my home for the next eighty-four hours was waiting.

After thanking Walter, I climbed on board and found a window seat on the left side towards the back of the bus. Considering that I was about to spend the next three and a half days in that seat, I was certainly travelling light. My suitcase and my trunk were safely stowed away somewhere underneath the bus and, other than the documents and money that I was carrying in a flat leather pouch hidden underneath my shirt, the only other items I had on board were my toilet articles, a small German-English dictionary, a notebook, and a pen, all of which fit into a small briefcase that was stashed into the seat pocket in front of me.

Soon after the bus pulled out of the Port Authority, we drove through the Lincoln Tunnel and emerged in the State of New Jersey. "Good evening, folks!" said a friendly voice over the loudspeaker.

"This is your driver speaking. If you want a last glimpse of the Manhattan skyline, here's your chance." The sun was starting to set in the West, but behind me midtown New York glimmered in an unearthly reddish light. *How could anyone live in a place like that,* I wondered? *No trees, just jostling crowds surrounded by forbidding towers of concrete.* After taking in the view, I settled back in my seat and stretched out my long legs as best I could. The driver dimmed the lights in the bus forcing several passengers to turn on their overhead reading lamps. I fell asleep dreaming of a new life in sunny California.

****

A little over three weeks later, crushed and humiliated after an unsuccessful job hunt in San Francisco, I said good-bye to the Proctor family and boarded the bus for the trip back to New York City. I had wondered how anyone could live there. Now I was about to find out.

CHAPTER 2

*A*s soon as the bus pulled into the Port Authority Bus Terminal late on Wednesday afternoon I took a taxi to the Sloan House YMCA and booked an inexpensive room. After putting away my luggage and giving myself a quick wash, I headed back downstairs and peeked into the cafeteria to check on their daily specials. Only about half of the tables were occupied at that hour but there, towards the middle of the room, was Walter Licht, whom I had met on the S.S. *France*. He waved me over.

"I'm surprised you're still here," I said.

"If you'd come back a few days later you would have missed me. I'm about to move out. I take it you didn't get a job in San Francisco."

"Not unless you call washing Volkswagens a job."

Walter shook his head. "Arrogant bastards! With all your business training! If you ask me, you'll have a much better chance here anyway. New York's where the action is. Get yourself a bite to eat and then we can talk."

"I've been thinking," Walter said when I sat back down a few minutes later with a heaping portion of franks and beans. "I've landed a good job as a jewelry designer and I've just signed a lease for a

9

furnished apartment at 806 Madison Avenue near 67th Street. It's a large studio with cooking facilities and a shower on the second floor of a solid old building and the rent is only $140 a month. Still, I could use a roommate to split the cost. Why don't you move in with me while you look for a job? It's gotta be better than hanging around here."

I quickly calculated what was left of my original $400.00, being sure to allow enough leeway to get me back to Germany if I had to. It would be tight, but I thought I could manage it. I reached across the table to shake Walter's hand. "Count me in! You've got a deal."

****

Even though there were still a few days left until the first of the month, the Cerutti sisters, who owned the building, gave us permission to move in the next evening. Both in their early fifties, the sisters also managed an upscale children's clothing store on the ground floor where expensively dressed mothers and children in chauffeured limousines came to shop, together with their nannies.

Our second-floor walk-up apartment had one extra-narrow twin bed on the right side by the entrance and another extra-narrow twin bed on the left side of the room. Between two upholstered chairs, a brown couch and a low wooden table were set back in an alcove with large bay windows overlooking Madison Avenue. Although a year or two later it was changed to a one-way street, at that time traffic on Madison Avenue ran in both directions and city buses rumbled by day and night. It was clear that we would have to choose between sweltering with the windows closed or letting in diesel fumes and traffic noise with them open.

Opposite the windows, a large closet took up most of the wall. Instead of a separate kitchen, the gas stove, a small sink, and a refrigerator filled a recess in the wall near the bathroom at the far end of the room.

"You can take the bed near the door and I'll take the one on the far wall, if that's okay with you," Walter suggested. "Oh, and tomorrow morning I'll arrange to get our phone turned on. With everything we have to do around here, it's a good thing I don't have to start work until next week."

We had just started to unpack when there was a knock at the door. Our visitor was an extremely tall, broad-shouldered Negro man in a three-piece business suit. "Hi! I'm Quincy. Hope you don't mind my stopping by unannounced," he said in an unusually deep voice. "I'm your upstairs neighbor. Miss Cerutti mentioned that you'd be moving in today." He reached out to shake my hand.

We introduced ourselves. "The place is a mess," Walter said apologetically, "because we've just started to unpack. But you're welcome to come in for a while if you have time."

"I'd be glad to. Give me a few minutes to change into more comfortable clothes and I'll be right back."

By the time Quincy returned we had cleared away some of our things to make the apartment a bit more hospitable. Walter sat down on one of the chairs and I sat on the other, but Quincy startled us by taking a seat on the floor in front of the couch. He leaned back, spread his arms out across the seat cushions behind him, and stretched out his long legs under the table. "It's been a long day" was his only explanation.

We soon learned that Quincy was the director of a museum in Brooklyn. After serving in the American army, he had used the GI Bill to earn a BA in Economics and a Masters in History. Afterwards he had lived for several years in Paris. In addition to being fluent in French, he even knew a little German.

When I began to tell Quincy about my unsuccessful job search in California, he listened intently for a few minutes. Then he asked Walter for paper and a pen and began to scribble some notes. "Tell me again about your education in Germany. You say you didn't go to a university?"

"The Russians caught us after the War, so from 1945 to 1948 I only had a few months of school. By the time I got back to West Germany it was too late to get on a university track."

Quincy shook his head. "Is that what you've been telling people? Making excuses for yourself? No one's going to care about your sad childhood. You have to sound confident and *sell yourself*! Let's start again from the beginning. What education *did* you have that would help you get a job? What was your job experience in Germany?"

I told Quincy about my apprenticeship in the administration of an aluminum company, my coursework at a business school in Cologne, my adventures hitchhiking around Europe, my year of service in the *Bundeswehr*, and the various trainee positions I had in food-related companies up until the time I sailed to America.

"That's more like it," he said when I had answered all of his questions. "And while you've been talking, I've already blocked out a one-page résumé for you. I'll type it up tonight and slip it under your door tomorrow when I leave for work. All you'll need to do is have photocopies made and you'll be ready to hit the pavement."

"Should I bring these along, too?" I handed Quincy my English translations of letters of recommendation from my German employers.

He looked them over and shook his head. "I wouldn't, if I were you. First off, no one will have heard of any of these companies. And besides, they sound so good, people are going to think you made them up yourself."

"Another thing," Walter said. "I've been telling Günter to drop the 'umlaut' in his name. Otherwise Americans won't have a clue how to pronounce it."

Quincy nodded. "I was going to change that anyway because there's no 'umlaut' on my typewriter." He turned to me. "So, my new friend, are you ready to be just plain Gunter?"

When I decided to bring my small Olivetti travel typewriter with me from Germany I had never considered the possibility that American keyboards would be different from the one I used.

"Sure," I agreed. "If it's easier to be Gunter, then Gunter it will be."

"I'll bet people won't know how to pronounce it either way," Walter joked.

"Maybe so," Quincy agreed, "but at least now they'll be able to spell it." He slowly uncoiled himself from under the table and stood up to leave. "Well, it's been nice meeting you both. I'll have that résumé under the door in the morning. Good luck tomorrow, Gunter!"

"Thank you, sir," I replied.

"None of that 'sir' stuff do you hear? We're neighbors. Just call me Quincy."

CHAPTER 3

First thing in the morning I had copies made of the résumé Quincy prepared for me. Then, after sending off postcards with my new address to my parents in Germany, to the Proctors in California, and, after some hesitation, also to Charlotte, I stopped in at the offices of the German American Chamber of Commerce to get some leads. I jotted down information about German firms with offices in Manhattan and I also made a list of employment agencies. Following Walter's suggestion, I bought a supply of 15¢ tokens for the subway and the bus and set out to make the rounds.

Nothing turned up on that Friday, or on Monday, or on Tuesday. By Tuesday evening, feeling totally discouraged, I ran into Quincy in the stairway of our apartment building. I was wearing my dark blue suit, a white shirt, a red tie, and my dressiest shoes.

Quincy looked me over from head to toe and whooped with laughter. "Don't tell me that's the way you've been looking for a job?" he asked when he finally caught his breath.

"It's my best outfit. Why? What's wrong with it?"

"Because you look like a damn fag!" he exclaimed. "Just look at your shoes! No straight man would wear pointy shoes like that."

"Everyone's wearing them in Germany now. They're in style."

"You want a job, right? Trust me, it's hard enough to get one without going around looking like you're homosexual. Drop off your briefcase and let's go get you some decent footwear."

Minutes later Quincy brought me to a Florsheim shoe store a few blocks further down on Madison Avenue. The shoes he picked out for me were clumpy, round-toed monstrosities decorated with dozens of tiny holes punched into the leather. I'd have worn shoes like that in Cologne at my peril. Even worse, they would set me back a whopping $19.95.

The salesman slipped the shoes on me and tied the skinny laces. "These wingtips are our latest model, sir," he said. "I know you'll be very happy with them."

"You sure about this?" I asked Quincy, looking down at my feet doubtfully.

"Trust me," he said again.

"But . . ."

Quincy turned to the salesman. "Wrap them up!" he said. "He'll take them."

****

I'll never be sure whether those ugly shoes did the trick but, to my amazement, the very next day I landed a job. An employment agency had arranged an appointment for me with Mr. Lush, a Senior Vice President of the produce buying division of the Great Atlantic & Pacific Tea Company. To reach his office in Lower Manhattan, I rode the Lexington Avenue subway all the way down to Wall Street and then wound my way along a maze of narrow, crooked streets near the old Trinity Church.

The produce buying division occupied an entire floor of a towering skyscraper. When the elevator door opened, I was in an enormous high-ceilinged room where more than two hundred desks and chairs stood back-to-back in rows leaving barely enough room to walk between them. Except for the women who sat off to the side in one tight cluster of desks, which I assumed to be the secretarial pool, all of the employees I saw were men.

A cleared passageway led from the elevators directly to a four-foot-high platform about two-thirds of the way back across the floor. And there, with a perfect view of the clerks seated to all sides below them, were the A&P executives. I approached the platform, walked up the steps to present myself to Mr. Lush, and then, like a well-brought-up German, I gave him a little bow.

Mr. Lush stood up to welcome me. He had gray hair; there were deep laugh lines around the corners of his eyes; he spoke slowly and deliberately with a gravelly voice. At 5'4" he was nearly a foot shorter than I was, yet he left no doubt that of the six men who shared the platform, he was the one in charge.

"Well, young man, I see that you've already had some experience in the food industry," he remarked after glancing over my résumé. "But what we do here may be a bit different from what you're used to. Everyone you see down there is buying freight cars full of perishable fruits and vegetables from all fifty states and from Mexico. Now, every so often, one of those railroad cars goes missing. Your job, in a nutshell, is to trace the missing cars and get them back on the right track. Am I clear so far?"

"Yes, sir, absolutely."

"The job pays $80 a week plus health insurance and, of course, you'll be entitled to five vacation days after your first year. So what do you think? Can you start tomorrow morning at 7:45?"

"Of course, Mr. Lush," I replied. "I can't wait to get started!" and we shook hands.

Granted, after the generous vacations I'd enjoyed in Germany, getting only five days off, and that only after waiting a year, was disappointing. Still, it was all I could do to keep from singing on my way down in the elevator. Now I didn't have to go back to Germany. And $80 a week would be more than enough to let me pay my share of the rent and the phone bill. To add icing to the cake, our apartment was only a short walk from the 68th Street entrance to the Lexington Avenue subway that would take me to work. I couldn't wait to share the news with Walter and Quincy.

****

That same evening, to celebrate, I splurged by treating Walter and Quincy to a few beers at a neighborhood tavern. As the evening wore on, Quincy regaled us with one boastful story after another about his conquests in Paris, in Harlem, and in Greenwich Village.

"Blondes, redheads, brunettes. All races. All shapes. All sizes. For some reason they're all attracted to me. And, to be honest, it's sometimes more than I can handle," he groused after his third or fourth beer. "It's like a curse."

My patience finally ran out. "If it's such a problem, why don't you just settle down with one of them and get married?"

"Are you crazy? How could I ever pick one when they're all so different? Anyway, I'm not the marrying type!"

"But what if one of them gets pregnant?" (How often had I worried that Charlotte would try to trap me into marrying her that way?)

Quincy sneered, "The way I look at it, that'd be her problem, not mine. I figure with the pill and all the other stuff that's on the market a woman should be smart enough to protect herself. So why should I let that spoil my fun?"

"Are you serious?" Walter snapped. "How could you not take some of the responsibility?"

"The only person I take responsibility for is myself. Here's the way I see it. There are three rules a man has to follow if he wants to keep out of trouble. First, never invite a woman over to your own place. Your home is your castle and it's always off limits. Second, never travel with a woman or she'll think you're ready to settle down. And third, never let her give you the key to her apartment or you'll end up getting stuck with the rent. Those are the rules I live by and if a woman doesn't like to live by my rules, well then she can just go find herself another man."

Since this was supposed to be a night of celebration, I tried to make light of things. "You know, Quincy reminds me of my Uncle Helmut who's a real ladies' man. Whenever the subject of marriage came up, he would say, 'You don't have to buy the whole cow if you want to drink a glass of milk.'"

"I like that," Quincy said. "And it sounds even better in French: *'Si vous voulez boire un verre de lait, vous n'êtes pas obligé d'acheter une vache entière!'* That's going to be my official motto from now on."

But I wasn't thinking about Uncle Helmut's comment as we walked back home shortly before midnight. I was thinking about the expression Quincy had used earlier when he had said: 'I'm not the marrying type.' I was sure, as I moved forward with my Charlotte-free life in America, that that phrase would come in very handy.

CHAPTER 4

Despite the lack of sleep the night before, I was up, showered, dressed, and out the door by 6:35 a.m. on my first day on the job. Following the directions Walter had written out for me before he had left for work, I took the #6 local train at the 68th Street 'Hunter College' station towards Brooklyn Bridge and then transferred to the #4 Express at 59th Street, arriving at the Wall Street stop with plenty of time to spare. After walking several times around the block to calm my nerves, I reported to Mr. Lush promptly at 7:45 a.m. He was already deep in conversation with two of the vice presidents on the platform but, as soon as he saw me, he made a quick phone call and a short, stout man came up the steps behind me.

"Joe, meet Gunter Nitsch, your new man. Gunter, this is Joe Coletta who's going to teach you the ropes. Once he shows you what to do, I'm sure you'll get the hang of things in no time."

Joe Coletta wore a dark blue suit, a white shirt, and a red tie. Since his slacks were an inch too short, I could see that he had on white socks and black shoes. He had straight, silver-gray hair. The thick lenses in the round metal eyeglass frames perched on his prominent nose gave him a professorial look.

Joe shook my hand. "Welcome aboard, Gunter. If you follow me I'll introduce you to Greg Draskovic, the other member of our team." He led me to a desk just two rows back from the passageway leading from the door to the platform. "You've got the desk right next to Greg's," Joe explained. He turned to Greg. "Gunter's the German guy Mr. Lush was telling me about. I'll leave him in your good hands for now. If either of you need anything, just gimme a holler." He took his seat at the desk behind ours.

Greg also had gray hair, but his was curly, not straight. However, unlike Joe, Greg was tall and lean; his baggy clothes looked to be a size too big. He had the hangdog expression of someone who had forgotten to drink his morning coffee. "So you're from Germany?" Greg said when Joe returned to his desk. "You certainly look the part. Tall, blond and blue eyes."

"They're gray," I corrected him.

"Are they? If you say so. Did Joe happen to mention that we're both World War II vets? Joe was an interpreter for the American forces in Italy. That's where his folks are from. As for me, I saw action on the European front." He dropped his voice. "Joe was an enlisted man." After a pause he added, "And I was a first lieutenant." Although he didn't say it, I could tell that he was thinking, "And look at me now."

"I spent a year as a private in the German army, but of course that was much later. When I was twenty in 1958, I was in the first group after the War to be drafted into the new German Army, what we call the *Bundeswehr*. We even had some of our maneuvers with American soldiers at Baumholder."

"Did you, really?" Greg glanced back at Joe Coletta who was impatiently tapping his pencil on his desk. He turned to me with a sigh. "I guess that's enough chitchat for now. Let's get right to it. Just to give you a better idea of what we do around here, most of the men at the other desks are produce buyers. Say they order five carloads of cantaloupes from Mexico to be shipped from Laredo via El Paso, Texas, but somewhere along the line one of the carloads gets shunted off onto the wrong track. Then it's up to us to get on the phone with the railroad officials to straighten things out before the missing shipment rots. This morning we're tracing a lost shipment of apples from Washington State. But the worst are the strawberries. They'll spoil on you before you can turn around. When we make our phone calls today you should listen in to see how it's done. And if you have any time to spare, you may as well start with these." He handed me a long list of names. "You'll need to familiarize yourself with these freight lines because they come up all the time on the routing sheets for the missing railroad cars. Take your time. There are quite a few of them."

That was an understatement. There were literally hundreds of them, many with strange, unpronounceable names like Bangor & Aroostook and Erie Lackawanna. Since I was spending so much time listening in on phone calls, I decided to take the list to study at home. Whenever things quieted down, I practiced my touch-typing on the unfamiliar American keyboard on my desk.

Towards the end of the first week, Joe would often introduce me to railroad clerks over the telephone. He had an easy rapport with the people on the other end of the line, with some of whom he'd been dealing for many years. "Hey, Pete, how's the better half?" he would ask. "Did your son graduate from high school yet? My family? Wife and kids are fine, thanks. Still waiting for grandchildren though. Listen, the reason I called. I'm going to let you talk with Gunter because you'll be dealing with him from now on. Gunter's from Germany and he's only been in this country for a few weeks. So be patient with him, okay? If you don't mind, either Greg or I will be

21

listening in at first so there may be more than one of us on the line. And in case you're wondering, Gunter's really tall, at least 6'4."

Even though I had told Joe that I was only a little over 6'2", he always insisted on exaggerating my height whenever he described me to someone over the phone. "They'll respect you more," he explained. Since he was unusually short, I soon noticed that Joe was self-conscious when it came to his own small stature. For example, when he wasn't on the phone he often sat with his hands folded behind his head and his elbows jutting out to either side. Or if he was standing at the side of the room, he would prop himself up against the wall with one arm raised way above his head. Still, it didn't seem to bother Joe that I was so much taller than he was. He may even have been proud of the fact that he was the boss of the tallest employee working on that entire floor.

****

All morning long, from their vantage point high above us on the platform, Mr. Lush and his Vice Presidents kept their eagle eyes on their staff. However, about half an hour before noon every day the six of them would head out for business lunches with executives from other companies. And, no sooner had the elevator doors closed behind them, than all of the employees let down their guard and relaxed.

It was during one of these breaks that Joe Coletta came by my desk. He leaned over close to my ear and confided, "You know I'm Italian Catholic, right? What you probably haven't been here long enough to notice is that most of the top guys are Catholics, too. It's the same at A&P headquarters. Pretty much all of them are Catholics." He waited for me to digest that bit of information. "You Catholic?"

"No, I'm not. I'm Protestant."

"Well, then it probably helped that you're a German. Most of the top honchos are the children of immigrants from Ireland, Italy, and Germany. It's almost like an Irish-Italian-German Mafia. I know as an Italian-American I shouldn't say that, but that's the way it is." His voice became normal again. "I want you to know that I've been working here a long time but we've never had an actual foreigner like you until now. You are the very first one. Not that I mind. Now if they were to hire a Nigger or a spic, that would be another thing entirely."

Greg interrupted him. "C'mon, Joe. Gunter is trying to learn proper English. You shouldn't say Nigger; you should say 'colored person'."

"Don't be such a fusspot," Joe chided. "Nigger, colored person, it's all the same to me. Hey, Gunter, see the fellow with the slick black hair way back in that corner? In a city full of Jews that's Paul, our only Jew out of a staff of more than two hundred people."

Greg nodded. "Joe's right. We have no idea who hired him but we sure could've done without him."

As soon as Walter got home that evening I told him about what Joe and Greg had said. "Are they nuts? How can they talk like that? And what bothered me most was that they assumed I would agree with them."

"Well, I'm glad you didn't speak up. It might've cost you your job. With me it's just the reverse. Where I work top management and most of the white-collar employees are Jewish and the eight hundred people in production are a good mix of whites, Negroes, and Latinos from all over the world. It's like a miniature United Nations. And the diamond district on 47th Street where I worked before? Almost 100% Jewish."

"Except for Paul and one man in a company where I worked in Germany, I don't think I've ever seen a Jew up close."

"I bet you have and you just didn't know it. New York's full of them and they look pretty much like everyone else."

CHAPTER 5

*A*fter a few weeks at the A&P I could practically trace missing railcars in my sleep and I began to have nightmares about shipments of fruits and vegetables lost on freight carriers with barely pronounceable names. My life had settled into a routine when I came home one evening and Walter held up four letters.

"Aren't you the popular one? One's from your parents but the other three! Just get a whiff of that perfume. Who's the mystery lady, may I ask?"

I reached over for the letters and opened the one from my mother first. She hadn't written much, just a short note to congratulate me on getting a job, but when I unfolded the letter, a photograph my brother Hubert had taken fell out. Walter swooped down to pick it up.

"Wow! She's a beauty. Are those your folks standing next to her?" he asked as he handed the picture back to me. "So what's the story?"

"Her name's Charlotte. And, how shall I put it? You know when people talk about the girl you left behind? Well, she's it." I turned the other envelopes over in my hands. Two of them had been addressed to me in California, and had been forwarded on to me by the Proctors. The third one had been sent directly to my New York address. All three were written in dark blue ink on light blue paper. And all three had the unmistakable scent of *L'Air du Temps*.

"All joking aside," Walter said, "just take your time and read them and then we can talk. I've got to buy a few things at the market so I'll leave you alone for a while."

Charlotte's letters read like diary entries in which she recounted, in great detail, everything she'd done since I left Cologne. I could picture her going off to work in her office near the Cologne Cathedral, or visiting her aunt, or sewing herself a new outfit. There was no mention of parties or dates or fun of any kind. *You see, I haven't thought of anyone but you*, she wrote. *I can't wait until you come back. I miss you more every day.*

By the time Walter returned with the groceries, I was close to tears.

"So how bad is it?" Walter asked. "Are you tempted to go back to Charlotte? Because, if you are, I've got a better suggestion for you. It seems to me you need to have a change of scenery. So I was thinking. You once mentioned that your Continental Trailways bus ticket is good for ninety-nine days?"

"Right. The deal was $99 for ninety-nine days."

"Well, then, why waste it? Let's go down to Washington D.C. for the day before your ticket runs out."

"Sounds good," I agreed, feeling suddenly better. "At least that would give me something to write back to Charlotte about other than my dull life tracing cauliflower and cabbages for the A&P."

****

On Saturday July 4th Walter and I left from the Port Authority Bus Terminal long before sunrise. The holiday weekend had started the day before so there wasn't much traffic. A little more than four hours later we stepped off the air-conditioned bus into the sweltering heat and humidity of Washington, D.C. While I had dozed on the bus, Walter had been busy reading *The New York Times*.

"We picked an interesting weekend to come down," he told me as we walked from the grounds of the U.S. Capitol building along the Mall towards the Washington Monument and the White House. "President Johnson just signed the Civil Rights Act on Thursday and not everyone's going to be happy about it."

Sure enough, even though we were still a few blocks from the White House, we could hear angry chants.

"Maybe we should keep a safe distance," I suggested.

"Don't worry. I'm sure they're harmless," Walter assured me. "People were protesting the last time I was down here, too."

But even Walter was stunned when we got close enough to see the demonstrators. Nearly fifty men in khaki uniforms, dark sunglasses, and paratrooper boots were strutting, lockstep, in a tight circle. Every single one of them wore a red armband on his left sleeve. In the center of each armband was a jagged black swastika in a white circle.

"Down with the Jewish communists in America!" they screamed into their bullhorns. "No integration with Niggers!" "Rid America of all Jews and Niggers!"

Aghast, I turned to Walter. "Are they actors in a movie? They can't be serious. If they did that back home, they'd all be arrested on the spot!"

"Trust me, they're deadly serious. I read about these guys in *The New York Times*. Their so-called '*Führer*' is a nut named George Lincoln Rockwell who, believe it or not, wants to be elected President in November."

I looked down at the literature one of the storm trooper types had just handed me. Each horrific pamphlet was covered in swastikas. One advertised a 'Coon-Ard' Lines boat ticket to Africa with such amenities as 'All the bananas and choice cuts of Missionary desired' and 'Barrel of axle grease for hair. Delicately scented with nigger-sweat.' Another provided a pass to gas 'Jewish Communist Traitors' complete with 'extra large-size, giant kosher nose-plugs, to avoid that gassy odor until the end.'

This kind of garbage could've been printed in Germany in the nineteen-thirties. But this was 1964! In the middle of Washington, D.C.!

Walter and I both snapped photos of the Neo-Nazis. "See, what did I tell you?" Walter said as we slowly made our way back to the bus station in the late afternoon. "You have to get out every once in a while to see what's going on in this country."

"Well, now I really do have a story for the folks back home," I replied. "But I'm not sure they're going to believe what I tell them."

CHAPTER 6

*W*alter had recently met Anne, a young teacher from Edinburgh who was working as an *au pair* for a well-to-do family over on Central Park West. She was a pretty blonde, about 5'7" tall, and she trilled the letter 'r' with a charming Scottish burr.

"Here's another idea," Walter said to me a week or so after our excursion to Washington. "If you want to forget Charlotte, you should start dating again. Anne's been telling me about her Irish friend, Brenda, who's working as an *au pair* for an Austrian couple. The four of us could double date. What do you say?"

As it turned out, Brenda was even taller than Anne but she weighed considerably less. She may have thought of herself as fashionably thin but to me, she looked downright scrawny. And, of course, I couldn't help comparing her with Charlotte, who had a gorgeous figure. More bothersome than her looks was the fact that Brenda had little interest in books or current events. When she was off-duty her favorite activity was to plunk herself down in front of the television and watch soap operas. But she was pleasant enough to be with and, since I had no one else, I took her on a couple of dates. She was, I figured, better than nothing.

One Sunday in July, Brenda and I packed towels and bathing suits and headed out to Rockaway Beach. We took turns swimming so that one of us could keep an eye on our things and then we strolled for a while along the five-mile-long boardwalk. As much as I tried to get a conversation going, it proved hopeless. No matter what subject I brought up, Brenda replied in monosyllables interspersed with throwaway phrases like 'you know' and 'I guess.' By that time we were a long way from the subway and I was desperate to find the shortest way back to Manhattan. Brenda, it turned out, had the unfortunate effect of making me miss Charlotte even more.

I approached three elderly men who were all wearing little black round caps and asked them for directions. But, rather than answer my question, one of them began to cross-examine me. "You German?"

"Yes, sir."

"How long have you been here?"

"In New York? Just a few weeks."

"How old are you?"

"I'm twenty-six. Why do you ask?"

He turned to the others and scoffed. "He wants to know why I'm asking. Imagine that." Then he turned back to me. "From which town?"

"I was born in Königsberg but then later . . . ."

One of the other men interrupted me. "Did you say Königsberg? Ever hear of the Stutthof concentration camp?"

"Yes, sir, I have."

Brenda was tugging on my arm to pull me away but I wanted to hear the men out. "The six million Jews killed. You know about that? Six million! How could your people let it happen? Tell me that. How could it happen? How? The Germans. The most educated people in all

29

of Europe, and they couldn't see that this was wrong? Explain that to me if you can!"

"C'mon, Gunter," Brenda pleaded. "You don't need to stand here and take this crap." Then she glared at the three old men. "Gunter had nothing to do with all that," she snapped as she pulled me away. "What creeps!" she groused once we were out of earshot. "Just ignore them. My boss tells me he gets blamed for the War all the time and he's sick of it." It was the most she had said at one time all day.

"They weren't blaming me. They just wanted to be sure I knew about it."

"Oh really?" She shook her head. "Then after you told them you did, why didn't they just give you the directions you asked for, huh?" It was a question I couldn't answer.

"I'm not going to see Brenda again," I told Walter when I got back.

"I guess she's not the brightest bulb is she?"

But when I described to Walter what had happened at Rockaway Beach his response surprised me. "I hate to admit it, but Brenda was right," he said. "As long as you live in this town, you're going to run into people who'll blame you for the Holocaust. So you may as well get used to it."

CHAPTER 7

y weekly paycheck from the A & P was only a few pennies more than $66 after taxes. After paying for rent, subway tokens, and food, there wasn't much left. That first summer I had also used up almost half of the $400 reserve I'd brought with me from Germany by taking weekend trips, one to Niagara Falls and one to Montreal, before my free bus rides ran out. Since the cheapest flight home on Icelandic Airlines would cost roughly $150, I panicked at the thought that my funds would dip below that margin.

Aside from needing the money, I was also looking for a way to keep busy on weekends. Walter and Anne were now spending quite a bit of time together. In addition, now and then Walter was asked to come in on a Saturday or a Sunday when there was a backlog of work at his jewelry company. To fill in the time, I was spending far too many weekend afternoons in cheap movie houses on West 42nd Street, where for a dollar I could watch two double features in a row. The sickening smell of greasy hotdogs turning round and round on grills in the lobby permeated the theaters and I had to change seats from time to time to avoid sitting near the dozing, urine-soaked derelicts who occasionally roused themselves just long enough to yell obscenities at the actors on the screen. My feeble excuse for these pathetic excursions was that the movies improved my English. In fact, I was just terribly lonely.

Our upstairs neighbor, Quincy, suggested that I could solve both of these problems at once by earning some additional money taking inventory in a supermarket at night over the weekend. Following his advice I went for an interview at a Grand Union supermarket on the West Side of Manhattan. Sure enough, they had a job for me at one of their stores in the South Bronx. The hours were from Saturday at 10 p.m. to Sunday at 7 a.m. The pay was a pitiful $1.15 per hour. But I needed the money and, besides, I was hoping to meet some people with whom I could speak English, since Walter and I always conversed in German.

The part of the South Bronx where the Grand Union was located might just as well have been in Cuba or in Puerto Rico. The laundromat, which was still busy at that late hour, was a Lavandería, the butcher shop was a Carnecería, and the little all-night corner grocery store was a Bodega. Wherever I walked I could hear the bouncy Latin beat of pachanga music blaring from radios in open apartment windows.

The twenty of us who showed up at 10 p.m. for our job assignments were also an international group. Most of my co-workers came from Latin America or from Eastern Europe and, to my dismay, my English was far better than most of theirs. The supervisor on duty handed out merchandise printouts and divided us up two to a team. One team member had to count and the other had to write down the quantities. To break the tedium we were told to reverse roles every ten minutes or so.

My partner was Richard, a Negro man from Harlem, and he and I got right to work. While Richard waited with the inventory list, I carefully counted more than one hundred stacked cans of Chicken of the Sea tuna. After he wrote the number down, Richard then tackled the Bumblebee brand. Despite our best efforts it was hard to concentrate because the team just down the aisle from us suddenly got into a violent argument. As best I could tell, the dispute was over whose turn it was to count. Since my Spanish was pretty much limited to ordering a beer, I wasn't quite sure.

"*Cabrón!*" shouted one. "*Carajo!*" the other yelled back. By that time the first man had put his co-worker in a stranglehold and screamed, "*Hijo de puta!*" Just when it looked as though there would be bloodshed, the supervisor came by and calmed things down.

"All in a night's work," Richard joked. "From your expression I gather this is your first time here. But don't worry. I doubt we're in any real danger. I wouldn't mind washing out their mouths with soap, though."

"How many times have you done this, then?"

"Just since last week. My dad was a dentist and things got tough when he passed away a few months ago. I've got an office job during the day but I figured this was as good a way as any to bring home a little extra money for my mom. How about you?"

"That's too bad about your dad. And it's the same with me. I have a job downtown but it's barely enough to get by on."

"Cheer up! It could be worse. At least you're only working nights on weekends," Richard said. "I also take evening classes during the week at City College. It keeps me out of mischief, I suppose."

The next weekend Richard and I teamed up again for two nights in a row but when we finally got our paltry net paychecks on Sunday morning both of us decided to quit. Taking into consideration the travel time, the risk of violence, and the skimpy reward, the job simply wasn't worth it. Still, I was glad to have met Richard and, before we parted ways I invited him to come to our studio apartment the following Saturday afternoon to meet Walter and Quincy.

CHAPTER 8

*O*n the appointed day, Quincy came downstairs shortly before Richard was due to arrive and I took the opportunity to ask him about a subject that was troubling me.

"You're asking me why I don't like the term 'Negro'? It's because it makes me think of segregated schools and segregated water fountains. Did you know that the Supreme Court used the word 'Negro' eighteen times in *Brown v. Board of Education*? Well, isn't it about time we moved on? Call me 'African-American' or call me 'Black.' Those are terms I can relate to."

"As long as we're on the subject, why do you call Walter and me 'white'?" I looked down at my arm. "I'm more of a yellow-pink shade except when I'm embarrassed and I turn red."

"Same here," Walter agreed and he held up his arm.

Just then Richard arrived and we invited him to join in the conversation.

Quincy shot back. "C'mon, Gunter. Don't give me that. Germans use the terms 'Weisse' and 'Schwarze' don't they?"

"I guess so," I admitted, "But even so, I'm no more white than you are black. A sheet of paper is white. Some of the keys on a piano are black. If there really were white people and black people and they had children, wouldn't their children be gray?"

Both Richard and Quincy chuckled at my remark. "You're a funny man, Gunter," Quincy said. "And in a way what you say makes sense. But try telling that to a white racist and you're liable to get your face bashed in."

Richard chimed in, "If you don't like being called white, how about Caucasian?"

"But I'm not from the Caucasus. That's part of Russia. I'm German."

"Just the same, some people call white folks Caucasian. And this'll blow your mind. That's also what they call people from India. Go figure!"

"I guess we haven't really cleared anything up, have we?" Walter asked. "To be honest, I'm more confused than ever."

"Same here, but I'll try not to use the word Negro any more if it bothers Quincy that much," I added.

"Thanks," Quincy said. "And in return I won't call you Caucasian!"

Richard turned to me. "Before I forget, a good friend of mine is giving a big party down in Greenwich Village later on tonight and I was wondering if you'd like to come along."

"Sure, that sounds like a great idea."

"Can I use your phone to call her and see if she would mind?"

He dialed the number and made his request. After giving me a thumbs up, he handed me the receiver. "She'd like to say hello to you."

"You haven't told me her name."

"Carol."

"Hello, Carol," I said. "I'm looking forward to your party."

Richard took back the phone and listened to Carol for a minute. Then he stifled a laugh. Covering the receiver with his hand he whispered, "She asked me *'where in Africa is your friend from?'*"

On hearing this, Quincy slapped his thighs and doubled over with laughter. Richard had to bite his lip before he replied. "You've got the wrong continent. My friend's a tall guy from Germany." Suddenly Richard stopped smiling. "Oh, okay then. I won't bring him along. I'll come by myself. See you later."

"Let me guess," Walter said when Richard hung up the phone. "She must be Jewish."

"How'd you know?"

Walter shrugged. "I can't really explain it. After a while, you just know."

"Talking about Jews," Quincy said, "hasn't the West German government forked over vast sums of money to Jewish Holocaust survivors?"

Walter and I exchanged puzzled glances. "Of course they have," Walter said. "What's that have to do with anything?"

"I'll get to that, but first I'd like to know how you feel about it," Quincy persisted.

After some hesitation, Walter replied, "Well, some older folks in West Germany aren't happy about it of course. But I think the people directly affected by the Holocaust should get back their property and additional compensation besides."

I nodded in agreement and chimed in, "So do I. But what bothers me is that they call it *Wiedergutmachung*, which literally means 'to make things good again.' No amount of money can ever repair what was done to the Jews during those years."

"Well, I'm glad you both think that way," Quincy said as he stretched his legs even further under the coffee table and leaned back against the edge of the couch, "and let me tell you why. Slavery was a crime against humanity just like the Holocaust. So if the Germans can pay billions of dollars to the Jews for twelve years of injustice, then why shouldn't the American government compensate African-Americans for two hundred fifty years of slavery?"

"Are you serious?" Richard asked.

Walter held up his hand. "And where, my fine man, may I ask, would the U.S. government get the funds to do that?"

Quincy sneered. "That's easy! By raising taxes on all white Americans. After all, the profits from slavery have been passed down from generation to generation, so why shouldn't they pay their share?"

"Hold on a minute!" I said. "Are you also including people like Walter and me who've only been here a few months?"

"Darn right I am! You're taking advantage of the American economy, aren't you?"

"Now you listen to me, Quincy." Walter was standing now. "If anyone has benefitted from the American economy, it's you. You have two college degrees; you have a good job. It's all nonsense to single out people just because they're white. At least with Germany's *Wiedergutmachung*, we know for sure who was responsible."

"Don't kid yourself," Quincy replied as he crawled out from under the coffee table and got up to leave. "We know who's responsible here, too. And, one of these days, they're going to pay for it."

When Richard had also left a few minutes later, Walter, who was usually a calm person, exploded. "That guy really gets on my nerves some times! I was just waiting for him to take up a collection!"

CHAPTER 9

O n that Monday morning I woke up with a jolt and I instantly knew that my alarm clock had not gone off. It was 7: 35 a.m. and I had barely 25 minutes to get to my office. I jumped up, shaved, skipped my shower, gulped down a glass of orange juice, washed my face, got dressed, and took the subway to Wall Street. The normally overcrowded elevator in my office building was empty except for the redheaded elevator operator with a blue anchor tattooed just above his right wrist. "Running late today, are you, sir?" he said, looking me up and down. "If I were you, I think you should button the middle button on your shirt before I let you out on your floor."

I left the elevator with the uncanny feeling that two hundred people were glaring at me as I strode up to the platform to meet my fate.

Even though Mr. Lush was busy talking with three of his Vice Presidents, I breathlessly blurted out, "Pardon me, Mr. Lush. I'm awfully sorry I'm late today but I slept over because . . . ."

The three Vice Presidents started to snigger but Mr. Lush held up his hand to stop them and looked down at me. Then, in a solemn voice, he asked, "So tell me, Gunter. How old was she?" before his serious face broke into a smile.

By then I had realized my mistake. Feeling the color rising in my cheeks, I stammered, "What I meant to say is that I *overslept* because my alarm clock didn't go off."

"That's all right," he said. "Just make sure that it doesn't happen again."

"Thank you, Mr. Lush."

Of course, when I got back to my desk Joe and Greg insisted on knowing what was so funny and, before long, the whole office was in on the joke. For weeks afterwards, some smart aleck in the crowded morning elevator would ask me, "So, Gunter, did you sleep over again last night?"

I always forced myself to laugh right along with them, but considering the sorry state of my social life, I found it hard to see the humor in it.

****

Quincy smiled as he listened to the story about my mix-up of 'slept over' and 'over slept.' But then, he suddenly got serious. "You know, Gunter, it sounds like you need to work a bit on your English. I'd suggest you look into taking a free evening class."

As a result I enrolled in a six-week-long summer course at Washington Irving High School. We met Monday through Friday from 7 p.m. to 9 p.m. Since the school was located on Irving Place about half way between the A&P and my apartment, if the weather was good I generally wolfed down a 15¢ slice of pizza or bought a cheap sandwich at Chock Full o'Nuts and ate my supper on a bench in nearby Union Square Park. Nearly all of my fellow students were African-Americans and Latin Americans in their late teens. At twenty-six I was at least seven years older than they were. I was also the only person in the class from Europe.

Our teacher, Mr. Bernstein, was a tall, elderly man whose long gray hair covered the collar of his white dress shirt. He had a loud voice but, even so, some of the students managed to doze off during class. Other students spoke with such heavy accents that I wasn't sure if they were speaking English or some other unknown language.

At the beginning of the second week we were each assigned to write a short essay and read it aloud the following day. My topic was my trip to America on the *France*. After pointing out a few grammatical mistakes, Mr. Bernstein congratulated me on my command of English. His compliment brought a few snickers and some catcalls from the rest of the class.

Before long Mr. Bernstein made a habit of interrupting other students who were reading their essays. "Hold on just a minute!" he would say and then he would turn in my direction and ask, "What's wrong?" or "What does our European friend say to that?" At other times he would say, "Does our German friend agree with that sentence?" and I would reply, "Double negative" or "The wrong preposition" or "The wrong tense." Needless to say, my classmates did not find this at all endearing. Mr. Bernstein was not helping me win any popularity contests but he was certainly boosting my self-confidence.

On the last day of class I asked Mr. Bernstein when the next session would start. "Let me tell you straight out," he replied. "I don't ever want to see you back here. You're wasting your time with this bunch of misfits. If you want my advice, you should be in college."

"Do you really think so, Mr. Bernstein?"

"I wouldn't suggest it if I didn't."

"Do you have a particular college in mind?"

"Where do you live?"

"Madison Avenue near 67th Street."

"Perfect, you're right near Hunter College. That's where you should go. But you'd better hurry because classes start in September."

****

The next evening as I walked over to the admissions office of Hunter College, I wondered whether Mr. Bernstein's advice would have been different if he had known more about me. To start with, I had never seen the inside of a German high school. My education in Germany consisted of one year of elementary school in 1944 followed by four years without school in Russian-occupied East Prussia after the War. In 1947, as other ten-year-old children in Germany were being tested to see whether they would qualify for a higher education, I was busy stealing potatoes, chopping wood, and begging for food. When I finally got back to West Germany in 1948 at the age of eleven, I was functionally illiterate.

After three more years of elementary school and two years in a commercial school, I graduated from a two-year business program in Cologne. Except for Mr. Bernstein, in all that time no one had ever told me I was a good student.

The lady behind the counter in the admissions office looked up from a pile of papers on her desk. "May I help you?"

"Yes, please. Is this where I can register for an English course and a course in economics?"

"Do you have a high school diploma?"

My heart sank. "No, I don't."

"Well, what kind of education do you have?"

"I completed a two year business course in Cologne, Germany."

"And what did you study there?"

"Economics, business administration, accounting, French . . ."

"Hold it right there!" she said. She jotted a name and a room number on a slip of paper and handed it to me. "Go see this gentleman. He's the head of the French Department and he may be able to help you." As I left her office, she was dialing the phone.

The door was open and a middle-aged man in a gray suit wearing horned-rimmed glasses looked up at me.

"Good evening, sir. My name is Gunter Nitsch."

He interrupted me. "*Comment vous appelez-vous?*"

"*Je m'appelle Gunter Nitsch, Monsieur.*"

"*Très bien. Et où êtes-vous né?*"

"*Je suis né en Allemagne en Décembre 1937.*"

"Well, young man," he said with a smile, "you've passed the test." He signed the little slip of paper and gave it back to me. "Bring this to the admissions office and they'll let you enroll as a non-matriculated student. If you get a few credits under your belt and earn good grades, you'll be able to matriculate."

"*Merci beaucoup, Monsieur, et au revoir!*"

I couldn't believe my luck. Starting in September, I would be going to college!

CHAPTER 10

*O*ne morning on my way to work I cut across Trinity Church Cemetery and ran into Paul, 'the only Jew in our office' as Joe had so crassly put it. It turned out that Paul was only two years my senior and we had a lot in common. He was an avid reader. He had spent time in both Paris and London. Best of all, he was a dedicated jazz fan. Despite Joe's evident disapproval, Paul and I went to lunch together now and then, always stopping in the cemetery on our way back for a short history lesson. It was from Paul that I learned about John James Audubon's wonderful paintings of birds, about Alexander Hamilton's fatal duel with Aaron Burr, and about the enormously wealthy John Jacob Astor, all of whom were buried there. But I was stunned when Paul recited a few lines from *Twas the Night Before Christmas* in front of the grave of its author, Clement Moore. From what little I knew about Jews, I was pretty sure they didn't celebrate Christmas.

"Are you surprised I know the words?" he asked me. "Don't be. Jewish kids grew up with that poem the same as we liked to sing 'Rudolph the Red-Nosed Reindeer' and 'Jingle Bells'," and he proceeded to hum both tunes until we reached the lobby of our building.

Shortly before the workday started one Monday morning, Greg, Joe and I were getting settled at our desks when Paul walked over to us with a big wooden cigar box and offered each of us a long, thick cigar.

"Help me celebrate!" he exclaimed. "I got married over the weekend."

Joe and Greg accepted their cigars with a smile but when I hesitated Joe threw up his hands. "So Goody Two-Shoes here doesn't smoke? For God's sake Gunter take it! I wouldn't mind having two."

Paul handed Joe the cigar he had taken out for me before he returned to his desk. Joe held up one of the cigars and read aloud the words printed on the gold band: *Paul and Rachel Forever.* "Well, would you look at that?" he mocked. "How fancy can you get? Personalized cigars!" He sniffed the tobacco. "And good quality, too. Their wedding must've cost a fortune if they could afford to give away expensive stuff like this. What do I always tell you? The Jews must all be rolling in dough."

****

I had gotten to know Paul fairly well and I was certainly aware of Joe's outrageous opinions. Greg, on the other hand, remained a mystery. He never mentioned his family. I didn't even know whether he was married or single. And, at times I even wondered whether something inside of him had snapped after the War. It unnerved me that he would line up marching platoons of paperclips on his desk in three precise groups of twelve each and then mutter under his breath, "Christ, I hate this job," before carefully sweeping the clips back into their box. "I once led platoons like these," he groused to me. I

45

recognized the bitterness, of course, since there were thousands upon thousands of veterans in Germany who still felt just as lost.

On this particular day, shortly before noon, Greg asked me whether I wanted to go with him to buy a sandwich at a nearby Chock full o'Nuts restaurant and then join him on a bench in Battery Park where we could watch the boats in New York Harbor. We both liked the Chock full o'Nuts cream cheese sandwiches, which were a bargain at only 35¢. Besides, as Greg was quick to remind me, the restaurant didn't allow tipping.

We arrived at a busy time. The place was packed and the line for take-out orders was long. Greg and I took a spot at what we thought was the end of the line when suddenly a giant African-American man roughly tapped me on the shoulder. "Hey, man," he snarled. "I's waiting here!"

Startled, my English momentarily failed me and I blurted out, "Is you?" at which everyone within earshot, including Greg, laughed out loud at my mistake. Meanwhile the angry giant muttered a few unintelligible curses under his breath as he defiantly took his place in front of me in line.

Once we were back outside with our sandwiches and our coffee, Greg shook his head. "You know you could've gotten us both killed in there, don't you? I'm sure that Nigger thought you were making fun of him. It doesn't take much to set a darky like that off."

"Sorry. I realized my mistake the minute I said it."

"Still, it sure as hell was funny. What did he say? 'I's waiting here.' What kind of English is that?"

Back at the A&P I took a small notebook out of my briefcase and added 'darky' to the long list of inappropriate words I was learning from Joe and Greg.

Yet despite his prejudices and occasional crude language, Greg considered himself to be a sophisticated and well-educated man, whereas he viewed me as an ignorant immigrant. One day, out of the blue, apparently to test me, he asked me whether I had ever heard of Gweth or Baitch.

"Neither one rings a bell," I replied to Greg's obvious satisfaction.

"You said you didn't have a good education but I thought you'd know at least that much about your culture!"

Suddenly a light bulb went off in my head. "Hold on just a second," I said. "Would you mind writing those two names down?"

Greg was glad to oblige. He neatly printed the words 'Goethe' and 'Bach' on his notepad. Joe, who had been following our conversation, looked over Greg's shoulder and began to chuckle. "Now I know why Gunter didn't recognize those names the way you pronounced them. Tell him, Gunter!"

I grinned. "'Goethe' is pronounced 'Gurt-ah.' 'Bach' sounds like 'Bock.' And, of course I know who they are. But 'Gweth' and 'Baitch'? Like I said. Never heard of them!"

CHAPTER 11

Meanwhile the letters from Charlotte kept coming. Several times a week there would be another new light-blue perfumed envelope in our mailbox. Where in New York, I began to wonder, could I ever find someone who cared for me as much as Charlotte did? All of the reasons I had run from her in the first place—the way her constant demands for attention took over my life, the endless pressure to get married, her pathetic suicide attempt when I had first tried to break things off—all these were forgotten as she reminded me in page after page of the deliciously sweet times the two of us had shared together.

I caved in. During my lunch hour on a hot, sticky day in late August, I found a telephone service near Wall Street where, for an exorbitant fee, I could place a long-distance call to Cologne. As soon as I heard Charlotte's voice all of my doubts fell away and I was sure that I was still in love with her. How could I have been so stupid? The thought that I had almost let her slip through my fingers left me totally distraught. Two sleepless nights later, I phoned Charlotte again to tell her that I was coming home.

The next morning I bought a ticket from Icelandic Airlines. My flight would arrive in Luxembourg on Saturday morning. From there, it would be a three-hour train ride back to Cologne. When I called Charlotte with the news, she insisted on traveling to Luxembourg to meet me at the airport.

With only twenty-four hours until my late Friday evening departure, I began packing the minute I got home from work. Walter walked in as I was folding my clothing into my trunk.

"Going somewhere?" he mocked.

"I feel bad leaving you on the hook for the rent," I began, "but I've decided to go back to Germany for good."

"Don't worry about the rent," Walter assured me. "But do you really mean you're going back for good or are you going back for Charlotte?"

"You probably think I'm crazy."

"Well, since you asked, I think you're about to make a total ass of yourself. After one week in Cologne, you'll be bored to death and the laughing-stock of just about everyone you know except Charlotte. Can't you see how she's got you wrapped around her little finger?"

"Maybe you're right, but I have to find out for myself."

The only reason I went to work on Friday was to get my last paycheck. For most of the day I sulked at my desk overcome with guilt because I had decided not to tell anyone I was leaving. As the day wore on I became less and less sure what to do.

As I was getting ready to leave the office at 5 p.m., I felt like two cents when Joe and Greg both wished me a great weekend.

Walter was reading *The New York Times* when I got home. He looked up at me and grinned. "So have you changed your mind?"

I shook my head and defiantly started to pack a few remaining toilet articles. My bus for the airport would leave in a little over an hour.

"Listen," Walter said. "Let me be blunt. You're not thinking with your brain! You've told me you dreamed about coming to America since you were a little kid, right? Well, you've finally made it! You have a real future here. You're about to start classes at Hunter College. Are you going to throw it all away just like that? It may be hard right now but in one or two more years at the most you'll have enough experience under your belt to succeed here." He paused and then he added, "And I guarantee you this, if you leave now you'll regret it for the rest of your life."

While Walter was talking I was clutching one of my plastic shoe trees, trying to decide whether to take them with me or leave them behind, when I suddenly realized that, if I couldn't even decide a simple thing like that, I was clearly in no frame of mind to decide anything else. All of the pressure I'd been under since my first phone call to Charlotte welled up inside me and, in frustration, I struck the shoe tree with such force against the wooden table that it split apart.

Walter stopped speaking and looked at me with genuine concern. "I didn't mean to get you so upset," he said apologetically. "You should do whatever you think is best."

"*VERDAMMTER MIST!*" I swore at the top of my lungs. "I'm an idiot. That's it! I'm not going anywhere!"

My hands were shaking so hard I had to ask Walter to dial the number of Icelandic Airlines so that I could cancel my flight.

"I'm supposed to go out with Anne tonight," Walter said once I'd made my call. "Let me phone her and postpone our date until tomorrow. I think you, Quincy, and I should go out for a night of bar hopping."

A few hours later, when all of us had had far too many beers, I suddenly sat up in a panic. "I completely forgot that Charlotte was going to meet me at the Luxembourg airport!"

"Forget Charlotte! You know what you need?" Quincy poked me in the chest. "You need to get yourself some tail! That's my advice to you. Put yourself out there. There's plenty of fish in the pond. Get my drift?" I stared at him in surprise. Bob had said the exact same thing when I was in California.

"What I think Quincy means is to start dating," Walter explained. "There are mixers where you can meet nice girls. I'll give you some suggestions tomorrow."

"Hey!" Quincy exclaimed. "I didn't necessarily mean 'nice girls' but it's a start. And listen to someone who knows about women. When you do talk to Charlotte, DON'T GIVE IN!"

****

Late on Saturday morning I dialed Charlotte's number. As the phone rang in far-away Cologne I could visualize the apartment where Mrs. Sorge had once walked in on her daughter and me as we slept together on the living room floor and Charlotte had defiantly refused to budge. Now, to my dismay, it was Mrs. Sorge who answered the phone. "Oh, it's you!" Her tone was icy. "You'd better have a good explanation. She's inconsolable." After a short pause I heard her yell, "Charlotte, it's for you. Günter from New York!"

"Are you all right?" Charlotte gasped between sobs as she took the receiver from her mother. "When you weren't on the plane I was sure you must've been in some kind of terrible accident!"

"Listen, Charlotte, there's no easy way to say it," I began, "and I hope you can forgive me, but I've decided to stay in New York, at least for another year."

"But you *promised!*"

"I know I did, and I feel bad about it, I really do."

I heard Mrs. Sorge's angry voice in the background. "So what's his crazy excuse? Dragging you all the way to Luxembourg for nothing! You have to stand up for yourself!"

There was a long silence on the other end of the line. "I still love you," Charlotte whispered and she hung up the phone.

****

Quincy stopped by our apartment a short while later. Walter had long since left to spend the day with Anne. "Just the man I'm looking for," he said as he handed me two books. "Since you're going to stay in New York I thought you should do some reading. These are both by James Baldwin. He writes pretty damn well for a fag, you know."

"What are they about?"

"Life in Harlem. The black struggle for freedom. Things you've been asking me about."

"Thanks. Maybe they'll help take my mind off things."

As he was about to leave, Quincy added, "I guess you already spoke to Charlotte?" I nodded. "It must be tough, but I'm glad you stuck to your guns. Call me if you need company. I'll be upstairs most of the afternoon." He turned back when he reached the door and grinned. "Anyway, what I really wanted to say is welcome home!"

CHAPTER 12

I was wracked with guilt. What if Charlotte really did take her own life this time? How could I ever live with that? But finally, at Walter's insistence that I focus on other things, I began to buy copies of the Friday edition of *The New York Post* to look through the ads for singles mixers at downtown hotels. From then on, once the weekend rolled around I would put on my best suit and attend one or another of these events. There were always more women than men so I had no trouble finding dance partners. Some of the girls were even interesting to talk to. But when I compared them to Charlotte, they all came up short.

Finally one Friday night I danced for several hours with Rose, a high school English and history teacher from Brooklyn who, I guessed, was in her early thirties. At the end of the evening, Rose suggested that we meet in the Egyptian Wing of the Brooklyn Museum that Sunday afternoon. From the moment I arrived, she impressed me with her extensive knowledge of ancient Egypt and the history of the pyramids. Whereas Charlotte's reading had mostly been limited to glossy movie magazines and cookbooks, in Rose, at least, I had found someone with real intellectual curiosity.

After several hours in the museum, I invited Rose to dinner in a small Italian restaurant. It was the first time I had treated a young woman to a meal in New York. Up until then, except for the young college girls at my table on the *France*, the only meals I had shared with any Americans had been sandwiches or pizza with my co-workers at the A&P. As I had been taught in Germany, I held my fork in my left hand and my knife in my right hand throughout dinner. So it came as a shock when Rose proceeded to cut her entire veal cutlet into bite-size pieces. Even more surprising, when she was through cutting her meat, she put down her knife, switched her fork to her right hand and ate the rest of her meal while her left hand rested in her lap.

Despite being taken aback by her strange table manners, when Rose invited me back to her nearby apartment for coffee and a piece of cake, I agreed to go. We were both relaxed after several glasses of wine and I was looking forward to a cozy, romantic evening. Unfortunately Rose had something else in mind. Every surface of her apartment was covered with model Egyptian pyramids. There were hundreds of them. Some were made of marble; others were of wood, or metal or plastic. The tallest pyramid was about two feet high and the tiniest no more than a quarter of an inch. Paintings and posters of pyramids covered the walls.

"You probably find it odd that I'm so in love with pyramids," she said while she served me a piece of cake.

"Oh no, not at all." I tried my best to look sincere. If Rose had cut the cake into the shape of a pyramid I wouldn't have been the least bit surprised.

"Oh, good!" she replied with enthusiasm. "I don't often get to talk about my collection." She then proceeded to bombard me with facts about the pyramids and the Egyptians until I was nearly cross-eyed.

Using the excuse that Monday was a workday, I finally managed to escape totally exhausted around 11 p.m.

Walter was still up when I got back home. "So," he teased when I told him about Rose's apartment, "are you going to see her again?"

"Not if I can help it. Anyway, it wasn't just that she's loony about pyramids. I also thought her table manners were appalling."

Walter grinned. "She switched hands, didn't she? She's an American. What do you expect? Know where that custom comes from?"

"No idea."

"I heard that in the Wild West men had to keep their left hands free so they could hold their Colts in their laps."

"You're making this up!"

"No, that's really what I was told."

"Look, I grew up reading about cowboys like Billy Jenkins and I'm pretty sure if a cowboy had to hold his gun in his lap he'd use his right hand to do it."

"I hadn't thought of that. But, whatever the reason for it is, it sure looks funny."

****

I had to think again of my conversation with Walter when, a few days later, Mr. Lush invited me to join him and three of his vice presidents for lunch in the historic Fraunces Tavern on Pearl Street. Joe was especially taken aback.

"Hey, Gunter, what's so special about you? Mr. Lush has never asked any of us to lunch!"

Although I didn't say so, I could only imagine that my being the only 'exotic' foreigner on the staff may have been the reason. The executives probably wanted to see what I was like up close.

Frances Tavern was an impressive redbrick building with a long history. As Mr. Lush explained it, I was in good company since George Washington himself had once eaten there.

During lunch Mr. Lush peppered me with questions about my life in Germany, both during and after the War. Then he and his colleagues got into a heated discussion about the produce industry to which I only half listened. While they talked I watched in astonishment as all four gentlemen switched their knives and forks back and forth in the same crazy crisscross style my pyramid date had used.

As we walked back to the office after lunch, Mr. Lush turned to the three vice presidents. "I'll come with Gunter in a minute. Why don't you go on ahead?" Once the two of us were alone he turned to me. "Listen Gunter," he said, "I watched you eating your lunch and I just wanted to warn you. If you want to go places in the A&P, you'll have to give up your strange table manners and start eating like a civilized American."

It was all I could do to keep a straight face.

CHAPTER 13

On Quincy's recommendation Walter and I went to the Roseland Ballroom on West 52nd Street. Walter would normally not have come along but he had had a fight with his girlfriend, Anne.

From the outside the nondescript three-story building gave no hint of what to expect. Inside, the scale of the place surpassed our wildest expectations. At least five thousand people could stand comfortably around three sides of the rectangular hall. On a raised platform at one end of the room, a twenty-piece orchestra in formal attire was playing a Viennese waltz for the overwhelmingly white crowd. The dance floor had ample room for twenty-five hundred people, many of whom were now twirling to the music. I felt as though I were in Vienna and not in New York City.

"We're idiots! How come we haven't been here before?" I asked in bewilderment. "This is the place to meet girls."

"I'm amazed Quincy even knew about it. I can count the number of blacks on the fingers of one hand," Walter glumly replied.

"Cheer up! Forget about Anne for one night. Let's have some fun!"

"Maybe you'll get lucky but I'm not much of a dancer anyway. I'm going to get myself a beer."

Screwing up all my courage, I danced with several young women with whom I exchanged a few pleasantries but that was all. Walter had started on his third beer when the emcee announced "Ladies' choice!" over the loudspeaker. Seconds later a tall, beautiful girl with long, pitch-black hair came over to where we were standing and asked me to dance. It was a slow waltz and I held her close.

"I haven't seen you around here before," she said. "Out of all these people I rarely find someone I can dance with cheek to cheek."

"It's my first time at Roseland. I wish I'd found out about this place sooner."

"You've got such a cute accent. Are you Scandinavian?"

"No, but you're pretty close. I'm from Cologne, Germany."

She pulled away from me and her smile froze. "You're from Germany? How long have you been here?"

"Just a few months." At that moment the music stopped. "May I have the next dance so we have a chance to get better acquainted?"

"No, I'd rather not," she replied and she rushed over to the far side of the room.

Disappointed, I went back to where Walter was standing. "Well, that was odd!" I exclaimed. "We seemed to be hitting it off and then she dumped me just like that."

He grinned, "I saw what was coming the minute she walked up to you. Did you happen to notice her necklace? She was wearing a *chai* pendant on a silver chain."

"A what?"

"A lot of the Jewish women in my office wear them. *Chai* means 'life' in Hebrew. But, if you're German, in a place like this it also means keep your distance."

"But wait a minute, I was seven years old when the war was over. I had nothing to do with it."

"I know that, and you know that. But don't forget what happened to you on Rockaway Beach. That's just the way things are."

"And I'd better get used to it, right?"

"You're starting to catch on," Walter said. "Let me buy you a beer!"

CHAPTER 14

Meanwhile, my classes at Hunter College had started at the beginning of September. Professor Hanley, a spirited lecturer with seemingly infinite patience, taught an English course called Elementary Exposition. There were twenty-two young women in the class and nine young men, myself included. Most of my fellow students were only slightly older than the ones who had attended my night school class at Washington Irving High School. But this time, at least, I wasn't the only European. Sitting one row in front of me was Jacques Feder, a Belgian with a strong French accent; he had a day job as a diamond cutter in the Diamond District on West 47th Street.

On the second day of class, Jacques addressed Professor Hanley as 'Madame' to which she gently corrected him. "May I remind you that we speak English in this class, Mr. Feder." The next few times Jacques called her 'Madame,' her objections became more and more shrill. "English! Mr. Feder. This is an ENGLISH class!"

One day Prof. Hanley had just recommended that we each buy a copy of *The Elements of Style* when Jacques Feder raised his hand. "Madame," he asked, "I have heard about this book. Do you have a special edition in mind?"

Now Professor Hanley's patience gave out. "MR. FEDER, for the umpteenth time, DO NOT address me with 'Madame.' I'm not running a whorehouse! I'm a professor of English! Say 'Ma'am' when you speak to me. But DO NOT say Madame. DO I MAKE MYSELF CLEAR?"

As our entire class sat, stunned, by the vehemence of her attack, Jacques' face flushed and his temples began to throb. "Yes, Ma'am. It won't happen again," after which Professor Hanley calmly continued her lesson as if nothing unusual had happened.

Jacques was still steaming when he and I walked down to the basement cafeteria together. "Stupid Americans! They use a French word, but pronounce it so no one can understand it. Had you heard the word 'Ma'am' before?"

"You're asking the wrong guy. First of all I'm German and, besides, your English is probably better than mine."

"I know you're German. And it's not just your accent. It's your looks. You could have been a poster boy for the SS."

"Hey, don't you start. You're not the first one to say that and, quite frankly, I don't like it one bit. In case you're wondering, I was born in December 1937 and the Germans ran World War II without any help from me."

"Hey, calm down. I didn't mean to rub you the wrong way. It's just that I'm also more than a little sensitive when it comes to that topic. I was born in 1936 in Poland. My family was Jewish and both my parents were killed by the Nazis. After that, some good people somehow managed to smuggle me from Poland to Belgium where I was adopted by a rabbi and his wife. How the three of us survived through the rest of the war, I'll never know. But anyway, here I am."

I felt a chill down my spine as I listened to Jacques' story. "But, why weren't you raised by relatives? Shouldn't you have been reunited with the rest of your family after the war?"

He was quiet for a moment. "I don't talk about this with many people," he finally said, "but I feel like I can trust you. Truth is, I'm all alone in the world. The Nazis killed them all: both sets of grandparents, all of my aunts, uncles, and cousins, every last one of them." I reached over to put my arm around his shoulder as he paused for a moment and swallowed hard. Then, in a barely audible voice, he added, "So now you know."

****

In my American Economic Systems class I met another European, John Vanderbosch, whose father was a Dutch diplomat. John had curly dirty-blond hair, clear blue eyes, a wicked grin, and the athletic build of a football player. Girls swarmed around him before and after class like flies around a honeypot. Despite the fact that he had only just turned twenty-one, he had already flunked out of several different American colleges, a fact in which he took inordinate pride. Now, after his father had cut off his allowance and forced him to take a full-time job in a printing company, John was starting over with evening classes at Hunter. Judging by his nonchalant attitude toward his studies, I guessed it would only be a matter of time before Hunter became the next school to eject him.

Although he was careful not to mention it to the young women in class, John had a steady girlfriend. Ronnie was a tall, long-legged blonde who lived alone in a studio apartment on the Upper East Side. I joined the two of them occasionally in a nearby coffee shop and couldn't help noticing that whenever it came time to pay, Ronnie reluctantly picked up John's tab. One day she boiled over.

"I'm getting tired of footing the bill for you, John. Money doesn't grow on trees you know. Have you any idea how much you owe me already?"

"Chill out, honey," John replied. "If I get my hands on the money somehow, I'd rather spend it with you than pay you back."

It was at the coffee shop that I also met Ronnie's best friend, Yvonne, a strikingly beautiful young woman from Egypt. She was pleasingly plump and had short pitch-black hair, a pale complexion as smooth as white porcelain, and the deepest blue eyes I'd ever seen. She wore revealing, low-cut sweaters and, I couldn't help noticing, she had a *chai* pendant on the gold chain around her neck. Yvonne was fluent in Arabic and spoke English with a charming French accent. I presumed that she also knew Hebrew, but didn't dare to ask. The more she talked, the more I liked her, even though she was clearly way out of my league.

****

On a Saturday in the middle of October Quincy stopped by our apartment just as I was getting ready to go out. He looked me up and down approvingly.

"So where are you headed, all slicked up like that?"

"Remember I told you about that guy John? He invited me and his girlfriend to lunch at his parents' home in Darien?"

"Darien, Connecticut? Then I'm willing to bet that that Egyptian beauty you were telling me about won't be there."

"How did you know? I was kind of disappointed that she wasn't invited."

"Listen up, my young friend," Quincy said, "and let me teach you some new vocabulary. Darien is what they call a restricted community. That means no Jews, probably no Catholics, and definitely no blacks. When you get back I'll loan you my copy of *Gentlemen's Agreement* and you'll see exactly what I mean."

John's parents lived in a palatial house set back on a beautifully landscaped estate. I had read about autumn in New England but was still amazed by the profusion of bright yellow, red, and orange leaves on the trees lining the long driveway. A late model Mercedes was parked by the front door. The interior of the house was even more magnificent. In the dining room an enormous crystal chandelier hung over the massive mahogany dining table and a thick red and black oriental rug covered most of the floor. I was surprised that no one suggested we take off our shoes before going in.

"Welcome to Darien!" John's father greeted me. He and his wife both spoke English with a distinctly British accent since he had previously been stationed for many years in London. "Don't be too impressed with the house. We rented it furnished and it is not exactly our taste."

Lunch was a multi-course affair: first a thick squash soup, followed by a crisp green salad, then prime rib of beef and, finally chocolate ice cream sundaes for dessert. After the last dishes were cleared the conversation turned to the upcoming American elections.

"I shouldn't say this as a diplomat," Mr. Vanderbosch confided, "but if I could vote it would be for Barry Goldwater. He likes the status quo and so do I."

His wife, John, and Ronnie all strongly disagreed. "Are you for real? He isn't for the status quo," John insisted. "He wants to turn back the clock. What do you suppose would happen to the Civil Rights Act if he got in?"

"Well, it doesn't really matter what I think," his father went on, "since I'm pretty sure Lyndon Johnson is going to win in a landslide."

"Let's hope so," his wife said. "Goldwater is too rightwing even for me."

Suddenly Mr. Vanderbosch changed the subject. "I almost forgot. There's a Dutch book about Cologne in my office that I want to show to Gunter. If you'll excuse us for a minute . . ."

Mr. Vanderbosch closed the door to his office behind us. "Forget about the book. I really just wanted to talk to you alone. Listen, I've been observing you during lunch and you seem to be the first mature person my son has associated with in a long time. I'm worried sick that John is going to flunk out of college again. He's probably told you he's had a terrible track record in that respect." He stopped and cleared his throat. "I assume I can talk to you in confidence? Look, let me be frank. My son speaks very highly of you so I was hoping that if you set a good example by finishing out this term successfully, he might too."

I took a minute to think over his astonishing request before replying. "With all due respect Mr. Vanderbosch, John and I are only in one class together at Hunter. Anyway, I'm struggling a bit myself to keep up with all the reading. Since I'm not even sure whether I'll survive this semester, how could I be of any help to your son?"

"I understand," he said. "I guess it wasn't fair of me to ask. But still, if you could keep an eye on him for me, I'd really appreciate it." He turned to one of the shelves behind him, then handed me a slim volume. "Anyway, here is the book I mentioned. I bought it at a little shop near the Cathedral on our last visit to Cologne. You can borrow it if you like and send it back to me with John next time he's home for a visit."

Mr. Vanderbosch clearly meant well. He could hardly know that the last thing I wanted right then was a picture book showing all the places where Charlotte and I had been together. Still, I couldn't very well refuse, so I thanked him and slipped the book into my jacket pocket. A week or so later I returned it to John unread.

****

Over the next few weeks I saw Yvonne again whenever she, John, Ronnie, and I would get together at Ronnie's apartment, but there was never an opportunity for the two of us to be alone. After a while I began to suspect that Yvonne might even be attracted to me. Still I didn't dare ask her out on a date for fear of being rejected.

"So when are you going to make a real move on her?" John teased me. "You know you want to. Don't forget what they used to say about Goldwater before the election: 'In your heart you know *she's* right.'"

"And just look what happened to Goldwater," I retorted. "He got crushed at the polls. I guess your dad wasn't too happy about that."

"There you go changing the subject again," John scolded. "But I won't give up!"

CHAPTER 15

Christmas approached. Small children pressed against store windows along Fifth Avenue to admire the colorful mechanical holiday displays inside. The giant tree in Rockefeller Center towered over ice skaters in the rink far below. Members of the Salvation Army blew trumpets and rang bells throughout Midtown. Shoppers laden down with parcels of expensive toys from F.A.O. Schwarz jostled one another in crowded busses on their way home. Yet I had never felt quite so alone.

On December 3rd, Walter and Quincy treated me to a meal in a coffee shop to celebrate my twenty-seventh birthday. The very next day, I found another light-blue envelope from Charlotte in our mailbox, but this time the envelope had an American postage stamp and a New York City postmark. She was here!

My heart was pounding as I read her letter. *"Dear Günter,"* she wrote, *"I'm writing to you from a departure lounge at Kennedy Airport. I've been trying all afternoon to get up enough courage to call you. But I realize now that it would be a mistake. You would just be angry and I would get hurt again. So I'm going back to Cologne tonight. They're about to call my flight. Please forgive me. I love you, Charlotte."*

Walter came home from work and found me staring out the window at the crowded busses rumbling by on Madison Avenue. When I turned around he took one look at my face and asked, "Hey, what's wrong with you? Did someone die? Did you get fired?"

"Can you believe it? Charlotte was in New York for a day and she just turned around and flew home again without so much as a phone call!"

"What gave you that crazy idea?"

"Never mind crazy. Look at this postmark. How could she do this to me, come to New York and not see me?"

Walter glanced at the envelope. Then he handed it back to me and smiled. "You want to know what I think? I don't believe for one minute that she was here. She wrote the letter in Cologne and got someone to mail it for her in New York. Trust me. She wasn't here. This was her revenge because you cancelled your flight to Luxembourg last summer! Pretty devious of her, I'd say."

"I suppose you're right," I admitted, suddenly feeling more foolish than angry. "It's the only explanation that makes sense. Women are complicated creatures, aren't they?"

"And what makes you think you're any less complicated? Tell me that!"

I didn't bother to reply. We both knew the answer.

****

When I got home from class late one evening, Walter was in an unusually bad mood. "She's leaving." He practically spat out the words.

"Who's leaving? If you calm down and tell me what happened, maybe I can help."

"Anne, that's who. She's going back to Scotland to take a teaching job."

"Well, at least you had a couple of wonderful weeks together. You always knew she'd go back one day didn't you?"

"You don't get it, do you? I wanted to marry her."

"Oh. That's different. Did you ever tell her how you felt?"

"I guess I hinted at it. I never asked her straight out, if that's what you mean, but she must have known."

"Well, if she didn't appreciate you, then she's not worth stewing over. The best thing for you is to find someone who'll love you back."

"You're one to talk. You've been mooning around here over Charlotte for almost a year now and you're giving *me* advice?"

"It's different," I protested. "You want to get married and I don't."

****

Since Walter was earning twice as much as I was, he could afford to enroll in an expensive private language institute to improve his English. As luck would have it, during his first class he had met Julia, a raving beauty from Chile. From then on, Walter and Julia were nearly inseparable and Anne was quickly forgotten.

One day Walter arranged a date for me with Julia's former roommate, a short, dark-haired Israeli woman named Tamara, and the four of us went out together for dinner. Tamara had a caustic sense of humor, starting with her greeting when she met me: "*Oy vey*! That's what I call *chutzpah*, fixing me up with a guy who looks even more German than Walter." She smiled at me. "Just trying to be funny. Don't take me too seriously." I hardly knew what to respond when Tamara started in again. "Did Walter tell you that I know a few words in German? How's my pronunciation? *Gesundheit! Danke schön. Hallo! Wiedergutmachung.*"

"How come you know the word *Wiedergutmachung?*" I asked. "You pronounce it like a native. I don't even know the exact English translation."

"It means reparations for the Holocaust and, believe me, there isn't a Jew in Israel who doesn't know that word."

Walter shifted uneasily in his chair. The conversation was making him uncomfortable. "Let's change the subject, shall we? Have any of you heard the new Beatles' recording?" and, from there, we switched to movies, current events, and the weather, to Walter's evident relief.

After dinner Walter took Julia home and I escorted Tamara back to her apartment on the West Side. Maybe I had a bit too much to drink, but when we reached Tamara's building I suddenly worked up the courage to ask if I could come upstairs. Then I bent down to give her a kiss. She pushed me away.

"Are you *meshugge?*" she shouted, much to the amusement of several passersby and a doorman. "What do you take me for? You men are all alike!" and she turned her back and stormed inside. I wished I could disappear into the sidewalk.

When I slunk home like a beaten dog, Walter was still up. "So, how do you like Tamara? She's a bundle of energy, isn't she? Are you going to see her again?"

"She's a bundle of energy, all right, but she may be a bit more than I can handle. Maybe I came on too strong for a first date but the bottom line is, I don't think we'll be seeing each other again."

"And Julia, what did you think of her? I guess compared to Tamara she's somewhat reserved."

"Julia? She's a knockout and she knows it," I commented. "I hope things work out for you this time."

****

Walter and Julia asked me to go out with them to dinner and a late movie on Christmas Eve, but I decided to stay home by myself and sulk. All the holiday cheer had put me in a bad mood. I hadn't replied to Charlotte's last letter, the one she had supposedly sent from New York. How do you answer a letter like that? I'd asked Walter for advice but he had no suggestions. Even Quincy was stumped. Charlotte had played me for a fool and I guess it served me right.

I reached up to take a can of franks and beans from the shelf and was just about to light the stove when the telephone rang.

"Hi," a woman said. "This is Yvonne. Remember me?"

"Yes of course, forgive me. I didn't recognize your voice for a second. How did you get my number?"

"John gave it to me. Listen, I'm in your neighborhood. May I stop by?"

"Sure! I'd love to see you."

"Are you alone?"

"I've got the place to myself right now. My roommate's got a date."

"Great, see you soon," and she hung up.

My heart was racing as I rushed to put Charlotte's letters away into a drawer, straightened up the magazines on the coffee table, and put the unopened can of franks and beans back on the shelf. Then I brushed my teeth, tucked in my shirt, and waited. Ten minutes went by, then fifteen. *Maybe* I thought *she and John were just playing a mean joke on me.* For at least the tenth time I peeked out the window

71

onto the street below when the intercom bell rang and I buzzed to let her into the lobby. I could smell her lavender perfume even before she got to the top of the stairs. She was wearing a brown winter coat with a matching fur-lined hood. When I reached over to help her off with her coat, she kissed me right on the mouth.

"Sorry I took so long. I stopped to buy us a bottle of wine!"

"Thanks, but there was no need to do that." I found a corkscrew, opened the bottle, and poured the wine into two glasses. "Shall we toast to Christmas?"

"I don't celebrate Christmas, as you know. I was hoping to celebrate that we met and are finally alone." As we lifted our glasses Yvonne flashed an alluring smile and her eyes sparkled. She had never looked more attractive. "To us. Let's do what we've both been dreaming of!"

But whatever Yvonne and I had been dreaming of never happened and it was all my fault. I was devastated. *What I wondered must Yvonne think of me? Even worse, what would she tell John and Ronnie?*

As we lay side by side on my bed Yvonne was surprisingly sympathetic. "I guess you're still not over your German girlfriend," she said with a sigh. "I was sure enough time had gone by for you to get over her, but I suppose I was wrong."

"I'm so sorry. Really I am. I feel like an idiot."

Yvonne was about to reply when the phone rang. "Just ignore it," she urged, but it didn't stop ringing. I finally jumped out of bed and fumbled for the receiver.

"Hey, Gunter, Merry Christmas!" boomed John's voice on the other end of the line. "How're you enjoying the delicious present I arranged for you?" Then he snickered and hung up.

"Don't tell me," Yvonne said. "That was John, wasn't it? What a jerk! For the life of me I can't understand why Ronnie doesn't dump him."

Shortly before midnight I brought Yvonne down to Madison Avenue to hail her a cab. She kissed me goodbye, this time just with a quick peck on my cheek. We had missed our chance and there would never be another one.

****

It was just a few weeks after my disastrous Christmas Eve visit from Yvonne that Walter and his Chilean girlfriend, Julia, broke up. "Can you believe it? I took her tonight to see *Fiddler on the Roof* and she waited until after the final curtain to announce that she didn't want to see me any more. And you want to know why? It turns out that she's Jewish! Now I ask you, if that was such a big problem for her, why didn't she say so in the first place? Anyway, she'll be on her way back to South America before the end of this month. I have the strangest luck with women! I seem to drive them all out of the country."

Walter bounced back fast. Within weeks after Julia dumped him, he began to dress up and go out on Saturday and Sunday evenings, often returning to our apartment in the wee hours of the morning when I was sound asleep. At first Walter refused to tell me who his new girlfriend was or how they had met. He said he was afraid it might jinx the relationship and he didn't want it to end like his previous ones. But after a few weeks he couldn't keep the secret any longer. "I don't know what you're going to make of it," he confessed with a sheepish grin. "It's Tamara. I'm crazy about her."

"She doesn't mind that you're German and she's Jewish?"

"I think we can work through that if we're going to have a future together."

"You're already thinking about marrying her? Aren't you rushing things a bit? It wasn't so long ago that you wanted to marry Anne."

"It's the real thing this time. I'm sure of it." After some hesitation, he continued, "She's asked me to convert to Judaism."

"It's that serious? And what did you tell her?"

"You'll probably think I'm crazy, but I'm going to do it. I only pay lip service to Catholicism anyway. I began to skip Mass when I was fourteen because I felt closer to God taking long hikes in the forest than I did in church. And then, when I went to Rome a few years later and saw the Vatican—the pomp, the fancy robes, the art, the gold, the silver, all those precious stones—I was totally disgusted. Is that what they were supporting with the money we put in the collection plate?"

"That's no reason to convert. Every religion asks for money. I'm sure the Jews do, too. And at least some of it must go to good causes."

"Well, all the same, I've decided to convert to Judaism. I'll have to study with a rabbi and start attending synagogue. That's the easy part."

"What's the hard part?"

He bit his lip before replying. "This is why I've been reluctant to talk to you about it. I'd have to get circumcised."

I instinctively grabbed my crotch. "You're kidding, right? There'd be no turning back after that."

"My mind's made up."

"I'm speechless. I don't know what to say."

Walter grinned. "If I can borrow a phase I learned from *Fiddler on the Roof,* how about *mazel tov?*"

CHAPTER 16

"I really need to improve my English," I confessed to Walter and Quincy a few weeks into the spring semester at Hunter. "It's hard to keep up with all the reading."

"Your problem with English reminds me of a joke I heard at my NYU reunion." Quincy said. "An old African-American professor received honorary degrees from several famous universities, mainly due to the bad conscience of the white man." Here he paused to check our reactions but, since neither of us blinked, he continued. "Anyhow this professor retires from Howard University and is interviewed by a TV reporter: 'Professor Washington, I understand you have honorary doctorates from the Sorbonne, from Oxford, and from Harvard,' and the professor smiles proudly and replies, 'Yes, sir, I does!'" Quincy turned to me and beamed, "So what should he have said?"

"Shouldn't he have said, 'Yes, sir, I do?'"

Quincy slapped his thigh. "I gotcha! It was a trick question. Have you forgotten what I've taught you? *No man should ever say 'I do!'*"

"Sorry, I don't get the joke."

"That's what you say when you get married," Walter explained.

"But the grammar?"

"Your grammar was just fine," Quincy assured me. "Listen, Gunter, all kidding aside, if I were you, I would sign up for English in Action. They match foreigners and native-born American speakers for weekly one-on-one conversations. In my book, there's no better way to learn."

"How on earth do you find out about all this stuff?"

"I keep my eyes and ears open, that's how. Anyway, if you decide to go to English in Action, let me know what you think of it."

****

The receptionist at English in Action assigned me to Mark Silverberg, a short, elderly gentleman with forward sloping shoulders and thick, snow-white hair. In our first hour together Mr. Silverberg told me that in 1912, when he was eighteen years old, his father, a manufacturer of children's apparel, had sent him first to Paris and then to Berlin to work as a sales representative for the family business. He had spent a year in each location and had become fluent in both French and German when, in 1914, with war on the horizon, he had sailed back home. After a few years in his father's New York City office, he had gone on the road as a travelling salesman for the company. As he put it, "If there was ever a road to drive on back in those days, I took it!"

When it was my turn to talk, I noticed that Mr. Silverberg cupped his ear and leaned forward to hear what I had to say over the din of a dozen other conversations going on all around us. At the end of the hour, he made a suggestion.

"You mentioned that you're taking another class with Professor Hanley this semester and an English for foreigners course at NYU but you must have at least one weeknight free."

"I don't have any classes on Wednesdays."

"Well, then, how about coming to my place on East 36th Street on Wednesday evenings? I usually get home from my office at 6 p.m. and you should be able to get uptown from the A&P by then. That way we'll have a quiet place to talk for an hour and then Esther, she's my colored housekeeper, can fix us both supper."

"That sounds great, Mr. Silverberg. I'll be there!"

"Please call me Mark," he said with a smile.

From then on I went to Mark Silverberg's apartment every Wednesday night. The routine was always the same. Mark would take the latest edition of *The New York Times* from his briefcase or he would open a copy of *Time* magazine, and then he would ask me to read articles aloud. He would listen attentively, occasionally correcting my pronunciation.

"Remember, Gunter," he would remind me, "it's *have* not *haf*." Or, again, "*Father* not *fatha*."

When I finished reading each article, Mark would challenge me to repeat the gist in my own words. His method not only improved my English, it also taught me a great deal about current events. For example, we went over President Johnson's inaugural address together line by line and Mark had me memorize the words, "*I do not believe that the Great Society is the ordered, changeless, and sterile battalion of the ants*," a phrase that I somehow found more creepy than inspiring. And, of course, we discussed the pros and cons of the escalating tensions in Vietnam. Mark was less interested in talking about the incipient struggle for civil rights in the South. For those details, I depended on Quincy to keep me up to date.

The whole time we were talking I could hear the clatter of pots and the soft sounds of hymns coming from the kitchen. Esther, Mark Silverberg's 'colored housekeeper' as he put it, was a petite woman with frizzled gray hair who had been born in a wooden shack somewhere in the Deep South. It was the highlight of the evening when she came into the living room to announce that dinner was ready. Esther's specialties were mouthwatering Southern fried chicken, chicken potpie, fried okra, black-eyed peas, cornbread, and peach or apple cobblers.

"Well, I sure am glad you're here, Mr. Gunter," she exclaimed to me later that first night as she returned from the kitchen to clear away my empty plate. "You know, that Mr. Silverberg, he don't eat hardly enough. I used to think it was my cookin'. But that sure ain't it, cause I see how much you like it."

Between my conversations with Mark Silverberg and Esther's dinners I was being nourished mind, body, and soul. And, what meant even more to me was that, despite our different backgrounds, they both saw me simply as a young man with a healthy appetite who was ready to learn.

CHAPTER 17

I was bored to death at my job in the A&P and one day I finally worked up the courage to request a better opportunity within the company. As a result, I was transferred to the Candy Department. My new office was in company headquarters in the Graybar Building on Lexington Avenue not far from Grand Central Station and within walking distance of my apartment. But by the second day there, I discovered that no one in that division had actually wanted me to be there. Someone higher up had brought pressure to bear and my presence was deeply resented.

The department's main function was to assign teams of five or six tasters to spend several hours a day evaluating assorted domestic and imported products: licorice, chocolates, caramels, jawbreakers, and jelly beans, just to name a few. Following the tasting, the team would meet to vote on the results. Then one person would be selected to write a memo to our supervisor, Mr. Brandon, who, it was soon apparent to me, preferred the taste of hard liquor to that of candy.

After two weeks on the job it fell to me to write the daily memo. Less than five minutes after the memo reached his desk, Mr. Brandon stormed over to where my group was sitting, held up the memo, hiccoughed loudly, and bellowed, "WHO WROTE THIS CRAP?" Clearly, this didn't bode well and when, a few days later, it was suggested to me that if things didn't work out for me in the Candy Department I could always work elsewhere in the company as a typist, I knew my days at the A&P were numbered.

The showdown came in the middle of March when Mr. Brandon urged me to take a position at one of the company's candy manufacturing plants somewhere in Pennsylvania. I turned him down and he fired me on the spot.

****

Since my parting of the ways with the A&P had come as no surprise, I had already contacted an employment agency about possible alternatives. I soon received a call from the agency setting up an appointment for me with William Ducat, the co-owner with his brother Joe of Brewster, Leeds & Company on West 38th Street. An hour later an elevator brought me to the fourth floor of their building and the door opened, not to a lobby, but to a large office, where roughly thirty people were sitting at their desks either making phone calls or typing. With the exception of the receptionist, no one bothered to look up when I walked in.

William Ducat was ensconced in a spacious, air-conditioned office behind thick double doors. He stood up when I came in, solemnly reached over to shake my hand, and offered me a seat. Of medium height, with a lanky frame, and balding, he wore a tailored gray suit, a dress shirt, and a silk tie. He spoke English with the heavy accent of his native Austria.

"I don't know what they told you at the agency," he began, "but just so you know, we are in the food export business. Based on your résumé I see that you've worked in the food industry both in Germany and here in New York, but our operation is probably unlike any place you've previously been. In simplest terms, we sell food from American manufacturers to importers and wholesalers in roughly fifty different countries."

"That sounds quite interesting, sir."

"Your job would be to process orders, taking into account quantities, prices, and rebates, and then to prepare the information for the typing pool. You'd also be spending considerable time on the telephone calling suppliers and shipping companies. Our hours are from 8 a.m. to 5 p.m. and then we all go home. I don't believe in the effectiveness of overtime. The pay is $100 a week. The possibility of your moving up to a sales job in the future is slim at best. I certainly wouldn't count on it. Listen, I've got to be honest with you. In my opinion, you're way overqualified for the job. You'd pick it up in a week and then it will turn into a mindless routine. So, now that you've heard me out, how does the position sound to you?"

The offer was hardly enticing, but I needed the money and the hours wouldn't interfere with my studies at Hunter. I swallowed hard and forced myself to smile. "If it's all right with you, sir, I'd like to take the job."

"Well, in that case, my brother would also like to meet you. I'm in charge of finances. Joe deals with marketing and sales."

William Ducat brought me to an adjoining office, which, unlike his own, had a simple wooden door. Joe Ducat was a heavyset, humorless man. He wore a white dress shirt with rolled up sleeves, a bright green tie, and brown suspenders to hold up his trousers over his bulging stomach. The few tufts of hair he had left appeared to be glued to the top of his scalp with a thick application of Brylcreem. He was helping himself to some brightly colored snacks when we came in. Quickly swallowing whatever it was he had been chewing on, he stood to greet us.

"One thing my brother may not have mentioned," he said, "is that the most lucrative aspect of our business is the export of closeout lots of discontinued food products from U.S. food manufacturers. If it is no longer selling here, we find a market for it overseas. We're the laxative of the American food industry. You do know what a closeout lot is, right?" I nodded and made a mental note to look up the words later. "You'll be the assistant to Mr. Leon so your desk will be in his office. If you don't have any questions, we'll expect you here bright and early and ready to roll on Thursday, April 1st."

Much to my relief, in contrast to the solemn Ducat brothers, Mr. Leon had a winning smile and a constant twinkle in his blue eyes. He was about forty-five years old, of medium build, with wide shoulders, and curly salt and pepper hair. "You have to have a good sense of humor around here," he explained to me on my first day. "After all, a big part of our job is to find buyers in third-world countries and convince them that they need vast quantities of cheese puffs or chewing gum or potato chips. Hell, we even sell frozen white bread to Saudi Arabia. And we import, too. Specialty items like chocolate-covered ants from Brazil and fried grasshoppers from Mexico. Don't look so disgusted. There's a market for that stuff."

The products were interesting and varied. My job was not. Mr. Leon was on the telephone more than half of the time while I prepared long, detailed reports. Since I spent my time in Mr. Leon's office, I didn't have much of a chance to interact with other members of the staff, a diverse group, which included African-Americans, Cubans, Puerto Ricans, Nicaraguans, and Panamanians. For the first few days, I went out alone for lunch. Then, one day Andy, a chubby, bespectacled young man from the typing pool asked if I would like to join him at a Cuban restaurant that sold inexpensive sandwiches.

"So," he asked me quite out of the blue as we sat down to our meal, "you're not Jewish are you?"

"No. Why do you ask?"

"Well, I was wondering what it's like for you to work for a Jew like Mr. Leon. You do know that he's Jewish, right? Same for his cousins, the Ducats."

"No, I didn't know. But anyway why should that make a difference?"

Andy's face flushed. "I guess it doesn't," he mumbled and he quickly changed the subject.

Actually, I couldn't have had a nicer boss than Mr. Leon who, during rare moments of down time, spoke to me in German about his life.

"I may as well tell you that my real name is Leon Begleiter. Most Americans get tongue-tied when they try to pronounce my last name so it's just easier to go by 'Mr. Leon.'"

"Am I right that, judging from your accent, you're not from Austria?"

"You've got a good ear. I was born in Germany, in Dortmund to be exact, where my father owned a shoe store before the war. Back in 1933, when I was fourteen and attending the Gymnasium, I was damned if I was going to glorify the Storm Troopers so I refused to sing the 'Horst Wessel' song with the rest of my class. Well, my teacher called my father to warn him that he wouldn't be able to protect me from the authorities. And my father shipped me off to work as a farmhand for friends of his in Holland."

"I'm sorry that you had to go through all that," I said.

"Look, I know that none of this had anything to do with you. You weren't even born then!"

"But then the Germans invaded Holland."

"But not until 1940 and by then I'd been living in Palestine for a year. That's where I learned Hebrew while working on a Kibbutz. I guess you don't know what that is. A Kibbutz is a kind of socialistic farm where everyone shares in everything. Then from 1939 until 1943 I served in the British Army in Palestine and afterwards I had a succession of odd jobs in Israeli restaurants until I came to the United States in 1948."

"Is that when you started working for your cousins?"

"Not at first. I was a waiter at the Vienna Café over on West 77th Street near the Museum of Natural History before starting here."

"You should write a book!"

"Believe me, I've mailed off some stories to publishers but I never heard back from any of them." He grinned. "Nobody gives a damn about a German Jewish boy from Dortmund. There are way too many stories like mine."

CHAPTER 18

Shortly after my conversation with Leon Begleiter, a young French couple from my English for Foreigners class at NYU told me about a party being given by a French professor on the Upper West Side. "Why don't you join us?" they suggested. "There'll be at least fifty people there so one more won't make a difference."

The French professor lived in a three-story brownstone on a side street just off of West End Avenue. When I arrived shortly after 8 p.m. I could see through the open windows on every floor that the party was already in full swing. I worked my way up to the top floor but didn't find my classmates or anyone else I knew for that matter.

On the second floor landing a petite lady with a charming French accent tapped me on the shoulder. I guessed she was about ten years my senior. "I seem to have lost my friends in this crowd. It looks like you're trying to find someone, too."

"I've given up," I replied. "I'll never find them with all these people."

"Excuse me, but are you German?"

"Yes. How did you know?"

"Your accent. It's a dead giveaway. We New Yorkers have good antennas for that sort of thing."

"I've only been here about a year so I'm still learning."

"Mind telling me how old you are?"

I touched my sideburns, which had recently turned prematurely gray. *She's probably hoping I'm closer to her age* I thought. "I'm twenty-seven, why?"

"Oh just so." She smiled. Apparently my answer had satisfied her because for the next hour we stood apart from the other guests and chatted about a wide range of topics: the sumptuous menu on the S.S. *France*, museums in Paris and New York, favorite movies. Despite the difference in our ages, I was considering asking her for a date when she reached up to put her empty wine glass on a nearby shelf. Her sleeve slid back to reveal the concentration camp number tattooed on her forearm.

Instinctively, I reached over to touch her arm. My hand was shaking and I felt sick to my stomach. "Are you upset about this?" she asked, pointing to her arm. "It's a souvenir from my forced vacation in Poland during the war."

"It's just . . . I mean . . . It's just that I've never seen anyone before with that, with that . . . I'm sorry."

"I didn't mean to get you so upset," she said. "And I certainly don't blame you for what happened to me if that makes any difference. You were too young."

"It's more complicated than that. Listen, I hope you don't mind, but I think I should leave."

With so much to think about I decided to walk home through Central Park in the dark. I couldn't believe it. I had just spent an hour engaging in meaningless small talk with a beautiful young woman who had been in a concentration camp. I had read about those things, of course. And they'd been shown on German television not long before I left for America. But nothing prepared me for the shock of seeing that tattoo with its precise German-style crossed "7's."

I got teary-eyed as I thought about my mother's father, my beloved Opa, having been forced by the Russians to use his bare hands to unearth the bodies of Jewish women who had been slaughtered by the SS in the last days of the war. The experience broke his heart and his spirit and sent him to an early grave. I could have told her about that.

But then there were the things I couldn't talk about. There was my father, who bragged about his low membership number in the Nazi Party and fondly recalled the heads he had bashed at Communist rallies with his fellow Storm Troopers. And my Uncle Bruno, my father's brother, who cynically insisted that Jews had themselves tattooed after 1945 in order to collect money from the German government. There was even a joke in the family that Uncle Bruno slept with his arm stiffly raised in salute.

Like I said, it was definitely complicated.

CHAPTER 19

*T*owards the end of our lease term, our landlady at 807 Madison Avenue informed us that she needed our apartment for one of her employees. So, on June 1, 1965, Walter and I packed our things and moved into a house in Woodside, Queens, leaving behind our upstairs neighbor with all of his bravado about women and his wild dreams of restitution. At Walter's insistence, and despite my objections, we didn't give Quincy our new address.

The new place was close to the jewelry factory where Walter worked, but I was back to using the subway to get to my job at Brewster, Leeds. Our landlord was a master carpenter who was living the American dream, having managed to acquire half a dozen houses in Queens. He had recently retired to live off the rents. But Rudolf also had his dark side. He had been born in New York in 1930 to German immigrant parents, but shortly before the beginning of World War II, his father had moved the family back to Germany, joined the *Wehrmacht*, and fought for Hitler and the Fatherland. When Rudolf eventually returned to Queens, he did not look kindly on African-Americans and Jews.

Between the house Walter and I were in and another house our landlord owned next door, there were twelve of us altogether, eight in our building and four in the other. Our building had two units, each of which had a large living room, a kitchen, and two small bedrooms. We slept two to a room. I shared space in the apartment on the second floor of one of the buildings; Walter, who shared a room with another young German in the apartment downstairs, was away most of the time, either at work or with Tamara.

The three young men on my floor were a motley crew to say the least. My roommate, Earl Ferguson, was a tall, gangly, pipe-smoking, socially awkward twenty-year-old South Carolinian who worked as an NBC intern. Unfortunately for Earl, who aspired to be a stand-up comic, apart from his gawky appearance, there wasn't much that anyone found funny about him.

José Ortega, a student at a technical college in Manhattan, who had only recently arrived from Mexico City, and David Kohn, a college graduate from Connecticut who worked for AT&T, shared the other bedroom. When David talked, he looked up at the ceiling as his eyes rapidly darted back and forth. I was in his debt because he was willing to correct several of my papers for Hunter, so I gritted my teeth and put up with his habit of returning home after work, dropping his trousers onto the living room floor, guzzling a glass of orange juice, and plopping down in front of the TV in his boxer shorts. Despite this strange behavior, David had a steady girlfriend, a graduate student in German literature.

José, on the other hand, was a ladies' man. He regularly brought home one pretty coed after another. His routine never varied. First he would cook his latest flame a spicy Mexican meal, somehow managing to use every single pot in the kitchen. Then, blithely leaving behind a cluttered pile of unwashed dishes, he would often manage to cajole

David into spending the night on the living room couch so that José and his latest sweetheart could take over their bedroom.

When it came to keeping things clean around our apartment, my other roommates weren't much better than José. I was the only one who began to notice the small army of ants and the occasional cockroach feasting on the leftovers in our kitchen. No amount of arm-twisting could get my roommates to clean up the mess but, for that, I probably had myself to blame. They knew if they just waited long enough that I would end up doing it myself.

****

Since we lived in neighboring buildings, the tenants next door—Jochen Kleinman, a junior shipping company executive from Hamburg; William Exeter, an Englishman majoring in economics; and Stu Baxter who was originally from Rhode Island—were also part of our social group. Our landlord had recently placed an ad to find them a fourth roommate and they had already interviewed a prospective tenant from Brooklyn.

I had gone over to watch *The Ed Sullivan Show* with the three of them later that same day when our landlord, Rudolf, stormed in. "This will just take a minute," he said as William reluctantly reached over to turn off the TV. "We need to talk about that fat, red-headed what's-his-name Ira Birnbaum you met today. What do you think? I mean, if you want him to live here, fine. But quite frankly, I already have one Jew boy in the other house and now this one turns up? Before you know it they'll be taking over the entire building. As far as I'm concerned, if you want me to, I'll run the ad again."

"There's no need," William said sharply, "We all liked him."

"Yeah, don't bother," Jochen agreed. "He's a pre-med student and he made a good impression on us, right Stu? We've got nothing against his moving in."

Rudolph shook his head. "I won't argue with you but I sure as hell hope you boys know what you're doing."

I had to grin when I thought about Walter's planned conversion. He would make it three.

****

The living room in the neighboring house was double the size of ours and it also had a much larger kitchen. Since they had the space, William, Jochen, Stu, and Ira often threw parties on Friday and Saturday evenings to which we were each expected to contribute some food or a six-pack of beer. Woodside, Queens, wasn't far from LaGuardia Airport and, after the word got around, there were always a good number of stewardesses, ticket agents, and other airline personnel in attendance. There were always more women than men.

It was at one of those parties in early June that I met Carmen, a vivacious Ecuadorian girl with pitch-black hair and beautiful brown skin. She was fun to be with as well as a wonderful cook. But there was one small problem. By the middle of August, she had already brought up the subject of marriage and I started to look for a way to break things off. As it turned out, she made it easy for me.

"You keep telling me 'no' but I'm sure I can get you to say 'yes'," she insisted when I tried to change the subject once again. "When we go to Staten Island next Saturday I'll have a big surprise for you!"

But Carmen couldn't have been more wrong. When I came to pick her up for our date, I scarcely recognized her. She had dyed her lustrous black hair a ghastly shade of platinum blond.

"See! I figured out what was missing," she proudly announced as she spun around. "Now I look like a German girl."

"My God" I gasped. "What have you done?"

With tears in her eyes she asked, "You don't like it?"

"Listen, Carmen, believe me, you might as well have dyed your hair purple or green for all the difference it would make. I really meant it when I said that I'm just not the marrying type."

We still went to Staten Island where we took a long walk and had dinner in an Italian restaurant before we went back to her place on West 48th Street. The whole time we were together I was praying we wouldn't run into anyone I knew. I never called her again.

CHAPTER 20

*I*t was October, and nearly a year had passed since my visit to the Vanderbosch home in Darien, Connecticut. What would John's parents think of me now as I sat down with Ira Birnbaum to help him study French?

"I have to learn the language if I'm going to be able to study medicine in Brussels," he had explained to me. "But I'm having trouble getting the hang of it."

And no wonder, I thought. Ira pronounced each word phonetically. *Garçon* became gar-kon. *S'il vous plaît* sounded like sill voos plate. The result was a language no self-respecting Frenchman would recognize.

"That didn't sound right, did it?" Ira said after another failed attempt to repeat what I had said.

"Have you ever studied any other languages?" I finally asked in desperation.

"I know Yiddish. My parents speak it at home."

"Well, in that case, you'd have no trouble at all picking up German. I'm willing to bet you could be fluent in six months to a year.

So here's an idea. I can help you learn German and then you could study medicine in Germany. How about it? "

"You're joking, right? I wouldn't set one foot in Germany if you paid me."

Just then Jochen walked in from the kitchen apparently having overheard the last part of our conversation. "Hey, Ira! You don't know what you're missing. The war's been over for twenty years now and things have changed."

"For you maybe," Ira replied. "But not for a Jew from Brooklyn like me."

****

Later that same day, I returned to the house next door for a party. As I checked out the room for a possible replacement for Carmen, an unusually tall woman with long dark brown hair caught my eye. She had been standing off to one side, wine glass in hand, but now she pushed her way through the crowd and came over to me. "Hi I'm Jackie, Jackie Schmidt. And like just about everyone else around here, I work for an airline in Manhattan. And you are . . . ?"

"Gunter Nitsch."

"Hello, Gunter Nitsch," she said as she tossed back her head to finish off the rest of the wine. "Mind getting me another glass?"

Her bright smile didn't match up with her downcast eyes. She constantly twisted a loose strand of her hair or reached over to brush away an imaginary speck of dust from my jacket. She wasn't even especially pretty. And she drank like a fish. All the warning signs were there, but she had a gorgeous figure and when she asked me to come spend the night at her place, I chose to ignore them.

A thick layer of dust coated the surfaces of Jackie's studio apartment and the scatter rug nearest to the couch had several cigarette burns. When we walked in Jackie quickly gathered up the piles of dirty laundry strewn about on the floor and shoved them under her bed. Her refrigerator was stocked with beer and wine—and nothing else. And still I stayed. She had something to offer that I badly needed and I was intent on getting it.

Every week or so after that, I swallowed my pride and travelled to Manhattan to spend the night with Jackie. On Thanksgiving Day the two of us were invited to dinner by her brother, an executive with a Fortune 500 company, who lived in Westchester County with his wife and his three young children.

"So, we finally get to meet you!" Roger Schmidt enthused. "From what we've been hearing, the two of you are going to be a great match. And I can certainly see why. I'm sure you've noticed that my little sister is usually shy around men. It's because of her height, you know. And most men are also put off because we're all such neat freaks. Our family's originally from Germany, which is where *that* comes from I suppose. But you're from Prussia, I understand, so you know all about that."

I hardly knew how to respond. Was he talking about the same Jackie? "Well, she certainly is tall," I finally replied. "That's for sure."

"Forgive me. I'm being a bad host," Roger Schmidt continued. "Come in! Take off your coats! Let's have some turkey!"

****

"Why do the women I date always want to spoil things by bringing up marriage?" I complained to William and Jochen when the three of us went out for a beer on the Sunday after Thanksgiving. The two of them exchanged glances.

"Listen, Gunter," William said, "we've got to level with you." He stopped and looked over at Jochen.

"They all want to get married," Jochen continued. "Every last one of them. But with Jackie there's more to it than that. How much do you really know about her?"

"I know what she's good at, if that's what you mean."

"That's just it. How can I put this?" He fidgeted with his cocktail napkin.

William jumped in. "Let me come right out and say it. We're all pretty sure she hasn't bothered to tell you that she had a baby about a month or so before you moved in with us.

"Jackie has a child? I don't believe it."

"It's true. A little boy. She gave him up for adoption. And since that time she's slept with more of the guys who come to our parties than you want to know about."

"And everyone knew about this except me?"

"Pretty much." Jochen shook his head. "Sorry, man. We drew straws to decide who was going to break the news to you, and the two of us lost."

****

The next day I called Jackie at her office in Manhattan and asked if I could come over to see her right after work. "How nice! I'll be home by 6:00. See you then," she chirped.

As soon as she closed the door to her apartment I confronted her with what I'd heard. "Is what they told me true?"

She began to sob. "I haven't dated all that many guys. That's an outright lie!"

"And the baby?"

"Okay, it happened like this. I'd been going out with someone I met at work for almost a year when he was transferred to Chicago. A few weeks later I discovered I was pregnant so I called to tell him. 'Come on out to O'Hare. I'll meet you at the airport, and everything will work out just fine.' That's what he told me and I was dumb enough to think he was going to propose to me. But that bastard just handed me a couple of hundred dollars and the address where I could get an abortion and then he left me standing there at the gate."

"But you decided to keep the baby?"

"Do you know how many women die from those back-alley abortions? I may have been upset but I wasn't suicidal!" Her eyes narrowed. "My family was right to warn me about him. He was just a typical Jew who thought he could buy his way out of trouble." Then she dried her eyes and flashed me her most alluring smile. "That's why they were so glad I met you."

"You're telling me that it's all the fault of his religion. C'mon, whatever he did to you, I'm sure his religion had nothing to do with it."

"Boy, are you naïve. Of course it did. It had everything to do with it. Why else wouldn't he have wanted to marry me when he got me knocked up?"

At that moment I could think of at least a dozen good reasons and any one of them was reason enough to leave, which is exactly what I did.

CHAPTER 21

"**Y**ou sure know how to pick them," Leon Begleiter teased me when we chatted during a coffee break at Brewster, Leeds a few days later. "First that peroxide blonde bombshell from Latin America and then a complete neurotic. Have you ever tried to meet someone at the Lorelei on East 86th Street where all the Germans hang out? That's where you'll most likely find someone on your same wavelength."

Leon was certainly right. I felt at home on East 86th Street. At least once a week, on the days when I didn't have class, I went uptown after work to shop at Schaller & Weber, a German butcher store on the corner of Second Avenue to buy such mouthwatering delicacies as Black Forest ham, *Leberwurst*, and *Bauernschinken*. I often got some angry glares from hungry fellow passengers on the long, hot ride back to Queens as I carried my neatly wrapped bundle of meat, which gave off an alluring aroma, but I didn't care.

On all my excursions up to 86th Street, I passed right by the Lorelei dance hall and did not go in. To be honest, Leon Begleiter had hit a nerve when he had joked with me about my bad judgment in picking women. That Jackie had managed to keep such a huge secret from me was disturbing. That my roommates knew about Jackie's secret all along and didn't bother to tell me was even more so. At the same time I was beginning to doubt that I would ever find that most elusive of females: one who was attractive and emotionally stable, who had intellectual curiosity and a big heart, but who also, like me, had no interest in getting married.

So, for the next several months I threw myself into my coursework at Hunter and studiously avoided giving the least bit of encouragement to the women I met in class, at parties, and at Roseland. During that whole time the only highlight of my week was my Wednesday evening conversation with Mark Silverberg followed by Esther's fine Southern cooking. On May 18, 1966, Mark suggested that we discuss an article from *The New York Times* about the appointment of Stokley Carmichael as Chairman of the Student Non-Violent Coordinating Committee two days earlier.

"Racial unrest is the big story right now," he explained. "It was one thing for Congress to pass the Civil Rights Act but you can't just snap your fingers and make it a reality." He smiled at me. "I don't imagine you've had too much close contact with colored folks, am I right? Other than Esther, I mean."

"I've met a few since I've been here," I said, carefully avoiding his terminology. "And we've gotten along just fine."

"Well, unfortunately, not everyone does. But I guess you already know that."

****

The Saturday following my conversation with Mark Silverberg, I finally worked up the courage to find a 'nice German girl' at the Lorelei. I stepped inside the restaurant and immediately felt right at home. The waitresses were dressed in low-cut white blouses embroidered with flowers, dark-green dirndls, and red aprons. A strong smell of dark German beer hung in the air; and the small orchestra was playing "Du kannst nicht treu sein" ("You can't be true, dear") as everyone locked arms and swayed back and forth in time to the music.

When, a few minutes later, the orchestra switched to a tune with a bouncy Latin beat, a young woman with an hourglass figure, light brown skin, a towering beehive hairdo, and five-inch heels took to the floor and, when her partner was unable to keep up with her, she danced alone. From the minute she began to dance, she lit up the room. As soon as the music stopped, I pushed my way through the small crowd that had formed around her and asked her for the next dance.

Her name was Jeanine Rondeau and she spoke English with a charming French accent.

"Where did you learn to dance like that?" was the first question I asked her.

"As a teenager in Haiti. I was '*une danseuse folklorique,*' you understand? Oh! Listen! It's a merengue! Would you like me to teach you some steps?" and, with that, I let her take the lead.

After the third or fourth dance I was totally out of breath. Jeanine, on the other hand, was just as lively as she'd been when I first saw her. "You poor thing," she teased. "Am I wearing you out?"

"Well, when they play the Viennese waltz, I'll show you what I can do."

"Wonderful! Can you do the turn in both directions?" As I walked her back to the table she took three quick steps to the right and then three quick steps to the left, nearly knocking down another couple as she spun around. Was there anything this woman couldn't do?

"Would you mind giving me another lesson next Saturday?" I asked once we had sat down. "As my date, I mean."

"*Bien sûr, mon ami*! But first you must come to dinner at my house. Are you free on Wednesday? That way you can meet my sister Martine and her little boy who live with me."

"Would Thursday work just as well? I have my English lesson every Wednesday. I could come right after work and still get to my 8:30 class."

"Thursday would be fine. And, by the way, my sister is a wonderful cook as you'll soon find out."

When I made the arrangement with Jeanine, I'd completely forgotten that our Mexican roommate, José, was flying back home that Thursday morning and I had agreed to help him bring his luggage to Madison Avenue and 40th Street where he would catch the bus to the airport. That meant leaving Queens much earlier than usual. Add to that my job at Brewster, Leeds and my late evening class, it was going to be a very long day.

"What on earth do you have in here? Bricks?" I asked as José and I each dragged a heavy suitcase onto the subway.

"LPs. I just couldn't resist. Dylan, the Beatles, the Stones. You name it. I bought it." He grinned. "My parents are going to hate them, I'm afraid. They're more into Frank Sinatra and Bing Crosby. That stuff puts me to sleep. Oh, and before I forget, if you ever get down to Mexico City, be sure to look me up."

After my early morning start followed by my boring job at Brewster, Leeds, I was dragging my feet as I stopped to buy a bottle of white wine on my way up to Jeanine's West Side apartment, but as soon as she greeted me at the door, I was reenergized. No one, I was sure, could resist her smile. Jeanine lived with her sister and her five-year-old nephew in a spotless two-bedroom apartment on the tenth floor of a high-rise building. Colorful paintings of tropical fruits and palm trees hung on the living room walls and brightly glazed bowls with abstract patterns in yellow, black, and orange were neatly arranged on the coffee table.

Martine, Jeanine's older sister, came out of the kitchen to meet me. "*Mon Dieu!* I thought Jeanine was exaggerating when she told me how tall you are. But don't worry. I'm cooking a lot of food. We can eat in about half an hour." Martine then spoke to her sister for a few minutes in a language I couldn't understand before disappearing into the kitchen.

"Was that a kind of French? I thought I caught a few words."

"It's Creole. Some French, some African words, and a few other things mixed in. The nuns taught me French in Haiti. I even had four years of Latin. And what good does that do me here?"

Suddenly Jeanine turned to the little boy who was sitting on the couch in front of the television set. "Teddy! Come over here and say hello to Gunter." Without taking his eyes from the screen, Teddy gave a little wave in my direction. Jeanine went over to turn down the volume a bit. Then she and I sat down in the two armchairs to talk. "So," she began, "you've told me about your job in the food export company. Let me tell you what I do. I supervise the girls who model our dresses. When the buyers come in from all over the country, I make sure they look their best."

"You're looking pretty great yourself," I said.

"You like my dress? It's from my company." She stood up and slowly turned around. "I can't ask the models to look their best if I don't myself. Am I right?"

"Um, Jeanine," I interrupted, "do you know that Teddy is watching the news?"

"He watches everything. News, sports, cartoons, why?"

"Because they're showing a report about a Buddhist monk who set himself on fire in South Vietnam. Should he be watching that?"

"Martine lets him watch whatever he wants. She figures he'll learn about the world that way. Anyway, later on he'll be watching garbage like *Batman* and *F Troop*. It kind of balances itself out, don't you think?" She lowered her voice. "Besides, the TV is a cheap and easy babysitter. Otherwise Martine wouldn't get any time for herself, isn't that so?"

I glanced back over at the sullen child on the couch. "Give me a minute. I have an idea," I said and I reached into my briefcase and tore a sheet of paper from my class notebook.

"What are you going to do with that?"

"I'd like to make him a paper airplane."

"Did you hear that, Teddy?" Jeanine said. "Gunter's going to make you an airplane. Do you want to watch him?" Teddy firmly shook his head, his eyes still glued to the screen.

It was only when I finally let the paper airplane sail across the whole living room that Teddy's eyes lit up. "*Manman, manman,*" he shrieked in Creole. "Come and look!" Martine and Jeanine watched in amazement while Teddy let me show him how to throw the airplane to get the most distance. And then, while I took out another sheet of paper to teach him how to make his own airplane, Jeanine quietly walked over to the TV and turned it off.

****

Martine had cooked a delicious meal: chicken marinated in a lemon and tomato sauce and then sprinkled with cashew nuts; rice mixed with kidney beans; and buttery okra. "The chicken is a specialty from Cap-Haitien in the northern part of our country. We call it *poul ak nwa*. I hope you like it," Martine said.

"Everything's delicious. I just hope I don't fall asleep in class after all this rich food!"

"And the wine," Jeanine added as she refilled her sister's glass. Then she looked down at her place setting. "Martine! You forgot to bring us spoons for the ice cream!" and Martine dutifully returned to the kitchen to get them. "Martine only has a part-time job so she has time to pick up Teddy from kindergarten," Jeanine explained to me while her sister was in the other room. "And when she and Teddy get back home she does everything for me: cook, clean, wash laundry. Isn't she a gem?"

Martine returned from the kitchen with the spoons. Then she cleared away the supper dishes and brought back four heaping dishes of vanilla ice cream topped with shredded coconut. "You know," I said as I ate my dessert, "I couldn't help noticing that you eat like Europeans." (Except for Teddy, that was, but I didn't want to say so.)

"You mean the way we hold our forks and knives?" Martine smiled. "The way Americans do it, I just can't understand. It's complicated, yes?"

"Even the rich ones do it that way," Jeanine added. "I once tried to copy the way they were eating in an expensive French restaurant and I got all tangled up, I could never learn it!"

I looked at my watch. "Forgive me, ladies. I wish I could stay longer. But if I don't run for the cross-town bus now, I'm going to be late for class. Thanks for the wonderful meal, Martine. It was nice meeting you, Teddy."

Jeanine walked me to the door. "Shall I come pick you up on Saturday around 8 p.m.?" I asked.

"*À bientôt!* See you then," she replied and she gave me a quick kiss.

CHAPTER 22

*O*n Saturday, as planned, Jeanine and I went back to the Lorelei. After we were shown to a table and I had ordered *Sauerbraten* for both of us, Jeanine looked around at the crowd. "The few colored people who come here are all from the islands, you know," she confided. "I'm glad American Negroes haven't discovered the Lorelei."

"Wait a minute! How can you tell that they're not Americans if you can't hear what they're saying?"

"That's easy. It's the way they dance; the way they gesture; the way they dress."

"Are you're telling me that you don't like to be around African-Americans? I just assumed . . ."

"Because we're all black, that we'd all get along? Do all white people get along? Let me ask you that."

"No, of course not. But still . . . shouldn't you judge each person for himself?"

"It has nothing to do with skin color. I can't really explain it. I just feel more comfortable around people who come from my own culture, that's all."

"Speaking of skin color, can I ask you a personal question? Do you and Martine have the same parents? I mean, you're so much lighter."

"Because I'm *café au lait* and Martine is dark brown? You should see our younger sister, Jacqueline. Her skin's so light that people take her for Italian or Spanish. And, yes, we do have the same parents. When people in the Caribbean have children, they never know what they will get. For example, I have good hair, nearly straight, Jacqueline's hair is even better then mine. But you saw Martine. She's tried all kinds of straightening creams but her hair stays just as kinky. It's as if, with each child they had, we just got lighter and lighter. If they'd had another one, I've often wondered if she would have been an albino." She laughed. "Don't look so serious. I was just joking." Then she reached over to pull me up from my chair. "C'mon, let's dance!"

****

In the weeks that followed, my life fell into a regular pattern. On Thursday evenings I would have dinner with Jeanine, Martine, and Teddy in their apartment. Once the semester ended at Hunter and I didn't have to rush off to class, I usually didn't leave for home until 11 p.m. On Saturday evenings, Jeanine and I would go to the Lorelei, or to a Jamaican restaurant on the Upper West Side, or to a jazz club in Greenwich Village, and then we would spend the night together at her place.

Hanging two-deep on pink satin hangers hooked over the double rows of poles in Jeanine's walk-in bedroom closet was a colorful assortment of dresses, skirts, blouses, and tailored jackets in cotton, linen, silk, and wool. Neatly lined up below them in a special wire rack on the closet floor were eight pairs of stiletto-heeled shoes in shades of red, pink, yellow, and green. My feet hurt just to look at them.

Her dresser top was cluttered with powder compacts, eye shadow and eye liners, assorted shades of lipsticks and rouges, a dozen kinds of Revlon nail polish ranging from bright red to coral, and a selection of the finest French perfumes from Chanel, Guerlain, Christian Dior, Lancôme, and Givenchy, just to name a few. Jeanine wore a different sweet fragrance each week, often letting me choose one for her from her collection. Each time she asked, I deliberately avoided picking out *L'Air du Temps*. It was still too evocative of Charlotte.

On a sultry Saturday evening in July, I put on my dark blue suit, a white dress shirt with French cuffs, and a tie. For this special occasion, Jeanine was wearing a bright yellow cocktail dress, a pearl necklace, and lemon-colored heels. We both looked our best as we headed over to the Americana Hotel where I had made reservations for a performance by Trini Lopez. It was a special treat for Jeanine who was in the habit of humming "Lemon Tree" whenever we walked together in Central Park. Just to be on the safe side, we arrived more than forty-five minutes early to be sure to get good seats.

Only a few of the tables were already occupied. Even so the maitre d', with an air of disdain, briskly ushered us to a table on the far left side of the room directly behind a column and just outside the swinging doors to the kitchen.

"There must be some mistake," I protested. "Why on earth are you giving us the worst table in the entire place? We have a reservation!"

Jeanine pulled on my sleeve. "Gunter, don't you understand? It's because of me." She turned to the maitre d'. "Isn't that so, sir?"

Now my blood was boiling and I raised my voice loud enough to be heard throughout the room. *"If you think you can stick my girlfriend and me in this godforsaken corner, you are sadly mistaken.* I insist on talking to your supervisor!" During my tirade, the other early arrivals stopped their conversations and turned to stare at us.

"My apologies, sir," the maitre d' stammered, and he led us to a table near the stage. By that time, the place was starting to fill up and the maitre d' rushed back to his post. The other guests were mostly white, although there were a few Latino couples. With the exception of Jeanine, there were no other blacks in the audience.

The concert was wonderful and, at the end, when Trini Lopez sang "If I had a Hammer" as an encore, everyone sang along.

On our way out I glared at the maitre d'. "You're not still upset, are you?" Jeanine gently chided me.

"No, I guess not. I was just wondering if he was listening to the words. You know, the part about love between my brothers and my sisters all over this land."

"Do you really think it would make any difference if he had?"

"And it doesn't make you angry? Being treated that way, I mean?"

"*Écoute, mon chéri.* What good would it do? After a while, you just learn to let it go."

CHAPTER 23

The Rondeau sisters had a Haitian friend named Jerry who sometimes double-dated with Jeanine and me. He seldom came with the same girl twice. Jerry was the fifty-year-old owner of an electronics retail store in Lower Manhattan. A faint scent of coconut clung to his stringy black hair, which was plastered to his scalp with Murray's Super Light pomade. His success in business was evidenced by the jewel-studded silver belt buckle barely visible under his protruding stomach, the late model Cadillac de Ville he drove, and the thick wad of fifty-dollar bills held together by a red rubber band that he casually stuffed into his right-hand pants pocket. When we were out with Jerry, it was always his treat.

Jerry occasionally went to dances at the Lorelei, but his taste in entertainment ran more to the Cuban and Jamaican nightclubs in Harlem or the South Bronx where he generously tipped the musicians to sing multiple versions of the sexually explicit lyrics to his favorite song, "The Big Bamboo." On those occasions Jerry introduced me to his friends as "*mon ami allemand*." I was usually the only white person in the audience.

****

"Jerry has a crazy idea, and I was hoping you would say no," Jeanine announced to me over dinner at her apartment one Thursday towards the end of July. "He wants us to go with him to a cockfight!"

"That sounds good to me. It would be nice to get out of the city for a change."

Martine shook her head. "*Pauvre* Gunter. He has no idea."

"The kind of cockfight Jerry's talking about takes place in a basement somewhere in the South Bronx. Men go there to bet and get drunk while they watch the roosters tear each other apart." Jeanine shivered. "I've seen them fight in Haiti and I hate everything about it."

But if Jeanine had hoped to discourage me, she'd had just the opposite effect. I was intrigued. After all, when else would I have a chance to see a spectacle like that? "I hate to say it, but you've made me nosy and I'd really like to go."

"I was afraid you'd say that," Jeanine replied. "I guess it's a man's thing. Okay, then. I'll call Jerry."

The following Saturday around 8 p.m. Jerry, his latest Cuban girlfriend, Jeanine and I went out to eat at a Chinese restaurant located over a dry cleaners on Upper Broadway. The girls wore dressy outfits but Jerry and I were casually attired in jeans and sport shirts. Once we finished eating Jerry drove us up to the South Bronx where, just past rubble-strewn empty lots and abandoned buildings with broken windows, he pulled into a parking space behind several other black cars on a dark side street directly across from a seedy-looking red-brick apartment building.

"Are you sure it's safe to leave your car here?" I asked Jerry as the four of us got out.

"Don't worry. I've got it covered. See that guy over there?" He pointed to a wiry man dressed entirely in black who was slouching against a wall. "He'll watch it for us." Jerry peeled off a bill from the wad in his pocket, spoke to the man briefly in Spanish, and then led us across the street.

Jeanine held tight to my hand as we went inside and rode the elevator to the basement. A long, dimly lit, graffiti-covered corridor wound past a boiler room and four overflowing, foul-smelling garbage bins. I had long since regretted my decision to come along, but there was no backing out now.

At the end of the corridor, Jerry pushed open a stairway door and we followed him upstairs, across an empty lot, and into the basement of another building where two powerfully built men blocked our way. Jerry's wad of bills came back out and, after he had a brief conversation with the men in Spanish, we were allowed to pass. Ahead of us we could hear muffled shouts, which became louder and louder until we finally reached the cockfighting venue.

Amid the stench of thick cigar smoke, old sweat, and cheap beer, at least one hundred people, mostly men, were shrieking out their bets in Creole and in Spanish as they crowded around a small sand-filled circle enclosed by two-foot-high wooden boards. Large bills—twenties, fifties, and hundreds—rapidly changed hands. A dozen caged roosters cooped up nearby waited for their turn in the ring.

Suddenly an announcement was made and the first two birds were let loose upon each other. With a great squawking and flapping of wings they fought not only with their beaks but also with the sharp metal spurs attached to their claws. Jeanine hid her face in her hands, but I couldn't turn away. Drunken men all around me were on their feet, wildly waving their arms, and screaming for blood.

"He's getting killed!" I yelled into Jerry's ear as one of the birds got torn to pieces. "Shouldn't they stop the fight?"

He shook his head. "Too late for that!" he shouted back as the victorious bird was lifted up and angry men all around me tore up their betting slips and tossed the scraps into the air.

After two more cockfights the crowd had worked itself into a torrid frenzy and the ring was nearly obscured by the thick smoke. Jerry's girlfriend tugged on his sleeve. "Honey," she hollered, "let's leave now before they start throwing punches." He pointed to the exit and the three of us followed him back to his car by the same circuitous route we had taken earlier.

Jeanine sat trembling next to me on the back seat and I put my arms around her. "And they call that a sport!" she hissed through clenched teeth. I'd never seen her so angry. "Next time you can go without me."

"There won't be a next time," I assured her. I had already seen more than enough.

Chapter 24

Since, with the exception of Walter Licht, my roommates in Queens had expressed an aversion to 'colored people,' I never brought Jeanine to our apartment. Instead, she and I went out to dinner in Manhattan several times with Walter and Tamara. So it came as no surprise after Walter, who had been taking religious instruction from a Reform rabbi in New Jersey, completed his conversion to Judaism at the end of August 1966, that Jeanine and I received invitations to the wedding. All of the other guests were Tamara's friends and relatives.

On September 11th, I picked up Jeanine, who was wearing a scoop-necked, light-pink cocktail dress and matching stiletto shoes. The two of us headed over to West 48th Street to join the other guests at Gluckstern's kosher restaurant. The unusually short men and women clustered around the bride all turned to stare. I felt like Gulliver among the Lilliputians. We heard the whispered words '*schvartze*' and '*goy*' from every corner of the room as we went over to congratulate the bride and groom.

"Don't congratulate us yet," Tamara scolded. "*After* the ceremony, then you can say *mazel tov*." She was wearing a white dress and a white hat. Walter had on a tuxedo and a black yarmulke with white trim.

The rabbi, a skinny little man with a gray mustache, came over to us. Ignoring Jeanine, he looked me up and down as if he were measuring me for a suit. "Judging from your height, you must be Walter's friend from Germany," he finally said.

"Yes, sir, I am. I'm Gunter Nitsch and this is my girlfriend, Jeanine."

"Your girlfriend, you say?" He clasped his hands behind his back to avoid having to shake either of ours. "Yes. Well, all right then. Nice meeting you both. Let me find you a yarmulke before we head upstairs to the chapel."

Jeanine couldn't help giggling when she reached up to attach the little cap to my head with bobby pins. "What on earth is so funny?" I asked her.

"I was just thinking. If I weren't here, one of those tiny ladies would probably have to climb up on a chair to pin this on you. And they're all so short, I'm not even sure they can see it on the top of your head." She stood back to look at me. "Besides, I think you look silly."

"Well, try not to laugh, okay? I'm sure I look ridiculous, but it means a lot to Walter and Tamara."

Since most of the ceremony was performed in Hebrew, Jeanine and I could only guess what was going on. However, at the very end, it was clear to both of us from the murmurs of '*oy vey!*' and '*oy gevalt!*' that the crowd considered Walter's failure to shatter a glass with his foot on the first try a bad omen.

As soon as we left the chapel and started to walk back downstairs, Jeanine pulled me aside and whispered, "*Mon chéri, je n'aime pas ce petit chapeau,*" and, reaching up, she unpinned the yarmulke and put it in my jacket pocket.

The twenty-six other guests had gone ahead of us and were already seated in the restaurant. Tamara's parents had both been too frail to make the trip to New York from Israel so, other than two cousins who had flown in from Poland, everyone else was from the New York area. Even so, we hardly heard any English. Just about everyone was speaking in either Hebrew or Yiddish.

Walter and Tamara were seated at the head table with the rabbi and his wife. Ignoring the two empty chairs at one of the other tables, the waiter seated Jeanine and me by ourselves in an empty booth.

"Feel free to order whatever you like," he said haughtily, handing us each a menu.

Jeanine looked over the unfamiliar items and turned to me for help. "What are these things? Kasha varnishkes? Fried kreplach? Gefilte fish? Do you have any idea?"

"I'd suggest we start with the chopped herring and then have the Hungarian goulash. I've eaten both of those and I'm pretty sure you'll like them."

While we waited to be served, Jeanine looked over at the bride and groom and her eyes got a dreamy, far-away look. I was immediately on the alert!

"I love weddings!" she exclaimed. "Just look how happy Tamara is! A small wedding like this one is so much nicer, don't you think?"

"It's a shame that Tamara's parents couldn't be here," I replied, adeptly changing the subject. "Speaking of family, I was wondering how often you get back down to Haiti to visit your sister, Jacqueline?"

"Are you crazy? No one who gets out of there will ever go back as long as Papa Doc is in charge. Do you know anything about his soldiers? The *Tonton Macoutes*? They would chop me down with their machetes just like that," and she snapped her fingers. "Martine and I are hoping to bring Jacqueline up here. Maybe you will get to meet her one day." She took a forkful of chopped herring and wrinkled her nose.

"Don't you like it?"

"I don't like anything about this place. Did you hear them call me a *'schvartze'* when we walked in? Do they think I don't know what that means? If you work in the garment district like I do, you know when you're being insulted. *"Incroyable, c'est toujours la même chose."*

"They didn't exactly welcome me with open arms either, don't you forget. But, for Walter and Tamara's sake, let's try to enjoy ourselves."

"You're right," Jeanine agreed. "I'll do my best."

CHAPTER 25

I was nearly twenty-nine years old and had been working at Brewster, Leeds for more than two-and-a-half years. Surely, I thought, there must be a more meaningful job out there than arranging for the export of rattlesnake meat, overstocked Cheez Doodles, and kosher Dum Dum Pops to third-world countries. Since I had long planned to use the two weeks of vacation time I was owed to visit my parents in Germany, I decided to combine my trip home with a job search for a possible marketing position to start in January 1967. By the time I flew out of Kennedy Airport on Friday evening September 23rd, I had lined up five interviews with German subsidiaries of American firms.

Café Nitsch was crowded with customers who were waiting in line for fresh rolls, croissants and Danish pastry when I walked into the shop the following morning. As soon as she saw me, my mother took off her apron and left her place behind the counter. The two of us joined my father in the kitchen for a second breakfast.

"Who's the girl minding the cash register? She must be new."

"She's been here nearly six months now," my father replied. "We had to add another girl since our business has really picked up. Or did you think that life in Bergheim stood still just because you went to New York? Speaking of which, did your mother and I understand correctly from your letters? Even if you find a good job over here, you still plan on going back to America?"

"At least for a few months. I don't want to make any hasty decisions."

My father shook his head. "Is it because of that Haitian woman you've been dating? You're not actually considering marrying her are you?"

Before I could answer, my mother spoke up. "While we're on the subject, are you going to call Charlotte? She knows you're here."

"You told her I was coming?"

"She's such a lovely girl. Your father and I have always thought the two of you would make a wonderful couple."

"Well, since she already knows, I guess I have to give her a call," I said begrudgingly. Knowing how much my mother hoped to bring the two of us back together, I did not want to let on that I had intended to call Charlotte in any event.

Later that same afternoon, I stood waiting for Charlotte outside the Brauhaus Früh am Dom, a five-minute walk from the Cologne Cathedral. We had often eaten in the Brauhaus during the year and a half we were together and it was strange to think that now we had been apart for longer than that.

And then, suddenly, I was enveloped in the fragrance of *L'Air du Temps* and there she was.

"You're just as pretty as ever," I said and I leaned down to give her a peck on the cheek.

"I wasn't sure I could trust you to show up." Her tone was icy. "After all, you left me stranded at the airport in Luxembourg."

"Believe me, that's still on my conscience. But on the other hand, you came to New York and never contacted me," I countered.

"It was just my way of getting even. You didn't really think I would fly all the way over there just to mail a letter, did you?"

If Walter hadn't set me straight at the time, I would have gone on believing just that, but I certainly didn't want to admit it to Charlotte. "Of course not. But it did give me quite a start when I first saw the envelope, I'll grant you that."

When we had taken our seats in the restaurant, Charlotte grasped both of my hands. "Tell me the truth. How many American girlfriends have you had in the meantime?"

"One or two. Nothing really serious. What about you?"

"I'm dating someone right now, a young economist with a great job, but it's not like it was when I was with you. To be honest, when it comes to that topic, I really don't know what I want any more."

"But you still want to get married some day?"

"Oh, yes! With the right person, of course."

"Well, I don't. I may not know where I want to live or what kind of job I'd like to have. But one thing I'm sure of. I'm definitely not the marrying kind."

Charlotte sighed and let go of my hand. "So what are you going to do while you're here? Will you spend all your time with your parents in Bergheim?"

"I'll be doing a little traveling, too. There are some people I want to see." It was a white lie. If Charlotte knew that I was considering taking a job in Germany, there was no telling how much pressure she might bring to bear.

We talked for another hour, about Charlotte's job in an accounting firm and about my adventures in America, when suddenly jet lag caught up with me. I stifled a yawn and glanced at my wristwatch, trying to figure out what time it was back in New York. Charlotte grabbed my right hand with both of her hands. "So, will I see you again before you fly back?" she asked.

"Sure, why not? I'll give you a call to arrange it on October 8th when I get back to Cologne. That'll be my last Saturday before I leave for New York."

"I don't understand why you came all this way and you're only staying two weeks."

"The Americans aren't as generous with vacation time as the Germans are and, besides, I can't afford to miss any more classes or I'll flunk out."

I put my arm around Charlotte's shoulder in the tram on the way back to her apartment building. Neither of us spoke much during the ride. When we reached the entrance to her building, we hugged each other and she clung to me and cried. If her mother hadn't been upstairs waiting for her, I'm not sure what would have happened next. But with a resolve I didn't know I possessed, I stood back to watch Charlotte go inside and then I turned and walked away.

****

The Cologne railroad station was only a short distance from Hohe Strasse, the pedestrian shopping zone where my brother, Hubert, was managing a small self-service fast-food restaurant so, rather than head straight back to Café Nitsch, I decided to stop by and say hello. On the left side of the restaurant were six tall round tables, around each of which two or three customers could stand while they gulped down bratwursts on tiny rolls, or tossed back a stein of beer, or indulged in a Belgian waffle topped with a dollop of whipped cream. There were no chairs or utensils.

Behind the counter on the right side of the restaurant, giving instructions to the three young women who were heating up the sizzling bratwursts and sprinkling powdered sugar on the waffles, was Hubert, all 300 plus pounds of him. He was wearing a navy blue bib pocket apron that barely covered his bulging stomach and he was not making the least effort to smile at his customers.

Since he was extremely busy, I watched him for a few minutes from the doorway before finally stepping over to the counter to place my order. "May I have a waffle without whipped cream, please?" Hubert's face broke into a broad grin and he reached over the counter to shake my hand.

"Günter! I'm so glad you stopped by. Let me fix you a waffle and then we can go upstairs to talk."

Hubert had a one-bedroom apartment on the second floor directly over the restaurant. Dozens of cowboy novels with colorful covers filled the bookcases. Long-playing albums with songs by pop artists like Catarina Valente, Heino, and Freddy Quinn were strewn about. The minute we walked in, Hubert put one of the records on his turntable and ratcheted up the volume, making conversation difficult.

"Have things gotten any better between you and Vati?" I asked him once Hubert had washed his hands and sat down next to me. From my mother's letters I knew that an estrangement between my brother and my father had gone on for nearly a year because my father disapproved of Hubert's lifestyle.

"Now that my girlfriend, Irmgard, has moved out and she and I are planning to get married, things have calmed down. At least Mutti doesn't have to sneak over here to see me any more and I can go over to the Café whenever I want to, but I still think he's a hypocrite. With all the womanizing he did, who is he to tell me what's right and what's wrong?"

"We both know he's not going to change. That's just the way he is. Anyway, I'd better get back to Bergheim and catch up on my sleep. Will you have time to come out to the Café while I'm here?"

"I could always make the time but I'm not going to come. It's always the same when I'm there. No matter what I do, he finds fault, and I'm sick of it. Life's hard enough as it is." He turned off the music and put his apron back on. "I'd better get down to the shop. It's our busiest time."

"By the way," I said when I was about to leave for the train to Bergheim, "I saw Charlotte this afternoon."

"And?"

"I guess I've moved on."

CHAPTER 26

*T*he first four businessmen who interviewed me gave me only vague promises and not much hope. But it was different with the Pepsi-Cola executive who interviewed me in Frankfurt. He was an American, fluent in German, who had lived in Europe for a number of years. From the moment we met, the two of us hit it off. I got together with him twice, once in his office and, the following day, as his guest in an expensive restaurant where, over a meal of chicken cooked in white wine, he offered me a job selling his company's product line to the largest supermarket chains in Germany. The salary would have been more than triple what I was earning when I had left for the United States in April 1964.

"I assume you took the job," my father commented when I told my parents the news. "You'd be crazy to turn it down."

"Actually, I told him I'd think about it and send him my decision when I get back to New York."

"Sometimes I just don't understand where you're coming from," my father said. "Why did you bother to go on those interviews anyway if you weren't going to take a job?"

"To be honest, I really just wanted to know what my chances would be for the future. I mean, after I get my bachelor's degree from Hunter College. But now I regret that I got such a good offer right away because it forces me to make a decision."

"I think we should let Gunter figure this out for himself. Don't you?" my mother said. Then she clapped her hand to her head. I had a pretty good idea what was coming next. "Oh! I almost forgot to tell you. Charlotte phoned me yesterday to see when you were coming back. She said you were going to see her again before you leave for New York tomorrow."

"I called her from a phone booth in the railroad station on my way here this afternoon and her mother answered. When she heard my voice, she hung up on me. I actually dialed the number again. Same result."

"I guess you can't blame Mrs. Sorge," my mother said. "I would probably have done the same if she were my daughter. But you could have called Charlotte at her office yesterday and arranged to meet. Or didn't you think of that?"

Between my father's pressure on me to take the job with Pepsi-Cola and my mother's scheming to get me back together with Charlotte, I could see myself slipping right back where I had been two-and-a-half years before. I was more than ready to return to New York City.

On Sunday, October 9, 1966, early in the afternoon, just as I was about to leave for the airport, I leaned down to give my mother a hug. Then, as had always been our custom, I reached over to shake my father's hand. Instead, quite unexpectedly, my father threw his arms around me. In a voice choked with tears, he pleaded with me one last time: "*Um Gottes willen*, don't stay much longer in that awful country. Everything you need is right here."

It was the only time my father had ever embraced me. Looking back on that day years later, I've often wondered if he had sensed at that moment that he would never get another chance.

****

"So, how was your trip?" Mark Silverberg greeted me. "We have a lot to catch up on!"

There had been no classes due to Columbus Day and I had spent the day in the Hunter College library madly trying to catch up on the reading for my courses on American Economic Systems and on Prose Fiction. "I'm glad to be back," I admitted. "It was nice seeing my parents again, but I felt as though I'd get stuck in a rut if I stayed a minute longer."

"And the lovely Charlotte? Did you see her?"

"That's just it. I found her exactly where I'd left her. I've broadened my horizons. She's stuck in the same place."

"So you're over her?"

"I guess I am. But I'm not sure she's over me."

"And what about your job search? Did anything come up?"

I told Mark about the offer from Pepsi-Cola and my reluctance to accept it. He heard me out and then he smiled. "Well, if I were you, I'd stick it out here. You have the opportunity I never had to get a college education. And no matter how things may look now, once you get your degree, the world will open up to you. Besides, and forgive me for this really selfish reason, I'd miss our weekly conversations if you went back. Wouldn't you?"

Less than a week later, Esther phoned to tell me that Mark Silverberg had died of heart failure in his sleep. Treated as unwelcome outsiders by Mark's sons and their families at the funeral, Esther and I mourned together in a back pew. I had never had a chance to tell Mark that I turned down the job offer, but I think he had known, even before I did, what my decision would be.

CHAPTER 27

*I*n February 1967 Jeanine and I, together with Jerry and his latest girlfriend, went to the Haitian Ball at the Waldorf Astoria Hotel. Jeanine had been gushing about this event for weeks. She had even bought a strapless pale yellow ball gown especially for the occasion. On the big night hundreds of elegantly dressed guests were milling around in the lobby before heading up to the Grand Ballroom. About half the men were dressed, like me, in business suits. The rest wore either tuxedos or white tie and tails. The chic, low-cut dresses of the women were in a dazzling array of bright colors—reds, pinks, turquoise, peach, and green. Diamond necklaces sparkled around their necks and the scent of expensive French perfume filled the air.

Round tables elegantly set for parties of ten surrounded the polished dance floor in the four-story high ballroom. As I walked arm in arm with Jeanine to our assigned seats, surrounded by all of that provocative décolleté, she flashed me a smile and whispered, "Hey! Don't look at them. Look at me!"

But the attention I was paying to all of the beautiful women I saw was minimal compared to the attention I was attracting to myself. Judging from the quick scan I made of the room, among the roughly one thousand people in attendance at the ball there were about a dozen white women with their Haitian husbands or boyfriends and not a single man who looked like me.

We introduced ourselves to the other six people at our table who, as a concession to me, switched their conversation from Creole to English. I leaned over to Jeanine to make myself heard over the Latin beat of the twenty-two-piece orchestra. "Do you think pretty much everyone here is Haitian or are there also some Americans in the crowd?"

"You mean American Negroes? Maybe a few who are married to Haitians. Otherwise they couldn't afford the tickets. And you want to know why? Haitians have good jobs. They're doctors, lawyers, engineers, professors, businessmen. American Negroes live off welfare and their women spread their legs to have five babies by five different men! Isn't that so, Jerry?" He grinned and nodded in agreement.

This was the second time I had heard Jeanine express hostility towards African-Americans and it did not sit well with me. "Come on Jeanine. How can you stereotype people like that? I'm sure there are as many underprivileged Haitians in New York as successful ones, probably more. And there are certainly plenty of hard-working African-Americans."

She shook her head. "You won't change my mind," she said firmly. "Haitians are superior to American Negroes and that's the truth."

There was no time to pursue this topic further because, just then, the emcee made an announcement in Creole, the music became louder, and serious dancing began. Jeanine beamed at me as we moved to the rhythms of the Caribbean and, no matter what the musicians played, the crowd called out again and again in Creole for the 'Mereng!'

"When are they going to play a Viennese Waltz?" I asked to the amusement of everyone at our table.

"I'm sure they don't know how," Jeanine replied when the laughter had died down.

I pushed back my chair and stood up. "Well, I'm going to request one."

"Please don't," Jeanine pleaded. "We're attracting enough attention as it is."

"Don't listen to her," Jerry said as the other men at the table nodded in agreement. "Let's see how brave you are."

All eyes were on me as I strode over to the bandleader and, in my best French, said, "*Excusez-moi, Monsieur.* Do you have a moment? I'm from Germany and I was wondering if you would please play a Viennese waltz, perhaps the Blue Danube?"

He turned to consult the musicians in Creole before replying, "I can't promise, but we'll try."

"I was right, wasn't I?" Jeanine continued to insist when I got back to our table. "They don't know how." Before she finished the sentence the orchestra began to play another merengue. "*Voilà!* What did I tell you?" she gloated.

But the next time the music stopped, the conductor announced that, by special request, they would play a Viennese waltz. The few other couples who joined Jeanine and me quickly gave up, leaving the two of us alone to twirl around and around on the dance floor. Jeanine felt light as a feather in my arms and when the last note was played and she and I walked back to our table, one thousand Haitians rose to give us a standing ovation.

****

On the last Saturday in April 1967, exactly three years to the day since Walter and I had disembarked from the *France,* he and Tamara invited us to join them at a concert being given by an Israeli band in a club in Greenwich Village. Tamara looked especially radiant that night. She was almost eight months pregnant.

We were seated on long benches at a table near the wall with a good view of the stage. There were five musicians in the group, two of whom sang lively pop songs in English and in Hebrew, a language most of the other guests seemed to understand. Tamara did her best to translate the announcements made between each number.

About an hour into the performance, the lead singer took the microphone and spoke for the first time in heavily accented English. "Good evening ladies and gentlemen. We appreciate the warm welcome. How many of you here are from Israel?" There was loud applause from every corner of the room. "Any other countries? Don't be shy!"

Someone called out, "Lebanon!" and the announcer said, "Let's all give a hand to our guests from Lebanon!" The same thing happened as people spoke up from England, from France, from Mexico and several other countries. "Anyone else?" he asked when the applause died down.

"I'm from Germany!" I boomed.

"Did you say GERMANY?" The young man threw up his hands in mock astonishment. Then, pointing in my direction, he let loose a torrent of words in Hebrew at which people all around us roared with laughter.

"What did he say?" Walter asked Tamara, but she ignored him and, rising from her seat she screamed, "How DARE you insult our German guest! And my Jewish husband is also German, you stupid *hatichat harah*! You stupid piece of shit!"

The poor man tried to appease Tamara. He held out his hands to her, bit his lip, and mumbled into the mike, "C'mon, I was just joking. I didn't mean anything by it."

But it was too little, too late, as far as Tamara was concerned. Grabbing the loose folds of her maternity dress in one hand and holding onto Walter's shoulder for support with the other, she climbed up on the bench to hurl more insults at the man in Hebrew who, as best we could judge, began to reply in kind. The audience was no longer laughing. It was one thing to enjoy the joke when Germans were being attacked and quite another when the target was an Israeli expectant mother. By the time Walter coaxed Tamara back down from the bench, the guests at nearby tables were applauding her.

"Boy, I really let that sonofabitch have it!" she finally said when she had caught her breath. Then Tamara reached over to put Jeanine's hand on her stomach. "Can you feel the baby kicking? He's as angry as I am."

"So, Tamara, what on earth did you say to that poor man anyway?" Jeanine asked. "They're going off on a break and I'm not sure they're coming back."

"Maybe we should leave, too," I suggested. "What do you say?"

Walter was about to agree when Tamara stopped him. "And let him think he won?" she exclaimed. "Not on your life. I'm not budging until the end of the concert and that's that."

****

The minute Tamara let Jeanine feel the baby kicking, I knew that I was in trouble. Sure enough, the next time Jeanine and I got together she snuggled up to me and said, "If we get married and have a baby,

131

I'm sure he would look like you because you're not racially mixed like me. Don't you think so?"

"Well, I suppose we'll never know because I'm not going to get married." Before Jeanine could object, I added, "Oh, I forgot to tell you. There's a tall, beautiful young woman from Jamaica in one of my classes, who also wants to marry me."

She stiffened. "You never told me about her."

"I didn't say I was dating her. She came up to me out of the blue a few days ago with a nutty scheme. Would you believe she offered me $2,000 if I would marry her? And then, after a year or two, we'd get divorced. She thought I was a citizen who could help her get a Green Card. "

"So are you going to marry her?"

"No, of course not. And I told her so."

"Good, then let's forget about her and talk about us," Jeanine said. "I need to know, once and for all, whether you're planning to marry me."

"Jeanine, haven't you been listening to me? I've always said that I don't intend to get married, not to you nor to anyone else."

"Now you listen to me. We've been together for a year. That's a long time and I'm not getting any younger." She was on her feet now, pacing back and forth. "And, unlike you, I do want to get married. So I don't think we should keep on dating each other. I'll just have to find somebody else."

I got up from the couch to get my coat. "Then I guess I won't see you again?"

"No, no, don't say that. We're not enemies," Jeanine assured me. "We can stay friends. Please call me sometime." Then she smiled. "And when I do meet someone who wants to marry me, I'm going to invite you to my wedding!"

I grinned back and gave her a hug. "If you invite me, I'll be there!"

CHAPTER 28

*L*eon Begleiter was engrossed in *The New York Times* when I came in to work at Brewster, Leeds a few days later.

"Excuse me, Mr. Leon, but I need a really big favor," I began.

"Would you look at this?" Ignoring me, he handed me the paper. "If I read this right, Egypt is trying to wipe Israel off the map."

"I heard about it on the radio."

"Sorry, Gunter. I wasn't really paying attention to what you were saying. This news has me all rattled. What can I do for you?"

"Sven, one of my neighbors, is going home to Sweden in a few weeks, but before he leaves he wants to drive his brand-new Ford Mustang to Mexico and back."

"Does he want travel advice? I've been down there many times."

"No, actually, the thing is," I shifted from one foot to the other, "he wants a travel companion to help navigate and to share the price of gas and, I know it's less than a year since I went to Germany, but . . ."

"Well, it would mean bending the rules a bit, but an opportunity like that doesn't come along very often. So, by all means, go ahead and have some fun. Don't forget to buy yourself a little phrase book before you leave. The Spanish alphabet sounds pretty similar to the

German one so it should be easy for you. And you might want to buy yourself a Lufthansa bag before you go to let people know that you're from Germany. There are a lot of places south of the border where Americans don't get a particularly warm welcome."

****

Sven and I left at the crack of dawn the following Saturday morning and, after four solid days on the road, we checked into a low-priced motel in Nuevo Laredo, just across the border from Texas. A squeaky electric fan in the corner of our room only succeeded in circulating the hot air and there were cigarette burns in the sheets, but at least we had finally arrived in Mexico. While Sven, who had insisted on doing all of the driving himself, went straight to bed to catch up on his sleep for a few hours before dinner, I changed into my swim trunks, wrapped a towel around my shoulders, and headed outside to the pool.

Aside from a small green lizard clinging to the trunk of a nearby palm tree, there wasn't a single other living creature in sight. Even though it was already nearly 5 p.m., the sun was still beating down so hard on the plastic lounge chairs that my back burned when I tried to stretch out. Desperate to cool off, I put down my towel on the chair and went into the lukewarm pool.

Floating on my back, I closed my eyes and relaxed, only paddling every so often to keep my legs from sinking. It felt so good to bob gently on the water that I began to drift off to sleep. Perhaps, I daydreamed, when I open my eyes I'll be surrounded by a group of beautiful girls in bikinis.

Suddenly I heard the flutter of wings followed by a series of raspy, crackling sounds. Slowly opening my eyes, I was horrified to find at least three-dozen large vultures sitting along the edges of the pool gazing at me hungrily. I frantically kicked as hard as I could, but the ugly, naked-headed creatures merely backed off a few inches and then stood their ground. It was only when I got up and shouted at the top of my lungs while wildly splashing water in all directions that the birds reluctantly flew away. My screams woke up Sven who poked his head out of the door to our room.

"What the hell is going on out here?" he demanded.

All of the vultures were gone by now. Even the small, green lizard had skittered away into the shrubbery. There wasn't a single ripple of water in the pool. "You wouldn't believe me if I told you," I finally replied with a sigh.

****

Before Sven and I reached Mexico City, I had phoned José, my former roommate from Queens, to let him know where we would be staying. On our second day in the Mexican capital José picked us up in front of our hotel in a brand-new white Saab and drove us to the Floating Gardens in Xochimilco for a boat ride. Then, after we stopped back at our hotel to change from shorts to slacks while José waited for us in the car, we headed over to the Ortega family home for dinner.

In stark contrast to the tumbledown shacks with corrugated tin roofs in the slums through which we had been driving earlier in the day, José's family lived in a mansion surrounded by flowering trees in the trendy Polanco neighborhood, just off of Schiller Street near the vast Chapultepec Park. A large Mercedes and a sleek Porsche were parked in the driveway in front of a three-car garage.

José's parents escorted the three of us into their elegant dining room. Beneath the dark-timbered cathedral ceiling, twelve ornately carved, high-backed wooden chairs surrounded a massive dining table covered with a white lace tablecloth. Standing at attention behind each of the five chairs where there were place settings stood five very short, brown-skinned serving girls in identical white uniforms complete with matching gloves; each girl wore her black hair in a single long braid that reached half way down her back.

Throughout the meal the girls posted behind our chairs made sure that our water and wine glasses were always filled, while two other similarly uniformed girls brought out four different courses, starting with a spicy bean soup, then a leafy green salad, followed by mint flavored chicken served with mashed potatoes and squash, and, for dessert, crêpes in a thick caramel sauce.

By the time we retired to the living room after dinner to sip *rompope*, a Mexican egg liqueur, from crystal cordial glasses, I had a lot on my mind. Granted, José had once told me that his father was the Mexican representative for two different expensive brands of French perfume, but I had had no idea that his family was so well off. However, rather than be impressed with the family's obvious wealth, it made me uncomfortable. After all, I was perfectly capable of pouring myself a glass of water if I needed one, just as I could have placed my own napkin on my lap. I couldn't help wondering throughout the meal what those seven Mexican serving girls must have thought of the five of us. What I would have given if I could have listened in to their conversation as they made a meal of the leftovers in the kitchen later that evening.

It wasn't until shortly before 11 p.m. when Sven and I thanked Mr. and Mrs. Ortega for their hospitality. Then we climbed into José's Saab for the ride back to our hotel. But, a few minutes into the drive, José suddenly screeched to a stop and threw up his hands. *"Dios mío!* I totally forgot to show you our new Azteca Stadium!"

"Well, maybe we can get over there tomorrow," I suggested. "We still have a day left before we drive to Acapulco."

"Tomorrow? Why does everyone think Mexicans always put things off until *mañana*? No. We're going to go there *right now*."

For the next half hour I gripped the edge of my seat as José ran a series of red lights and drove the wrong way down one-way streets. When we dared to speak up, he brushed off our concerns. "There's no traffic at this hour, so who cares?"

In the darkness, only the silhouette of the vast Stadium was visible when José pulled into the parking lot. A single light bulb in a small guardhouse nearby, where several soldiers with rifles slung over their shoulders lounged against the wall smoking cigarettes, provided the only illumination. There was also a small store at the far end of the parking area whose owner was apparently getting ready to shut down for the night. Without a moment's hesitation, José ran over to the guardhouse and talked for a few minutes to the soldiers. Then he ran back to Sven and me.

"Guys, it's going to cost you five dollars. What do you say?"

"I don't want any part of this," Sven said and he turned to me for support. But, curious to see what would happen next, I handed José the money.

"Now you'll have to trust me for a few minutes," José said as ran to the little store and, from there, back to the guardhouse, before returning to where he had left us. "Hop in the car!" he yelled. "We don't have much time!"

And, just then, the huge gate swung open and one of the soldiers waved us inside as all of the floodlights in the 105,000-seat stadium came on. Sven and I gaped in astonishment as José drove one complete round of the field beneath the towering tiers of empty seats.

"How on earth did you manage that?" Sven was the first to ask once we got back outside and could see the lights shutting down behind us.

"All it took was a $5.00 bottle of tequila," José replied with a chuckle. He made a sharp turn within shouting distance of the guardhouse and yelled, "*Adios, compadres!*" before driving off at bone-rattling speed in the direction of our hotel.

****

After my terrifying encounter with the ravenous vultures and the life-threatening drives around Mexico City with José, I looked forward to a few quiet days in sunny Acapulco before flying back to New York. First taking a detour to Puebla to see a bullfight, Sven and I then headed south. The next few days were everything I had hoped for: sun, surf, and relaxation. Finally, I thought, this is a real vacation!

On the afternoon before my early-morning flight was scheduled to leave, my suitcase was packed and ready, and Sven and I were looking for one last thing we could do together before we went our separate ways. At the suggestion of some tourists from California whom Sven and I had met at lunch that day, we decided to make the twenty-minute drive along the coast west of Acapulco to nearby Sunset Beach. It was 4 p.m. and the sun was still high in the sky when, about a mile or so beyond the small town of Pie de la Cuesta, we reached the seemingly endless beach. On one side of the narrow strip of land was a tranquil, fresh-water lagoon. On the ocean-facing side, rolling breakers nearly 18-feet high thundered against the shore with a deafening roar and showered us with a salty spray.

Except for a husky young man in swim trunks who couldn't have stood more than 4'10" and a young girl with pitch-black hair who was carrying his pants, his shirt, and a small wicker basket full of mangos, we had the place to ourselves. It was my last chance to take a dip in the Pacific and I was sorely tempted, but Sven tried to dissuade me: "Don't be an idiot. If you get into trouble, there's no one around to help you."

Just then, the two young Mexicans approached us. First pointing to the ocean and then holding out his open hand towards me, the boy spoke in halting English. "Two dollars, I swim."

Now I felt challenged. *If this little pipsqueak can do it, so can I.* After all, hadn't I been able to hold my breath and swim more than fifty yards under water when I was in the German army in 1958? After wading up to my shoulders in the unexpectedly cold water, I swam out to meet the breaking wave. Then I took a deep breath and plunged under the turbulent surface of the water. But when I finally came back up, I could no longer see the beach and the next big wave was about to roll over me.

Trying not to panic, I decided to ride the crest of the wave in the hope that it would carry me towards the shore but, instead, it sucked me back under water. As I helplessly tossed about, I drew my knees into my chest and tucked in my head to form a giant ball. Now I was bobbing on the surface of the water, being pulled further and further from shore.

Had it really come to this? As a child I had survived almost four years of starvation under Russian occupation after World War II, followed by a hair-raising escape from East Germany. How ironic would it be to die from my own stupidity on a Mexican vacation? How would my obituary in the *Kölner Stadtanzeiger* read? "Günter Nitsch, born December 3, 1937, in Königsberg, East Prussia, drowned while showing off in Acapulco, age 29."

For the first time in many years I turned to prayer, "Dear God, You once saved me from drowning in an icy pond when I was seven. You brought me safely through the Russian times. I know I don't deserve it, but I'm asking for your help just one more time."

Just then I caught a glimpse of Sven and the two young Mexicans on the distant beach frantically signaling me to swim north, parallel to the shore, toward a spot where the land jutted out into the sea and the waves were somewhat calmer. With a new burst of energy and hope, I swam at least half a mile in that direction until I could break through the rough surf and get close enough for Sven and the young man to pull me out onto the sand. As I collapsed to my knees, trying to catch my breath, Sven was decidedly unsympathetic. "That," he said, "was one of the dumbest stunts I've ever seen."

"I realize that now."

"And one more thing. Why the hell didn't you look in our direction sooner? We've been trying to signal you for more than half an hour. I hope you realize how lucky you were to get out of there alive after all that time."

After all I'd been through, the thought of waiting around on Sunset Beach for another few hours to watch the sun go down was no longer appealing. Instead, I invited Sven and my two Mexican rescuers to have supper as my guests in a restaurant where Sven and I were the only outsiders. Afterwards, we drove the young man and his sister back home through a part of Acapulco that tourists never get to see, where pigs and chickens run loose on unpaved roads and where the kind of people who had just saved my life live in pitiful plywood shacks with hanging plastic strips instead of doors.

CHAPTER 29

As I squeezed into my seat for the flight home from Mexico, I couldn't escape two nagging thoughts. The first, of course, was how lucky I was to be returning at all after my near-death experience in Acapulco. The second was the inescapable fact that I had gotten fat. Over the past year my weight had ballooned up from 180 pounds to 210 forcing me to punch a new hole in my belt and to buy slacks several sizes wider in the waist. Part of the blame went to the enormous portions of chicken, goat, lamb, and fish that Jeanine's sister had cooked up in a giant iron pot filled with vegetable oil. Part was also due to the junk food I wolfed down between my job at Brewster, Leeds and my evening classes at Hunter College.

Still it was only when Tamara had eyed me up and down and announced that I looked pregnant that I decided to take off some weight. The very next day I gave my roommates my supply of Entenmann's Glazed Walnut Danish Rings as well as the two six-packs of Schaefer beer I always kept in the refrigerator. Then I went jogging. It was my first long run since I had been in the German Army and, after two miles, totally exhausted, I limped back home and collapsed. Despite hurting all over the next morning, I kept up my jogging, constantly increasing my distances. Three months later I was running six miles, three or four times a week, without any strain. The day finally came when my old slacks fit me again. It was only then that I decided it was high time to look for a new girlfriend.

****

My chance came at the end of August when Ira Birnbaum organized a farewell party for Jochen Kleinman, who was returning to his affluent family in Germany, and for William Exeter who, having just received a draft notice from the U.S. Army, had promptly decided that he would be far better off back home in England than he would be in Vietnam.

"You're not still seeing that Haitian woman, right?" my roommate Earl Ferguson asked me as we walked next door to the party. "I don't know why you bothered with someone like that. None of us did."

Comments like Earl's were the reason that I had never brought Jeanine out to Queens while we were dating. I was convinced that she would be made to feel uncomfortable if I had. In fact, in all the time that I had been living in Queens, I had never seen a black person at any of our parties. So it came as a surprise when the second group of women to arrive included an attractive African-American.

"Well, this is awkward," I heard Earl whisper to William in his Southern drawl. "They're all teachers. I met two of them when they took an NBC tour, but maybe I should've been more specific when I asked them to bring along some friends."

Yet, despite the fact that half the people in the room were gawking at her, the young woman looked perfectly composed as she chatted and laughed with her group of friends. She was just over 5'4" tall, with a bright smile, sparkling eyes, and high cheekbones. Her dark hair was parted in the middle and pulled back in a short ponytail tied with a black satin ribbon.

Just then Ira sat down at the upright piano in the corner of the living room. "Cheer up, everybody!" he shouted. "Let's give Jochen and our draft-dodging English pal a good send-off. How 'bout starting with some anti-war songs?" Without waiting for a reply, he launched into Bob Dylan's "Blowin' in the Wind." A few measures in, the five teachers came over to the piano, put their arms around each other's shoulders and sang along. They had beautiful voices; actually they were so good that everyone stopped talking and leaned forward to listen. Before long a few other people starting to sing along if they knew the words. By the time Ira played Pete Seeger's "Where Have All the Flowers Gone?" followed by "Michael Row the Boat Ashore," we had all joined in.

When the last note had died down, one of the teachers bent over and whispered into Ira's ear. "Really?" he asked. "She can do that?" He leafed through his sheet music. Then he turned to our African-American guest. "Victoria, is it? Your friend here wants you to sing 'Summertime.' What do you say?"

"If you can play it, I'd be glad to," she replied as her four fellow teachers dropped back and left her alone at the side of the piano.

And sing she did, with the voice of an angel. When she finished to thunderous rounds of applause, she caught a glimpse of me and smiled as I wiped the tears from my eyes.

When she stepped away from the piano, I walked over to her and introduced myself. "Where on earth did you learn to sing like that? You sound like an opera star," I exclaimed.

"Don't I wish! No, actually I'm a teacher with a Head Start program up in Harlem. You know about Head Start? It's a fairly new program that prepares underprivileged children for kindergarten. By the way, my full name is Victoria Hoyt and I'm glad you liked my singing."

"Well, Victoria Hoyt," I replied. "Let's see if you can dance as well as you sing."

Much to my roommates' obvious discomfort, Victoria and I spent the next hour together, dancing and talking until, shortly before 11 p.m., she announced that she had to leave. She had promised to attend a Sunday morning picnic for the medical staff of Columbia Presbyterian Hospital, where her sister, Eve, was a nurse. She had to get to bed early.

"My sister and I are very close," she explained. "We've been to Europe together twice, once to France and once to Italy. Anyway, as much as I'd like to stay longer, I can't break my promise to her."

"Then at least let me bring you home," I replied.

"I'm afraid it's quite a bit out of your way. I'm all the way down in the East Village near Tompkins Square Park."

Ira had been standing nearby, listening to our conversation. "Tomkins Square? Then you must know Ratners Jewish Deli on Delancey Street. I just love their cheese blintzes!" Then, when Victoria went over to say good-bye to her fellow teachers, Ira muttered under his breath, just loud enough for me to hear, "Gunter, I gotta ask you. What the hell's up with you and the *Schvartzes*?" I ignored his question.

It was shortly after midnight when Victoria and I walked from the Astor Place subway station to 8th Street. She had recently moved into her sparsely furnished loft apartment and was still in the process of unpacking. Apart from two armchairs, a small table, and a large bed, there were three empty bookshelves and half a dozen cartons full of books.

"Let me light a candle so it won't look so bleak," she said as she turned off both of the lamps and poured us some white wine before we sat down to talk. Originally from Brunswick, Georgia, Victoria had moved to Peekskill, New York, with her mother and her two sisters after her parents' divorce. Besides working fulltime as a Head Start teacher she was also taking education courses at Baruch College.

"I want to apologize for the cool reception you got when you arrived at the party. My roommates are idiots."

"No need to apologize. I don't let things like that bother me any more. When you grow up in Georgia in the 1940s you develop a pretty strong backbone. Would you believe, when we were children there was only one day a week we were allowed to go to the park, not to mention having to sit in the balcony when we went to the movies! And of course there were the separate drinking fountains. I could go on and on but it's getting very late."

She reached over to take my hand and, without saying another word, we both knew that we were going to spend the night together.

****

After getting barely five hours of sleep, Victoria and I dragged ourselves out of bed early the next morning for the hour-long trip by subway and bus to the hospital picnic in Fort Tryon Park on the northern tip of Manhattan Island. Home to The Cloisters, the medieval wing of the Metropolitan Museum of Art, the Park has a commanding view of the Hudson River far below. It was the first time I'd been up there, but I was way too tired to appreciate it.

I glanced over the crowd of almost three-dozen nurses and more than a dozen young interns who were already gathered for the picnic to try to pick out Victoria's sister, but there was no one there who was at all like her. Instead, Eve was a short, stocky, gap-toothed, chain-smoking woman with glasses who maintained an air of dignified reserve on being introduced to me.

"You're German, I suppose, with that name?" she surmised. "It just so happens I'm on a German reading kick right now. I'm half way through Hermann Hesse's *Siddhartha* although I liked his *Steppenwolf* better. Which one do you prefer?"

Victoria had mentioned that her sister was a bookworm. Even so, her question took me by surprise. "My taste in reading runs more to *The Tin Drum* by Günter Grass," I admitted. "I only read Hesse because his books were assigned to us in school." Judging from her look of pity, if Eve had just put me to some kind of intellectual test, I was sure I had flunked.

Just then Victoria came back with two paper plates of sandwiches. She poked me with her elbow. "Well, it's your turn today. Have you noticed the attention we're getting from all the pasty-faced Jewish doctors? Eve tells me they work such long hours this may be the first time they've seen the sun in weeks. Wouldn't you just love to know what they're thinking when they see a black woman like me with a tall German guy like you? I bet they'll be talking about us for weeks."

"How d'you know they're Jewish?"

"Maybe not all of them, but just look at some of the name tags: Cohen, Shapiro, Goldberg. What else can they be?"

I pulled Victoria off to one side. "Frankly, I don't much care what they think. What bothers me is your sister. I don't think she likes me."

"I wouldn't let it worry you. Eve's a real introvert. And, please keep this under your hat; she once confided to me that she's always fantasized about meeting a Burt Lancaster type. Someone pretty much like you. So, she's probably just jealous that I found you first.

CHAPTER 30

Despite the fact that evening classes had started again for both of us, over the next three weeks Victoria and I spent as much time together as possible: sharing spring rolls and spicy orange peel chicken at a Chinese restaurant on the Upper West Side, mingling with the 'flower children' in Greenwich Village jazz clubs and, most fun of all, travelling out to meet Walter and Tamara's three-month-old son, Benjamin, in their apartment on Queens Boulevard.

"You know," I said to Victoria on a Friday evening in the middle of September, "I haven't really wanted to bring you back to my apartment after the chilly reception you got the first time, but I was wondering if you'd be willing to give it another try?"

"Sure. I'm game. What do you have in mind?"

"My roommates have organized a trip to Rockaway Beach for tomorrow morning. They'll provide the transportation and we can each bring along a date."

She cocked her head to one side and paused a moment. "Do they know that you and I are going out?"

"I don't think so. Why? What difference would that make?"

"It's just that . . ." Her voice trailed off and she was quiet for what seemed like a full minute. Then she smiled. "Let's do it" Victoria finally said. "It should be an interesting day."

First thing Saturday morning the two of us took the subway to Woodside, Queens, arriving at a quarter to ten. We hurried upstairs so that I could show Victoria where I lived while I quickly packed my swim trunks, a blanket, and a towel. Four cars were already parked in front of the apartment building next door when we came back outside.

Ira Birnbaum's car was the first in line, but when I asked him for a ride for the two of us, he shook his head. "Sorry, I'm all filled up." Just then another couple stepped in front of us and climbed in.

The next two cars also drove off without us despite having enough room for us to squeeze in. As the others drove off, Victoria and I were left standing on the sidewalk next to Stu Baxter's car. He and his young blond date already occupied the front seat. The back seat was empty. I reached down to open the car door but Stu stuck his arm out the window to hold me off.

"C'mon Stu, what's *your* excuse?" I snapped. "You clearly have room for two more." Stu looked over at his girlfriend for an out, but she was peering into a small, mirrored compact and studiously powdering her nose. "Well?" I pressed.

"Okay. Get in," he said. His tone was anything but cordial. As we drove in complete silence for the next ten minutes, Stu clutched the steering wheel so tightly that his knuckles turned white. I could see him glaring at me in the rearview mirror, his forehead wrinkled deep in thought. Without warning, he suddenly pulled over to the curb.

"Change of plans!" he announced. "We weren't all that keen on going to the beach anyway, were we honey?"

His date had just put on a fresh coat of lipstick and was blotting her lips with a tissue. "Huh?" was her only reply.

"So," Stu continued, twisting around to face us in the back seat, "I'll just drop the two of you off right here. I'm sure you'll find a subway."

"Are you out of your mind? Where the hell are we anyway?"

Victoria put her hand on my arm. "We'll manage somehow," she said as she opened the car door on the curb side and stepped out. I had no choice but to follow her, slamming the door behind me as I did so.

Stu made a quick U-turn and sped off, leaving us stranded somewhere in the middle of Queens.

"Try to calm down," Victoria said as we both watched our ride disappear around the next corner. "It could've been a lot worse."

"Worse? How could it be worse? Are they all nuts?"

"You think this is bad? You should've been with me two years ago when I was a Freedom Rider in Mississippi. Back then, if one of the white civil rights workers gave me a ride somewhere I'd have to duck down in my seat to avoid getting shot."

"What else don't I know about you?" I asked in amazement.

"Never mind that now. Let's just concentrate on getting to the beach."

"You still want to go?"

"Sure. Don't you?"

It wasn't easy, but after much trial and error, we finally found our way to Rockaway Beach. We stepped out on the sand to look for a place to spread our blanket. Victoria gave me a poke. "Don't look now," she said, "but all of your roommates are here."

"Including Stu?"

"How'd you guess? He just gave us a friendly wave."

"They make me sick, the whole bunch of them! I thought we were friends. And this is the way they act?"

"And it's all because of me."

149

"No, don't say that! This was a much-needed wake-up call for me. And my mind's made up. I'm going to find myself another place to live."

Victoria pulled me down beside her on the blanket so that she could slather some Coppertone lotion on my back, "Well," she said. "I did predict that it would be an interesting day, didn't I? And, boy, was I right!"

****

"You could always move in with me," Victoria suggested as we made our way back from the beach to her apartment in Manhattan. As tempting as her offer was, I hadn't forgotten Quincy's third rule: "Never let her give you the key to her apartment or you'll end up getting stuck with the rent."

"Thanks just the same, Victoria," I hastily replied. "But I really need my own space."

The very next day I bought a copy of the German-American newspaper *Aufbau* and, turning to the listings for 'Furnished Rooms to Rent,' I was intrigued by an ad placed by 'Frau Winter' for a large room on the tenth floor of a high-rise building at the corner of Broadway and 101st Street. Mrs. Winter was a petite, elderly lady with blue eyes, dimples in her cheeks, dyed blond hair, a raspy voice, and deep laugh lines at the outer corners of her eyes. She spoke to me in German with a thick Viennese accent as I followed her down a long corridor, passing the pay phone on the wall ("for my tenants," she explained), the kitchen where I would have cooking privileges, and the door to the room rented by Frau Apfel, her other tenant, to the room she had available at the far end of the hall. Directly opposite the door to the bathroom, the room had a bed against the far wall, a clothes closet and, in front of two windows with a view of 101st Street, two armchairs and a desk.

"Of course, I have my own apartment and my own bathroom," Frau Winter explained. "My apartment door is opposite Frau Apfel's room. But you would have to share the bathroom across the hall with Frau Apfel." I followed Frau Winter back down the hall and we stood outside the closed door to her apartment. "I expect rent to be paid weekly, in advance," she went on, "and you would be responsible for taking care of your own room, but I would provide you with fresh towels and bed linens every week. So what do you think?"

"It all sounds good to me." Actually, it sounded amazing. The rent was even less than I was paying in Woodside. "I'd like to take the room, if that's all right with you."

"Before you decide, there's just one more thing you should know. *I bin a Jidin.* If that doesn't bother you, then you're welcome to come."

"Excuse me, but I don't know that word, *Jidin.*"

She broke into a smile and said in high German, "*Ich bin Jüdin!*"

"Oh, now I understand. Well, I'm Lutheran, so if that doesn't bother *you* then we have deal."

Frau Winter giggled like a schoolgirl. "I think you and I are going to get along just fine," she said.

As I soon learned, my new landlady was the widow of a dentist, as was my fellow tenant, Frau Apfel, a short, dark-haired, frumpy-looking, cross-eyed woman with thick eyeglasses. Frau Winter and Frau Apfel had known each other for more than fifty years. Both women had fled Vienna with their husbands in 1938 and, after spending several years in Shanghai, had eventually settled in New York. After her husband's death, Frau Winter had begun taking in boarders to help cover the rent for her spacious apartment. When Frau Apfel's husband died, Frau Winter took her friend in as a paying tenant. Despite having known each other for more than half a century, I was never to hear the two of them call each other anything other than 'Frau Winter' and 'Frau Apfel.'

The next morning I piled my suitcase, my trunk, and two big cartons full of books into a taxi and, just as they had so recently done to me, I left my Queens roommates behind.

CHAPTER 31

*N*ow that I was living on the Upper West Side, the pattern of my life changed. In Hunter College I was taking three challenging courses: Introduction to Philosophy, Modern Drama, and Political Systems, the last of which was taught by Professor Michael Jaworskyj, who had the reputation of being quite a ladies' man. A passionately anti-communist Russian émigré in his forties with jet-black hair that was graying around the temples and the sharply chiseled features of the Marlboro Man, Professor Jaworskyj gave dazzling, albeit ungrammatical, lectures while impeccably dressed in a dark blue suit, a white dress shirt with French cuffs, and an expensive silk tie. It was no surprise that twenty-three of the twenty-eight students in our class were adoring young women, especially when their Professor reminded us from time to time that, "I don't care for older women. Eighteen years up to twenty-five years would be of interest. Twenty-six or thirty years old, no way."

Even before registering for his course, I had heard rumors that Professor Jaworskyj regularly chose one of his female students—the younger the better—to date during that semester. Within a few weeks we all had a pretty good idea whom he had selected from our class. Emma was a tall, shapely, pouty-lipped, ash-blonde Brigitte Bardot lookalike who came to class directly from her job as a fashion consultant at Bergdorf Goodman. She was one of the few women I had ever met who could look graceful while walking in 5" high-heeled shoes with cork platform soles. Emma wasn't only pretty, she was also smart. Whenever she gave the correct answer to one of Professor Jaworskyj's questions about political thinkers such as Aristotle, Maxim Gorky, Karl Marx, Charles Montesquieu, Oswald Spengler, or Henry David Thoreau, all of whom she could effortlessly quote from memory, he would flash her a rhapsodic smile.

Sometimes, Professor Jaworskyj didn't even give Emma a chance to answer his question. He would enthusiastically do so himself. "Do you know difference between Republican and Democratic Party?" he would ask and then, without a pause: "Ladies and gentlemen, there is no difference. Republican Party and Democratic Party are like Pepsi Cola and Coca Cola. If you taste without seeing bottle, you don't know difference!"

****

For reasons I could never understand, many of my professors at Hunter let us know as early as the first day of class that they were Jewish. Professor Albert, a fiery redhead who taught my course in Modern Drama and who was also an Old Testament scholar, was no exception. I had initially worried that my Jewish professors might be prejudiced against me for being German. However, since, as it turned out, they were often the ones who gave me even better grades than I thought I had deserved, I gradually let down my guard.

Professor Albert had a sadistic streak. When he handed back graded test papers he would first praise the three or four students with the highest marks. Then his tone would turn icy as he singled out the poorest performer for a public and humiliating rebuke.

One evening, a few days after we had sat for an exam on Ibsen's *The Master Builder*, Professor Albert waved one bluebook high in the air as he glared at each of us in turn. "As you all know," he hissed through clenched teeth, "I am a lover of the English language. So can you fathom, ladies and gentlemen, that we have a student in this class who had the brazen audacity to answer one of my test questions in GERMAN? Yes, you heard me correctly, in German, the language of Nazi Germany and the Holocaust! In an English class! It's absolutely beyond me how such a thing could have happened." With a trembling hand he pointed directly at me. "So tell me, Mr. Nitsch, no, tell all of us, what were you thinking when you wrote the answer to the question, 'Where did Master Builder Solness die?'"

"Dr. Albert," I replied as calmly as I could, "I knew the correct answer but at that moment the English word 'quarry' didn't come to my mind so I wrote the German word *Steinbruch* instead. I figured that answer would be better than none."

"Well, you figured wrong. Your explanation is nothing but a cheap excuse. Do I need to remind you that this is an English class?" But even Professor Albert must have had a softer side. Despite his mortifying tirade, he still gave me a 'B-' on the test."

****

Due to my late-night class schedule following a full day's work at Brewster Leeds, I usually just wolfed down a container of yogurt for supper in the college cafeteria around 5:40 p.m. I had long since discovered that if I ate anything more substantial, like a sandwich or a hamburger, I would fall asleep in class. Twice a week, on Mondays and Wednesdays, I didn't get back over to Frau Winter's apartment on the West Side until nearly 10 p.m. On those nights I would study my textbooks for an hour in my room and then, after fixing myself a cheese sandwich in the kitchen, I would head out to one of my two favorite bars.

One was a high-ceilinged Irish bar on Amsterdam Avenue and 101st Street that was patronized by white off-duty policemen and firemen. No matter how many times I had introduced myself to several of the men there, they only vaguely kept in mind that I was 'the German guy.' Much to my annoyance, to them I was always Karl, or Wolfgang, or Manfred, or Heinrich; anything, that is, except Gunter.

Paddy, the ruddy-cheeked bartender, deliberately kept the volume low on the black and white TV hanging on brackets above the bar in order not to drown out the conversation. I usually had a beer or two as I sat and listened to the men try to outdo each other with raunchy stories of their heroism in nabbing gun-toting perpetrators or dousing life-threatening fires.

Apart from the fact that they had such dangerous jobs, the patrons of the Irish bar were also united in their contempt for their "f—ing superiors" who kept denying them what they considered to be their well-deserved promotions. But nothing got all of them angrier than when they talked about 'the goddamned Niggers.' On the rare occasions when an unwary black man, perhaps new to the neighborhood, would wander in, all heads would turn in his direction, always causing him to beat a hasty retreat.

****

Many of the patrons of my other favorite bar, a smaller establishment on Broadway between 101st and 102nd Streets, only a short distance and a whole world away from the Irish bar, were black truck drivers from the garment district and black restaurant workers. They usually came in alone but, occasionally, they brought along their girlfriends or their wives.

Instead of a TV over the bar there was a jukebox in the corner from which blasted an amazing selection of songs by artists like Aretha Franklin, Ray Charles, Otis Redding, Marvin Gay and Stevie Wonder. Since the music was always played at top volume and the ceiling was low, patrons really had to speak up to be heard. The older one of the two bartenders, James, had spent some time as a GI in Germany and knew my name. But, to most of the regulars, I was once again just 'the German guy,' which is how I was always introduced to the newcomers who hadn't expected to see me there.

Aside from James the bartender, the only other person who at least attempted to remember my name was Charlie, a tall, skinny man who couldn't seem to hold a steady job. Charlie lived across the street from Frau Winter's building so we often ran into each other early in the morning as I left for work and also, occasionally, on weekends. Since I bought him a beer once in a while he made an effort to learn my name. He called me 'Gunner.'

One evening, as "Heatwave" by Martha and the Vandellas blared from the jukebox, I raised my voice to strike up a conversation with a high school English teacher I had met there a few days before.

"Excuse me, sir," I began. "I was hoping you could explain to me why, in all of my courses at Hunter College, there are, at most, only one or two black students out of a class of twenty-five."

"Wait a minute! You think that's low? Let me tell you, my naïve German friend. Up at City College on 138th Street in Harlem, in Harlem mind you, I've heard that only 2% of the entire student body is black. Only 2% in Harlem! That's outrageous. And you want to know why? The system stinks, that's why. It's stacked against us and always has been."

****

When I told Victoria about the two very different bars I frequented, she laughed. "Well, I'm glad you feel comfortable in both those places," she said. "But I'm willing to bet a million dollars, if the two of us were to come in together, we wouldn't be welcome in either one of them!"

CHAPTER 32

O n April 4, 1968, I had had an especially rough day at Brewster, Leeds. Leon Begleiter, who had just come back that morning from an extended business trip to Latin America, had swamped my desk with orders. "Do you want me to stay longer?" I asked shortly before 5:30 p.m. I had barely made a dent in the pile of documents on my desk.

"No, that's okay. The Ducats won't pay you for overtime anyway so you may as well go home and enjoy yourself."

Since it was a Thursday and I didn't have any evening classes, I rushed over to the uptown subway. But the minute I boarded the train I felt uneasy. Many of the white passengers, by glumly staring down at their shoes, were making an even greater effort than usual to avoid any direct eye contact with the other riders. Was it my imagination, or were several black passengers throwing hostile stares in my direction?

When I came up the stairs from the subway at Broadway and 96th Street, that normally bustling intersection was nearly deserted. Grabbing tighter hold of my briefcase I started to walk quickly towards Frau Winter's building when, without warning, two strapping young black men rushed at me and one of them punched me in the chest, nearly knocking me over. As I staggered backwards the taller of the two slowly rolled up his sleeves. "Let's finish off this motherfucker!" he snarled as I prepared to defend myself.

Then, just as the taller man was about to slug me again, my scrawny buddy Charlie from the 102nd Street bar appeared out of nowhere and held up his hand. "Hey, brother, leave this dude alone," he said. "Gunner's my friend from Germany. He ain't got nuthin' to do with this shit!"

To my astonishment, my two attackers shrugged and swaggered off without so much as a backward glance in our direction.

"What the hell was that all about?" I asked Charlie.

"Sorry, Gunner, but I guess you didn't hear about it yet. Some white dude just shot Dr. King down there in Tennessee."

"You mean Martin Luther King is *dead?*"

"They took him to the hospital but it don't look good. If I was you I'd keep off the street tonight. A lot of angry brothers are gonna be out fixin' for a fight."

"I guess I won't be joining you in the bar later," I said when we reached the entrance to my building. "Please tell everyone how bad I feel about what happened to Dr. King. And Charlie, thanks for saving my life."

"Forget it, man," he replied. "I know you'd do the same for me."

****

Normally when I got home Frau Winter acted as if she didn't hear me, but today she opened the door to her apartment. Her breath reeked of cigarette smoke and whiskey and her hands were shaking as she greeted me in the hallway. "Thank God you're safe!" she exclaimed.

"Did you hear about the idiot who shot that preacher King? Are they going to slaughter us in our beds tonight?"

"Yes, Frau Winter, I actually found out about it in a strange way," and I told her what had just happened.

"So two Negroes wanted to kill you and another one saved your life? Imagine that! The whole world's going crazy." She started to go back into her apartment, then suddenly turned to face me again. "You know, Mr. Nitsch, I'm glad you weren't hurt, but I don't know what a respectable young man like you is doing in that Negro bar. If you want my advice, I'd look for someplace else to have a drink."

CHAPTER 33

Despite Frau Winter's fears, thanks to the prompt intervention of Mayor John Lindsay, who sped up to Harlem right after the news of Dr. King's death came over the wires, New York City remained relatively calm. Still, at Victoria's suggestion, we decided not to see each other for a few days just to be on the safe side and, instead, kept in touch by phone.

"You know, I've seen this coming," Victoria had remarked when we spoke later that evening. "There are too many white people, especially here in the North, who claim to be liberal, but just let a black man stand up for his rights and their veneer of tolerance rubs right off."

"I've met plenty of them where there wasn't any veneer to begin with." *But it works both ways,* I thought to myself. *If I weren't German, would I still be welcome in Charlie's bar? I didn't think so.*

"Oh, I almost forgot!" Victoria went on. "My old high school friend Ruby just moved back to New York from Atlanta with her husband and we're invited over to their place on Sunday, April 24th. So please be sure to mark the date on your calendar!"

Ruby and her husband lived in one of The Bridge apartments, a group of four 32-story buildings straddling the Trans Manhattan

Expressway approach to the George Washington Bridge. I had read about The Bridge. Only five years old in 1968, it was the subject of a barrage of tenant complaints about traffic noise, fumes, and vibrations from the thousands of cars and trucks that drove under the complex day and night.

After checking in with the doorman, we took the elevator to the 21st floor.

As we stepped out into the hall, Ruby, a tall, slender woman with an enormous Afro, stared open-mouthed at me from the doorway of her apartment. She couldn't have looked more stunned if I had been Satan himself. Victoria, brightly smiling, led me over to her old friend. "So nice to see you again, Ruby! How long's it been? Nearly six years? And this is Gunter. I know you wanted to meet him and now here he is."

Ruby, still visibly shocked, reluctantly invited us inside and offered us seats on the big leather couch in the living room. Then she sat down on a leather armchair on the opposite side of the room, putting as much distance between herself and us as possible. "Isn't your husband at home?" Victoria asked. We both knew full well that he was. We had just seen him peek out from the next room and, just as quickly, disappear.

"George, don't you want to come and say hello," Ruby anxiously coaxed.

But George yelled back, "I'm busy!" Less than a minute later, in violent protest against his unwelcome visitors, the ear-drum-shattering staccato tones of George's saxophone burst upon us from the adjoining room.

Ruby had prepared ham and cheese sandwiches and a garden salad for our lunch and she invited Victoria and me to join her at the table. Before she sat down, she knocked on the bedroom door where her husband was still playing the saxophone. "Honey," she called out, "won't you join us?" and again he yelled back, "Leave me alone. I told you I'm busy!"

A minute later George rushed past us and went into the kitchen. He stacked three cheese sandwiches on a plate and helped himself to a frosty bottle of beer before storming back to the bedroom. Breaking the awkward silence that followed, Victoria mentioned for what must have been the third time that I was from Germany. To Ruby this obviously made no difference. To her I was just another honky, no matter where I came from.

Despite having planned to stay for the afternoon, Victoria and I beat a hasty retreat right after lunch. Once we were in the elevator, Victoria forced a smile. "Well, that was a great success don't you think?" she asked bitterly. "Seriously, I can't believe how much she's changed. I would never have expected her to act that way."

"Okay," I said. "Now I have to ask. What exactly had you told Ruby about me?"

"What I always tell people—that you're tall and handsome, that you're very kind, that you're working as a marketing assistant in an export company and going to Hunter College at night."

"That's it? You mean you didn't tell her that I'm . . ."

"Listen, Gunter. I don't see you as a 'white guy.' To me you're the man I'm in love with. I want people to judge you with an open mind when they meet you just like I did. If other people have a problem with that, it's too bad."

"So I don't suppose we'll be seeing Ruby and George again?" I asked coyly.

"No, I don't suppose we will."

****

Since we had some extra time on our way back to Greenwich Village, we stopped off on the Upper West Side to see the movie *Guess Who's Coming to Dinner?* It was an ironic choice under the circumstances. "What did I tell you?" Victoria said as we left the theater. "When it came right down to it, the white parents weren't really as liberal as they claimed to be. And I actually found it offensive that the black fiancé turned out to be a renowned physician, didn't you? I guess the liberal folks in Hollywood didn't think audiences would have bought the premise if he'd just been some ordinary nice guy who happened to be black."

It was already getting dark when we got back downtown. As we walked across Washington Square Park, two muscular young black men came towards us and blocked our path. Ignoring me completely, they both stared angrily at Victoria. "Hey, bitch," one of them sneered, "can't you get satisfied by a Nigger?"

Victoria gripped my hand hard and whispered, "Just keep going and don't say anything!"

When the two young men were out of earshot, I finally let off steam. "How can you stand it? The constant insults? George and his squawking saxophone were bad enough but now this? I didn't expect it here. How come no one seems to give a damn when black men come to the Village with their white girlfriends? Why should it be any different with us?"

"Calm down. Don't take it so personally," Victoria replied softly. "C'mon, let me fix you some supper."

****

It never ceased to amaze me how easily Victoria could ignore the stares and slurs directed at us wherever we went, but even she had her limits. In the middle of May 1968, only a few weeks after the unpleasant encounter in Washington Square Park, I had stayed over with Victoria the night before and we were talking and joking around as we walked hand in hand towards the Christopher Street subway station on our way to work. She was wearing a short flowery summer dress and her usual high-heeled shoes. I had on a light-gray summer suit, a white shirt and a tie.

Suddenly Victoria whispered, "Oh my God! Do you see that car with the windows rolled down? It's keeping pace with us and a man is making a movie!"

"What car?"

"The one with the Alabama plates! Please God don't let them shoot us!"

As Victoria clung to me in terror, my usual inclination would have been to yell at the two gawking elderly couples in the shiny Ford station wagon. But, then, I thought to myself, *don't get mad! Get even!*

Quickly dropping my briefcase, I grabbed Victoria's shapely derrière with my right hand and shoved my left leg between her legs. Then, gently pulling her head towards me with my left hand I bent down and kissed her on the mouth until I nearly ran out of air. Out of the corner of my eye I could see all four people in the car shaking their heads in disbelief as the movie camera kept rolling. Meanwhile the drivers in the cars the Ford was blocking began to honk.

After the Alabama car had finally sped away, Victoria doubled over, convulsed with laughter. Clutching her stomach, she was unable to talk for at least a minute before finally gasping, "You're too much. I thought they were going to have heart attacks! And when they show the movie to their friends . . ." She couldn't say another word.

I retrieved my briefcase and, as we continued on our way, Victoria was still giggling. As usual at that early hour the subway was crowded and we had to push our way inside. Since all the seats were already taken, I held on to a strap and my briefcase with one hand and clung to Victoria with the other. All around us, the other passengers had been staring glumly off into space. Yet each time I looked down at Victoria's face she had another laughing fit and, by the time I got off at 42nd Street and she continued on to her Head Start school near 125th Street, even though they weren't in on the joke, half the people in the car were smiling.

CHAPTER 34

*G*iven her cheerful personality, it wasn't at all surprising that Victoria had a wide circle of friends among the teachers and school administrators she knew, most of whom were either black or Jewish. As a result, she was frequently invited to parties in Greenwich Village and on the Upper West Side. Yet even in these large groups of self-proclaimed 'open-minded' people, when some of the guests discovered that the two of us were there together they couldn't disguise their shock or their disappointment.

Rather than let this upset us, we decided to have some perverse fun with it. As Victoria gleefully expressed it, "Let's smoke them out and see what happens!" From then on whenever we went to a party we followed a simple routine.

After first circulating in the crowd for an hour or so, we would split up to meet someone of the opposite sex. Since I was usually the tallest man there, I tended to attract unusually tall women of both races.

At one party, for example, Laura, a 5'10" redheaded teacher who lived on the Upper East Side, approached me and immediately launched into an excruciatingly detailed account of her entire life story. After ten minutes, as my eyes began to cross, I frantically looked around for Victoria and gave her the prearranged wink. Suddenly she was at my side.

"Hello, my darling," she cooed as she put her arm around my waist.

"Laura, I'd like you to meet my girlfriend, Victoria. She's a teacher, too . . . ."

"You idiot! You might have told me!" Laura snapped before angrily storming off.

Victoria, on the other hand, usually wound up with short, white, intellectual types whose hopes were dashed when I came to her rescue. In those instances it was never clear what the men found most disturbing—my height or my German accent.

We both knew that the game was cruel but, I'm ashamed to say, we enjoyed it.

****

In the middle of June the switchboard operator at Brewster, Leeds rang me. "Hi, Mr. Nitsch. I have Bob for you on the phone."

"Bob? Did he give you his last name?"

"He claims he's a friend of yours. Just a second; I'll connect you."

And suddenly I heard a familiar voice. "Hey, Stretch, this is Bob Proctor from San Rafael . . ."

I interrupted him. "I'll be darned. Great to hear from you! It's been ages since I heard that nickname. Are you calling from California?"

"No, we're staying with friends in Manhattan on the Upper West Side."

"That's were I live. But what do you mean by we? Are you here with your brother?"

"With my wife. Sue and I are newlyweds and we're staying with friends who recently moved to New York."

"Congratulations! We should get together while you're here. How about this? Let me take you and your wife out for dinner tonight or tomorrow, whatever works for you, and I'll bring my girlfriend along."

"I presume it's not Charlotte."

"Funny you should ask. Actually, I just got a letter from my mother. Charlotte got married about two weeks ago."

"Are you okay with that?"

"It's hard to believe, but I'm actually fine with it. Maybe that's because I'm dating someone special right now."

"Also German?"

"No, she's American. A teacher. So, when can we see you? Tonight? Tomorrow night?"

"Thanks for the restaurant idea but our friends have a huge place and they said they'd like to meet you, too. They're planning to order up some pizza tomorrow night and you and your girlfriend are more than welcome to join us."

The next evening Victoria and I stopped off in a liquor store to buy a bottle of Mosel wine. As we walked together to Bob's friends' apartment building, I boasted to Victoria about Bob. "He's one of the most open-minded, liberal people I've ever met," I began. "When I knew him in Germany, he said he felt ashamed after an African student wandered into the wrong bar and was beaten up by white American GIs. And he was always apologetic about the way whites in America treated 'Negroes'."

Victoria was quiet for a minute as we approached the building lobby. "I suppose," she finally said, "you didn't tell Bob that I'm black."

"I didn't see any reason why I should."

But the minute Bob opened the door to his friends' twelfth floor apartment to greet us, the color drained from his face and he shook our hands with great reluctance. The atmosphere was decidedly chilly as he ushered us into the sparsely furnished living room to meet his wife and their two friends whose unpainted étagère, splintery wooden bookshelves, outsized dining table, and six unmatched wooden chairs had all the charm of Salvation Army rejects. Apart from the television set in the corner, the only items that looked relatively new were four squashed-down black beanbags.

In the awkward silence that followed the introductions, I didn't have to glance over at Victoria to know what she was thinking. It didn't matter whether it was her black friends from Atlanta or my white friends from California; the message was the same.

"So, Bob," I finally said as nonchalantly as I could, "how're your parents doing?"

"They're doing okay."

"Your mom still runs the beauty parlor in San Rafael?"

"Yeah, she does."

"And your dad? Still working for the Customs Office?"

When Bob answered only with "Yep", Victoria excused herself and went to use the bathroom. She was gone for quite a while. During her absence from the room Bob and his wife discussed with their friends what else they should see in New York before flying back to San Francisco. All four of them acted as though I wasn't even there.

Suddenly Bob reached for the phone and said, "So should we order pizza?"

At that moment Victoria returned from the bathroom. She was clutching her head. "I'm awfully sorry," she blurted, "but I don't feel well at all. Gunter, would you mind bringing me home?"

Jumping up from my seat, I put my arm around her. Turning to our hosts, I mumbled, "It was nice meeting you all."

Bob followed us to the door. As he shook my hand he whispered under his breath, "I didn't expect this from you, of all people." Then, raising his voice, he added, "Take care!"

The elevator door had barely closed behind us when I gave Victoria an extra-long hug. "I apologize for putting you through that," I began. "I was so sure Bob would be happy for us both." Then I looked down at her face. "I hope you aren't really sick?"

"No, just sick at heart. I couldn't bear to stay there another second."

"What I can't figure out is whether Bob has changed that much or whether he was never really the person I thought he was."

Despite the warm weather Victoria shivered as we stepped out onto the street and headed for the subway. "Let's just forget about them," she said.

CHAPTER 35

Starting with my former roommates in Queens, ever since I had began dating Victoria my circle of friends had grown smaller and smaller. With the exception of Walter and Tamara, as time went on, nearly everyone I knew had snubbed me. So it came as a welcome relief when my former Haitian girlfriend, Jeanine, phoned to suggest that I come over to her apartment to meet the man she had been dating.

"Peter's German," she explained. "And he's lived in Cologne. So I thought you two should get to know each other."

"Hey, Jeanine, I'm happy you've found someone new. Is it serious?"

"*Mon Dieu, non!* He loves his booze way too much. The truth is I'm going to break up with him. But I wanted you to meet him before I did.

Born in Yugoslavia to a Serbian father and a German mother, Peter was a hard-drinking, big brute of a man whose upper arms were as thick as my thighs. He was so infatuated with all things German that he had changed his name from Wladimir Peter Vranjkovic to the decidedly more German-sounding Peter Vollmann when he had arrived in Cologne. Despite his protruding beer belly and the beginning of a double chin, I didn't doubt his claim that he had been a nationally known shot putter and hammer thrower during his university days.

Yet, for all his lack of polish I was glad to have Peter as a friend. He was the first person in several years with whom I could talk in German about my hometown. He was not at all nonplussed by my relationship with Victoria (or, as he more crudely put it, "As long as it's not a Scotsman, I'll date anyone wearing a skirt!"). As icing on the cake, he was willing to take me on as a tennis partner despite the fact that I had only recently started lessons at Hunter College.

From then on, whenever the weather was good, Peter and I played tennis on the public courts at 120th Street in Riverside Park nearly every Friday after work and early on Saturday and Sunday mornings. Even though I was a beginner, our games were nearly even. Although Peter could whack the ball much harder than I could, I easily outran him.

We soon fell into a pattern. On Friday evenings, when the sun went down and we could no longer see the ball, we would leave the courts and head over to the West End Bar on Broadway at 116th Street across from Columbia University, where I would eat a hamburger and drink a beer while Peter chugged down three or four beers in quick succession (his so-called 'liquid bread'). Then he drove back home to Brooklyn in his Ford Mustang.

Although Peter had earned a Mater's Degree in Business Administration from the University of Cologne, he was working full-time for a marble company 'to learn the trade', as he put it. His dream was to own his own business one day. "I do everything from operating the machinery to cutting and polishing the marble to transporting it," he would invariably confide in me after his third or fourth beer. "Right now I'm learning how to install marble in buildings and offices and how to sell the damned stuff. For two years I've been taking a load of crap from people who aren't half as smart as I am. And believe me, Gunter, once I learn the ropes, I'm going out on my own and they can all kiss my ass good-bye."

****

"The way you describe him, I don't know why you hang out with that character," Victoria chided me one day in late July when I phoned to tell her I'd probably get back later than usual from tennis. "Quite frankly, he scares the dickens out of me."

"Well, he may be a little rough around the edges," I countered, "but I'm sure he's harmless."

"A little rough? How many women has he gone out with since he stopped seeing Jeanine, tell me that?"

"I'm not keeping count but right now he's dating a biology professor from City College."

"That beats everything. When you discover what it is that all those women see in him, be sure to let me know," Victoria replied, "because I can't for the life of me figure it out! Anyway, I'll see you later!"

Peter was already waiting for me on the court when I got off the bus at 120th Street. "Hey, Gunter, I've got big news!"

"Don't tell me you've met someone new?"

"*That* wouldn't be big news. Women come; women go. It's all the same to me." He broke into a smile. "No, it's much bigger than that. I've just set up a corporation and on August 31st you and Victoria are invited to the grand opening celebration of my new company."

****

The grand opening took place in Peter's new showroom on lower Madison Avenue. Aside from the customary cheese tidbits and pigs-in-a-blanket, there was a seemingly endless supply of spicy Serbian meatballs catered by a nearby Yugoslavian restaurant. As we precariously balanced our food on paper plates, surrounded by hundreds of glistening marble samples on marble tables and on marble shelves attached to marble-covered walls, Peter gave a short welcoming speech to the assembled guests.

"See?" I whispered to Victoria. "You needn't have worried. He's really a nice guy."

A short time later Peter came over to where the two of us were standing.

"Too bad my girlfriend couldn't make it tonight 'cause I'd wanted to introduce her to you," he said. He paused to wave in two new arrivals. "Listen, you two. Once this party is over two of my friends are coming over to my place in Brooklyn with their girlfriends. Come join us. I'd like to show you where I live."

"Well," Victoria began, "I'm not sure that . . ."

"Of course we'll come," I quickly interjected before Victoria could finish her sentence.

"Great! The two of you can come out in my car. I've got plenty of room."

****

The living room of Peter's ground floor brownstone apartment near Prospect Park was furnished with an oversized, dark-brown wooden couch, three wooden chairs, and an enormous, marble-topped dining table.

"So what do you think?" Peter wiped his mouth with the back of his hand, having just single-handedly devoured one of the four large pepperoni pizzas he had had delivered, which he had quickly washed down with a bottle of Chianti. "Nice place, right? But now I want to show you where I spend most of my time. I call it my 'action room.'"

He got himself a bottle of Budweiser from his refrigerator, put his arms around the shoulders of his friends' dates, and led us into his bedroom. An unmade king size bed and two matching night tables filled most of the far wall. To the left was an open, walk in closet lined with neatly pressed suits and, on the opposite wall, a long bookshelf filled with brand-new hard cover books. I glanced at the titles. Some were in English, but most were in German. Nearly all of them dealt with World War II.

But, just as Peter must have expected, all of our eyes were drawn to a black and white poster on the wall above the bed. The huge photo showed a profile view of two steel-helmeted German soldiers, the one on the left crouching close to the ground clutching a rifle; the other supporting himself with his left arm as he was about to throw a potato masher grenade with his right.

We all stood gazing at the poster for a moment while Peter beamed. "You like it, huh?" Peter said. "I'll let you in on a little secret." He leaned forward and dropped his voice. "The soldier on the left was my brother!"

"Cut the crap, Peter," I said. "First of all, you told me you were an only child and, besides, I've seen the same picture in history books. That poster was made from a World War II postcard."

Before Peter could respond, Victoria spoke up. "Regardless of where it's from, what I want to know is why you have that awful poster in your bedroom of all places."

"You really wanna know? 'Cause when I bring Jewish girls in here, it impresses the hell out of them. That's why." He looked defiantly at each of us in turn. "You don't have to believe me, but it's true."

Victoria gave me a pleading glance. "It's getting awfully late," she announced. The other young women were quick to agree and they both soon left in disgust with their dates. Despite the late hour, the sensible thing would have been for Victoria and me to find the nearest subway, but when Peter offered to drive us back to Manhattan, I ignored the frantic signals from Victoria, and agreed to let him. After all, hadn't I driven with him several times before when he'd had a few drinks at the West End Bar?

That, as it turned out, was a big mistake. As Victoria cowered in the back seat and Peter chattered cheerfully about his new company, I watched in horror as the Mustang hurtled across the Brooklyn Bridge at more than sixty miles per hour and then screeched to an abrupt stop only inches from a concrete divider.

"Are you both okay?" Peter asked, suddenly contrite. "Good thing this baby is equipped with seat belts." As the angry drivers behind us honked with impatience, we practically crawled the rest of the way to Victoria's place on Eighth Street in Greenwich Village.

As soon we were in her apartment, Victoria exploded, "That guy is a lunatic and a drunk. How can you hang out with him? And that poster in his bedroom? Disgusting!"

"Look, he's not a bad guy when he's sober."

"So would it make it any better if he put that picture up when he was drunk?"

"Listen. It was my mistake to let us get into the car with him. And it won't happen again. Anyway, I should have known better. He's boasted about getting pulled over for drunk driving but I guess I didn't believe him. Apparently he keeps a fifty-dollar bill together with his driver's license and the cops let him off every time. Twice they even gave him a lift home."

She shook her head in disgust. "You knew all that and you still let us both get in that car?"

"I've got no excuse. It was an incredibly dumb thing to do."

"That was a first and last time for me," Victoria said. "You can bet on that!"

CHAPTER 36

*I*n early November I answered the pay phone at Frau Winter's apartment and heard a familiar voice. "Hello, Gunter, is that you? It's Jeanine! Remember when you promised to come to my wedding? Well, I'm calling to invite you. I'm getting married in two weeks and the reception will be held on Saturday the 16th."

"I'd love to come. Who's the lucky guy?"

"A high school history teacher. Giorgio's Italian-American and very nice and so are his parents. But they're all very short." She snickered. "You're going to tower over them. Oh, and before I forget! I know you have a new girlfriend, but would you mind being the escort for my younger sister, Jacqueline? She finally got out of Haiti."

"I'd be happy to. How old is Jacqueline by now?"

"She's seventeen. Much too young for you."

****

The wedding reception was held in the large party room in Jeanine's building. Jerry, who had managed to put on even more weight since I had last seen him, rushed over to greet me.

"*Mon ami allemand!* How long has it been? Come. Let me introduce you to Giorgio."

But Jeanine was already heading in my direction hand in hand with her new husband, an intellectual type with thick glasses and dark curly hair. In her high heels Jeanine was about an inch taller than he was. "Isn't he wonderful?" Jeanine exclaimed. "And so understanding! He doesn't mind at all that I invited you."

"Nice to meet you, Gunter. You're more than welcome," Giorgio said and he gave me a strong handshake. "After all," he added with a grin, "your loss is definitely my gain!"

"Now you must meet my sister Jacqueline," Jeanine said and she led me across the room to where her younger sister was standing. Jacqueline was tall and slender with straight, dark-brown hair pulled back into a ponytail. With her fair skin, her large brown eyes, long neck, and her perfect teeth, she reminded me of a young Audrey Hepburn. Before I even had a chance to speak, she was already telling me about her high school classes.

"You must be good in French," I said.

With a shy smile and a downward glance she softly replied, "In French I'm the best in class. But of course it helps that I come from Haiti." Then, after a pause, she added, even more softly, "and in Latin, too." *What a sweet, modest, gentle girl*, I thought to myself. I was impressed and I told her so.

Just then Jerry came over and asked me to help him get some cartons of liquor and wine from Jeanine's apartment. Promising Jacqueline that I'd be back soon, I followed Jerry down the hallway.

"I have to warn you," Jerry said as he turned the key in the door. "Jeanine has gone and married a real bookworm."

Despite the warning, I couldn't believe how much the place had been transformed. Floor to ceiling bookshelves packed with hundreds of books had been installed on both sides of the entry hall, barely leaving enough space for Jerry to go through without knocking anything down. Sadly, one thing still looked the same. Sitting morosely on the couch, glued to the television, Jeanine's little nephew Teddy didn't even bother to look up when we went to the kitchen to retrieve the cartons. If I had enough time, I would have made him a paper airplane. But the guests were waiting.

After a buffet dinner, a Haitian band played a slow waltz and, as everyone applauded, Giorgio led his bride into the center of the room to dance the first dance. All eyes were on the happy couple; all eyes, that is, except Jacqueline's. She kept sneaking glances at me instead.

When the music stopped, instead of inviting everyone to dance, Jeanine walked over to where Jacqueline and I were standing. "The band has a surprise for you!" she announced. Taking my hand, she led me onto the dance floor to the strains of the "Blue Danube Waltz." Once again the guests applauded, but this time it was for Jeanine and me. I caught glimpses of Giorgio's face as Jeanine and I twirled around and could only hope that he had approved of Jeanine's 'surprise' beforehand.

Then, to add insult to injury, just as the last notes of the waltz were being played, the 'lovely, demure' Jacqueline took a step forward, pointed at me, and shouted in English so that everyone could hear, "HE'S THE ONE MY SISTER REALLY WANTED TO MARRY!"

"Just ignore her," Jeanine said as I hurried her back to her husband. "She's probably had too much champagne. Isn't that right, *mon chéri?*" Jeanine added as she leaned over to give Giorgio a kiss.

Giorgio put his hand on my shoulder. "Cheer up, Gunter! Why the long face? I've got no hard feelings towards you, okay? This is the best day of my life and I'm not going to let Jacqueline spoil it. But," he continued after a short pause, "if you can talk some sense into that girl, I'm sure both Jeanine and I would appreciate it."

Easier said than done, I thought to myself as I reluctantly returned to Jacqueline's side and asked her for the next dance. "Jacqueline," I began as we stepped onto the dance floor, "don't you realize how hurtful your remark was?"

She snuggled closer to me, leaned her head back, and flashed me a wicked smile. "*Peut-être, mais c'est la vérité!*"

"How can you say that? I think Giorgio and Jeanine are a great match and I've never seen your sister happier."

Jacqueline stopped dancing. "All the same," she insisted, "she would've dropped him for you in a heartbeat." With a shrug of her shoulders, she stomped off to the far corner of the room and never looked back.

I glanced over at Giorgio and held up my hands in a gesture of defeat and he shrugged his shoulders and grinned. Jeanine was, indeed, lucky to have him.

CHAPTER 37

*E*ver since I had started taking classes at Hunter College I had been on a trial basis because I didn't have a German high school diploma. However, by the spring semester in 1969, my overall grade point average qualified me to enroll as a matriculated student. As such, I no longer had to pay tuition, much to my relief. Since I was eager to complete my undergraduate degree as quickly as possible, I took the plunge and registered for five courses.

It was a lot to take on, but I had no doubt that I could handle the work. After all, my track record was good. Except during my first year at Hunter when I had withdrawn from an economics course, I had completed every course in which I had enrolled. Victoria, on the other hand, had the unfortunate habit of registering for courses and then dropping them so late in the term that she couldn't even get back a fraction of the tuition. Just since we'd met, she had dropped one course in math, two courses in German and two in French. The waste of money and the fact that she gave up so easily disturbed me no end and we argued about it. Since I was living on a shoestring budget, it also aggravated me that Victoria had as many as twenty credit cards, among them credit cards from many of the leading New York department stores. And she was as nonchalant about spending beyond her means on clothes and shoes as she was about tuition money. (Her sister, Eve, had once warned me, "I learned the hard way. Don't ever lend her any money because you'll never get it back.")

When I told Victoria that I had registered for five courses, it was her turn to criticize me. "Now who's being irresponsible? And you, with a full-time job at Brewster, Leeds! You've taken on way too much and I'm willing to bet you'll regret it."

But, rather than discourage me, Victoria's comments made me more determined to succeed. I was going to show her how to take responsibility and stick things out, no matter how difficult. Still, it was not easy. Just for one of my five classes, a course on "Ethnic and Race Relations" taught by Luis Rodriguez-Abad, an inspiring lecturer from Ecuador, the readings included *Soul on Ice* by Eldridge Cleaver, *Black Skin—White Masks* by Frantz Fanon, *The Masters and Slaves* by Gilberto Freyre, and *Manchild in a Promised Land* by Jean Claude Brown.

"It's not just a problem in faraway places like Mississippi," Professor Rodriguez had stressed when he distributed the reading list. "Look in your own backyard and consider the injustice being done to brown and black people regarding higher education. Right now there are protests at Harvard, Cornell, NYU, Fordham, and Princeton. Even at some of the other City University campuses." We shifted uncomfortably in our seats as he looked around the room. There was only one black student in the class. "Mark my words, ladies and gentlemen. It's only a matter of time before the students at Hunter wake up, too."

This wasn't the first time I'd heard that militant message. A few years earlier, as I was on my way to my History of Art class, I had noticed an overflow crowd at the Hunter College Auditorium where a young African-American man was giving a rousing speech to the mostly white student audience. With an odd mixture of militant calls for Black Power, occasional sexual innuendoes, and, most surprising, considering the context, quotes from philosophers such as Immanuel Kant and Nietzsche, he held the crowd in the palm of his hand. *History of Art can wait*, I had decided and I had squeezed inside to take a place at the back.

"Who is he?" I asked one of the other students.

"Don't you recognize him? It's Stokely Carmichael!"

As he had been doing at college campuses around the country ever since he spoke these words at Berkeley three years earlier in late October 1966, Carmichael's speech was a call to student action:

> *There is then in a larger sense, what do you do on your university campus? . . . . Do you begin to relate to people outside of the ivory tower and university wall? Do you think you're capable of building those human relationships, as the country now stands?*

Professor Rodriguez was right. The winds of unrest were blowing and it was only a matter of time before they swept over all of us at Hunter College as well.

CHAPTER 38

On those weeknights when I had a class, I would get back to the Upper West Side around 10 p.m. After stopping into a nearby Jewish deli for a hot dog, I would hit the books until midnight. On Saturdays and Sundays, following an early morning run in Riverside Park, I would usually study until suppertime. Yet, even though I had less and less time for her on weekends, I stubbornly refused to admit to Victoria that I was barely keeping up with the reading for my five courses.

During that same time period, a different kind of problem was looming at Brewster, Leeds as well. On October 1, 1968, the longshoremen's union had gone out on strike. Despite a temporary injunction and court-ordered collective bargaining, the disruption to shipping was still ongoing in early 1969. For a company that relied on overseas exports for its survival, the impact was disastrous. With no end of the strike in sight, the Ducat brothers had already fired a typist and a clerk from the transportation department. I was sure that it was only a matter of time before I would be next.

Sure enough, late on a Friday afternoon in January 1969, Leon Begleiter handed me two weekly paychecks instead of the one I was expecting. "I hate to be the bearer of bad news," he said, "but our business has come to a standstill and we have to let two more employees go. Unfortunately, my cousins have decided you should be one of them."

"May I ask who the other person is? I'm guessing it must be David Goldberg since he's only been working here a few months."

"No, it's not him. The Ducat brothers are keeping David on. Their choice, not mine." Then he smiled and reached over to shake my hand. "I'm sure you'll find a much better job and you can certainly count on me for a good reference."

When I told Victoria how angry I was about what had happened, she only added fuel to the fire. "You know how it is with the Jews," she had remarked. "When it came down to a choice between you and one of theirs, you didn't stand a chance." Still, in a way, being fired by the Ducat brothers proved to be a blessing in disguise. After leaving my résumé with several employment agencies and investing in a portable typewriter with an American keyboard on which to write several upcoming term papers, I could now spend every day hunkered down in the Hunter College library catching up on my reading. Over the next few months, without a job to go to, I got my first and only luxurious taste of what it meant to live life as a full-time college student.

****

In spite of the reason for it, Victoria was delighted that I suddenly had so much extra time. When I met her for dinner on Valentine's Day (which, coincidentally, was also the day the longshoremen's strike finally ended) she asked if I would join her at a party being given the following weekend by Aleesa Leyland, the Director of her Head Start program. "She has a beautiful home in Harlem," Victoria explained, "and the guests will be mostly upper class blacks and a few Jewish teachers. You'll be very much in the minority. Are you okay with that? Are you sure it won't make you uncomfortable?"

"Not at all. You've really made me nosy. Would a business suit be good enough? Or do I need to be more formal?"

"A dark suit and tie will do just fine. And now that that's settled there's one more thing I want to ask you. We've talked a number of times about your coming to visit my Head Start class. So, now that you have some free time, how about joining me up in Harlem tomorrow? I think you should see that side of life up there before we go to Aleesa's party." It was arranged that I would come by around lunchtime.

The next day I rode the subway to 125th Street in Harlem and walked the few blocks to the Head Start school. Some of the twenty shabbily dressed boys and girls between the ages of three and five in Victoria's classroom were busy with building blocks and coloring books. Others had donned long green smocks and were sprawled on the floor doing finger painting. And several more were sitting cross-legged on a colorful, round carpet while Victoria read them a story.

Victoria got up from her stool and clapped her hands to get everyone's attention. "We have a special visitor today," she announced. "Let me introduce you to Mr. Nitsch. He's from a faraway place called Germany."

For the next two hours I did my best to help keep the children busy and happy. I clearly had no idea what I was getting myself into. My first mistake was to toss one of the boys into the air and catch him as he screamed with delight. When I set him back down, nineteen other children lined up for their turn to do the same. Then I got down on all fours to take one giggling child after another for a 'pony ride' on my back while Victoria held each of them in place. To catch my breath, I sat down on a tiny chair to make everyone a paper airplane. And, as the children attentively watched each step in the folding process, I somehow found enough energy to teach several of the little girls to count in German, "*Eins, zwei, drei, vier, fünf,*" all the way up to *zehn.*

When the mothers began to arrive at the end of the school day, six or seven little boys and girls took hold of my pants legs and begged, "Don't leave yet. Play some more with us please!" In fact they gripped me so tightly that Victoria had to pry them off in order to return them to their mothers.

"How do you have the energy to do that all day, every day?" I asked Victoria on our walk to the subway. "I haven't been this worn out since my days in basic training."

"The kids loved you, but I guess you already know that."

"But the way they clung to me at the end . . . it was kind of strange."

"Don't forget that the vast majority of the children are surrounded by women twenty-four hours a day. Only one of them, the little girl with the bright yellow farmer pants, has a father at home but, from what I hear, he has a drug problem. So you can understand why they were thrilled to have a man around if only for a few hours."

"Well, it's great what you're doing for them. I was really impressed."

"Don't be. My job pays well. But no matter what happens in the classroom, we only get to work with these kids six hours a day. The rest of the time they hear their mothers and their boyfriends talking ghetto English. You can't imagine how frustrating it is to send those boys and girls back out into that environment every day. I sometimes wonder if what I do is even worth it in the long run."

"Don't be so hard on yourself. You can't do more than you're doing for them. And I'm sure some of it must rub off."

"I hope so. That's what I keep telling myself. Anyway, this coming Saturday you'll see a totally different side of Harlem, I guarantee it."

CHAPTER 39

*A*leesa Leyland and her husband, a vice president with Chemical Bank, lived in a four-story brownstone home a few blocks from the City College campus in Harlem. As we walked that night from the subway to the Leyland residence, I tried not to show my nervousness. Here we were, Victoria in the elegant black pants suit she had just bought on credit at Saks Fifth Avenue and me, in my dark-blue suit. And from what little I had already seen of Harlem, I was sure we both had targets on our backs.

But this was not the Harlem I had expected. To begin with, judging from the Mercedes Benzes, Chryslers and Cadillacs parked on the street in front of the Leylands' brownstone, Victoria and I were, in all likelihood, the only couple to arrive on foot.

"Wow!" I said to Victoria as I took in the scene.

"What did I tell you?" she replied.

Despite the cool evening, several of the windows to the brightly lit rooms on the first and second floors were slightly ajar, and the sounds of a piano and of muffled conversations greeted us as we walked up the stone staircase to the front door. A young woman in a crisp black uniform and starched white apron took our coats and hats and directed us to the living room, which was furnished with ultra-modern leather and teak furniture. Clustered in groups around the perimeter of the room, expensively attired ladies and gentlemen were admiring the colorful African paintings and wall hangings.

Aleesa Leyland waved us both over to the far side of the room to meet her husband. Charles Leyland was my height and his wife was almost as tall in her stiletto shoes. In contrast to the bushy Afro hairstyles that many of the younger generation were now sporting, both Aleesa and Charles wore their hair closely cropped.

"I'm so glad you could come!" Aleesa exclaimed. "I hope you didn't have any trouble finding the place. Oh, and before I forget, Ruth Feigenbaum and her husband asked me to let them know the minute you arrived. I think you'll find them in the next room."

It was easy to spot Ruth and Saul Feigenbaum. They were one of only two white couples at the party. Ruth had been born and raised in Germany. Her husband was American born.

Ruth hurried to my side. "Gunter! I've been meaning to ask you. How did you like visiting Victoria's Head Start class the other day?"

"It was exhausting but I really enjoyed myself. Quite a contrast to the kind of work I normally do, that's for sure."

Ruth turned to Victoria. "Why don't you talk to Saul and let me borrow Gunter for a few minutes? I hope you don't mind?"

Switching to German, Ruth surreptitiously pointed to various couples and filled me in on who they were. Among them to my amazement were an assistant to Mayor John Lindsay, professors from City College and from Columbia University, the owner of a major car dealership, the pastor of one of Harlem's largest churches, a retired U.S. Army colonel, and a few well-known writers and musicians. "You look surprised. You shouldn't be. Harlem has its high society, too, you know."

"It's not that. I was just wondering what the heck I'm doing in this crowd. Look at me! I'm thirty-one years old, unemployed, still working on my college degree, and living in a furnished room."

"Don't sell yourself short," Ruth chided. "Victoria told me you'd lost your job, but I'm sure you'll land a new position soon."

"*Das hoffe ich sehr!*"

Just then Victoria interrupted us. "Enough with the German you two. C'mon Gunter. Let's go listen to the music." She took my hand and led me into an adjacent room where an odd mixture of French perfumes and heavy cigar smoke hung in the air despite the breeze from the open window. Seated at the grand piano in one corner of the room a heavy-set man in a tuxedo with a strong resemblance to jazz great Oscar Peterson was playing a medley of Cole Porter tunes. For a second I was tempted to ask him whether he really was 'the Oscar Peterson,' but I thought better of it lest I would make a fool of myself if he were not.

After stopping at the bar to get a glass of Chardonnay, we introduced ourselves to Leroy, a middle-aged man with a wide 'Einstein' moustache who was standing near the piano together with another Head Start teacher—a young woman in a tight red dress. While I enthused to the young woman about my course with Professor Rodriguez, her companion, who had been listening intently, suddenly startled me by speaking in German with a strong Bavarian accent. "Tell me, Gunter, where in Germany are you from? I can't figure it out from the way you speak English!"

Leroy, it turned out, had been stationed with the American Army in Würzburg where he had served as a logistics officer. Recently divorced from a Bavarian woman after a twelve-year marriage, he was now the sales manager for a General Motors dealership in the Bronx.

"How about you? What's your line of work?" he asked me.

"I guess you could say I'm between jobs right now. Several employment agencies have said they would get in touch once an opening turns up."

"Forget employment agencies! If you want an old man's advice, go to the German American Chamber of Commerce. They're much more likely to help you. Believe me."

While Victoria and I were riding home from the party hours later I thought over Leroy's suggestion. He might have been on to something. In the shock of losing my job at Brewster, Leeds I'd completely forgotten about having used the German American Chamber of Commerce as a resource back in 1964. If nothing else worked out, I decided, I would give the Chamber another try.

CHAPTER 40

*A*nd, in fact, nothing else *had* worked out. By the middle of March the little money I had managed to save up was dwindling fast and the luxury of having enough time for my classes was greatly outweighed by my lack of income. In desperation, I gathered together my updated German-language résumé and my references and, five years after first trying my luck there, I headed downtown to the 36th floor offices of the German American Chamber of Commerce in 666 Fifth Avenue, a fairly new, aluminum-paneled skyscraper between 52nd and 53rd Streets.

The receptionist eyed me quizzically. "My name is Gunter Nitsch. I don't have an appointment," I began, "but I was wondering if I could speak to someone for a few minutes about finding a job with a German company in New York City."

As I was talking to the receptionist a man who had come out of a nearby office stood off to one side listening to my request. He had thin lips, an aquiline nose, arched eyebrows, and a thick head of black hair that was graying at the temples. To my surprise, he addressed himself to me. "The name's Ledermann," he said in Berlin-accented German.

"I'm deputy manager of the Chamber. Please step into my office, Mr. Nitsch. Perhaps I can help you."

I followed Mr. Ledermann into his large, windowed office. After offering me a seat, Mr. Ledermann settled into a high-backed leather chair behind his large desk. "So," he said after looking over my résumé and hearing me out, "Brewster, Leeds let you go because of the longshoremen's strike?"

"Actually, there's more to it than that. They laid me off even though I'd been working there for four years, but they kept on someone who did the same kind of work who had only been there a few months."

"And you found this unjust? Do you want to tell me why?"

"Well, if it came down to a choice between Mr. Goldman and me, I thought for sure I'd be the one they'd keep on."

"When you say 'they,' whom do you mean? Who owns Brewster, Leeds?"

"Two brothers from Vienna who came to New York in the 1930's."

He leaned back, clasped his hands behind his head and said, "I'm beginning to get the picture. Tell me, do you have anything against Jews?"

It was only then that I realized how my comments must have sounded. "No sir, not at all," I hurried to reply. "It was just that I had so much more experience, that's all."

Now Mr. Ledermann smiled. "I thought not, but I just wanted to make sure."

After glancing over my German letters of recommendation again, he tapped his fingers on his desk, deep in thought. When he looked back up at me nothing could have prepared me for what he was about to say. "You know, Mr. Nitsch, I could give you the list of German companies you asked for, but I think we might have a position for you right here. Our Manager of Market Development is looking for an assistant. Your job would be to help German businessmen who need advice on how to market their products and services in the United States. Based on your education in Germany and your experience in both countries, I think you could handle the job. What do you think?"

"That sounds like a great opportunity, Mr. Ledermann. Of course, I'd like to know what the compensation would be."

"Before we talk about that, we have to ask Mr. Klingenberg, for whom you would be working, whether he agrees. Please wait here. I'll be right back."

Minutes later Mr. Ledermann returned with Rolf Klingenberg, a bespectacled young man of medium height with dirty blond hair and slightly bulging eyes. From his accent in German I knew right away that he was from the Stuttgart area. After asking me a few questions he took a quick glance at my résumé and then looked up. "I think Mr. Nitsch will do just fine," he said to Mr. Ledermann before hurrying off to a meeting elsewhere in the office.

To my amazement Mr. Ledermann now proposed a monthly salary that was substantially more than the amount I had been earning at Brewster, Leeds. "So, how does that sound?" Mr. Ledermann asked. "Would you like to accept the position?"

"I certainly would," I replied, as I tried to hide my excitement. "When can I start?"

"I'll expect you here on April first at 9 a.m." He got up, shook my hand and said, "Welcome aboard!"

Before I left, Mr. Ledermann also introduced me to the Manager of the Chamber. Mr. Henry Abt was a short, stout man with a strident voice and a full mane of straight snow-white hair. "Great news! Great news!" he practically shouted when he learned that I had just been hired. "Klingenberg can certainly use the help."

It was only when I returned to the ground floor that reality set in. As I came out of the elevator I noticed for the first time the floor-to-ceiling waterfall covering one side of the white marble T-shaped atrium-style lobby and the large marble slabs outlined in red, white and black on the lobby floor. A huge bookstore on two levels occupied one side of the main entrance to the building; an Alitalia Airlines office was on the other. And, when I stepped outside onto Fifth Avenue, I was just around the corner from the Museum of Modern Art and only a short walk from St. Patrick's Cathedral and Rockefeller Center. You couldn't get a better location than that! For someone whose career in New York had started off tracking lost shipments of cauliflower for the produce division of the A&P and who had gone on to process orders for chocolate-covered ants and rattlesnake meat at Brewster, Leeds, my new job with the German American Chamber of Commerce on the 36th floor of this beautiful building was an amazing leap forward.

****

Since a great way to catch up on German politics and economics in preparation for my new job was to read *Der Spiegel*, the leading German news magazine, the first thing I did when I left 666 Fifth Avenue was to splurge on the latest issue. Due to its high cover price, this was an indulgence I hadn't been able to afford during all the weeks I had been out of work.

With a copy of the magazine tucked under my arm, I headed over to East 51st Street to take the train down to the Astor Place stop. I knew that Victoria would be getting home around 3 p.m. this Friday afternoon and I couldn't wait to share my good news. At that hour the subway platform was nearly deserted and, when the train finally arrived, it was surprisingly empty. Three young black toughs in matching denim jackets and red, black and green knitted caps were the only other passengers.

Just as I was getting on board a tapping sound behind me made me turn around. Slowly making his way toward me on crutches was a one-legged man with a full Afro. To give the man time to board, I had positioned myself at the door to hold it open when, from inside the car, one of the young men yelled, "Hey motherfucker let go that door!" and he and his two companions all waved their fists in my direction.

Meanwhile the gentleman on crutches had hobbled onto the train and, after thanking me, he took a seat across from mine. Once I had assured myself that the three young men were no longer a threat, I opened up *Der Spiegel* and began to read the first article. But, at the same time, I couldn't help noticing that the one-legged man was staring at the magazine and at me with a great deal of interest.

After a few minutes he leaned forward and raised his voice over the noise of the train. "Excuse me, mister, I see what you're reading. Are you German?"

"I sure am," I replied. "Have you been over there?"

"I was stationed in Frankfurt for a few years when I was in the service. Best beer I've ever had. Boy do I miss that stuff! We had our maneuvers with the German Army at Baumholder. Do you know the place?"

"Baumholder? You bet. I was there with the *Bundeswehr*. That's where I ate my first hamburger and tasted my first ketchup! When were you there?"

Der Spiegel would have to wait as the one-legged man and I traded stories about our time in the military. A few stops later we were still deep in conversation when the three young men got up to leave the train. As we pulled into their station, the one who had hurled the insults turned to me and said, "Yo, man. We're really sorry!" and then they took off onto the platform.

"What was that all about?" the man with the crutches asked me. "Were those punks giving you a hard time?"

I was so stunned by the unexpected apology that it took me a few seconds to reply. "Oh, those guys? They were just a little impatient when I held the door open for you, that's all. Turns out they weren't anywhere near as bad as they looked."

"Glad to hear it, man," my companion said. "Very glad to hear it."

****

"Well, you've had quite a day so far!" Victoria exclaimed when I told her about the German American Chamber of Commerce and my adventure on the subway. "You know some teenagers wear those black power caps just to look intimidating. Others really mean business. It's lucky you ran into the first kind."

"Still, I wonder what their reaction would've been if I'd been there with you."

"Forget about them! Let's celebrate your new job. Didn't you promise me a ride on the Staten Island Ferry?"

The two of us went by subway to Lower Manhattan, paid the nickel fare, and joined the throngs of commuters heading home to Staten Island at the end of the work day. Stationing ourselves at the back of the boat, we watched the New York skyline get smaller and smaller as we headed out into the harbor.

"That's the best value for the money you can get in this town," Victoria said as we huddled together for warmth in the stiff breeze.

"You're shivering," I said. "Let's go back inside and get ready for the landing."

Just as we stepped off onto the dock I noticed Greg Draskovic in the crowd ahead of us. It had been years since I'd seen anyone from the A&P.

"Greg! Hello Greg! Remember me?" I shouted and I waved wildly with my left arm while holding tight to Victoria with my right. Greg turned to look in our direction, did a double take, and made a beeline for the exit. I yelled again, even louder than before. "Greg, I'd like to talk with you!" to no avail.

"Who on earth was that? He looked like he'd just seen a ghost," Victoria asked as we waited in the chilly departure area for the return ferry to Manhattan.

"Greg? He was one of my former bosses at the A&P. I can't believe he ran off like that. We always got along just fine. Maybe," I added, trying to put the best spin on things, "he was just in a hurry to get home"

"You know better than that, Gunter" Victoria retorted. "Don't kid yourself. It was because of us. It always is." Then she looked up at me with tears in her eyes and gave me a hug.

CHAPTER *41*

*O*n Tuesday, April 1, 1969, just two weeks after my excursion to Staten Island with Victoria, I strode past the waterfall in the marbled lobby and took the elevator back up to the 36th floor in 666 Fifth Avenue to start my new job. Rolf Klingenberg greeted me in the reception area and brought me into the office that he and I would share; it had a spectacular view looking south toward Rockefeller Center.

"I sit with my back to the window," he explained. "And you'll use the extended arm of the desk against the wall. That way we can easily communicate with each other."

"Thank you, Mr. Klingenberg," I said, setting down my briefcase in the assigned spot.

"Before we get started, there's one thing we should settle right away. I think the two of us should be on a first-name basis."

"Really? Are you sure? I've never done that in any German company I worked for."

"Well, I want you to do it with me. First of all, you're a year older than I am. Besides, I've been in this country since I was twenty. I served two years in the American army in Texas before moving to New York, getting a job, and earning my Bachelor's degree from Baruch

College at night. And right now I'm working on an MBA degree at NYU. You're also studying at night, right? So we have too much in common to stick to any rigid German formalities. Agreed?"

"Agreed!"

The phone rang. "That was Mr. Ledermann's secretary. He wants to see you in a few minutes, but before that, let me introduce you to a few colleagues."

After Rolf took me around to the Legal Department, the Trade Fair Department, and the Publications Department, he introduced me to Mrs. Bachhuber, the office manager, an exuberant, middle-aged lady with a Bavarian accent. In keeping with the age-old regional rivalry between people from the German province of Bavaria and Prussians like me, Mrs. Bachhuber looked me up and down and shook her head disapprovingly. "You do look every inch a Prussian," she said before breaking into a smile, "but I'll try my best to like you anyway. Seriously, Mr. Nitsch, if there's anything I can do to help, all you have to do is ask!"

****

"Good morning, Mr. Nitsch," Mr. Ledermann greeted me. "Please have a seat. I know all too well that the first day in a new place can be difficult, so I thought it might be helpful if I explained to you in more detail what we do around here. Our operations are partially financed by our parent organization, the Association of German Chambers of Industry and Commerce in Bonn, but the bulk of our budget comes from the fees we charge for our services and from representing German trade fairs. Here in New York we have a staff of twenty-four people, all of them bilingual. Our function is to help German companies with their marketing efforts in the United States. We have two publications:

The German American Trade News and *Amerika Handel*. Most importantly, we're a membership organization so one of your jobs will be to persuade the German and American companies that come to you for marketing advice to become members and pay us the annual fee. Any questions so far?"

"Well, I do have one. Mr. Klingenberg also introduced me to some people in the Trade Fair department. Will I have anything to do with them?"

"No, they're separate entities. The representatives for the Frankfurt, Cologne, and Düsseldorf trade fairs here in our office try to get American firms to exhibit at their German trade fairs." He waited to see if I had any other questions before continuing. "Now getting back to what you will be doing in marketing, here's the challenging part. It's our obligation to help everybody who contacts us for advice, be it by letter or in person. You'll find out soon enough that some of the inquiries we receive are rather outlandish. But no matter what's asked of us, we try to help. This may occasionally require a good bit of imagination!"

"Yes, sir."

"Oh, and one more thing! We also recommend experts such as lawyers, CPAs, consultants and executive recruiters to German companies. You should try to meet a few of them in person. But Mr. Klingenberg will help you with that. So, unless you have any more questions, that's it for today, Mr. Nitsch."

"Thank you Mr. Ledermann. I'm looking forward to getting started."

****

"Mr. Ledermann just gave me a nice overview about the Chamber, but I wasn't sure what he meant by 'outlandish' inquiries," I reported to Rolf when I returned from my short meeting.

"Before we get to the oddballs, let's start with the average inquiries, like the daily requests we get for lists of addresses of importers or wholesalers for a certain merchandise category. If the items the German company wants to export to the United States are machine tools, garden tools, sophisticated kitchen utensils, cheese, pickles, cookies, whatever, you can look up the addresses in those thick directories on the shelves against that wall. But for more practical advice, especially when it comes to technical equipment, we turn to experts with whom we have personal contacts."

"This may be a touchy question, but what's in it for them?"

"Around here one hand washes the other. Since we give them plenty of leads, they are only too willing to help out when we need help."

"Will I have a chance to meet contacts like that?"

"Of course. That's part of the job. But just so you don't get the wrong idea, the inquiries we get are not just about exports to the United States. Some German companies want to set up their own sales offices or even their own production companies here. We help them, too."

"And the 'oddballs' as you put it?"

"Let's see. Just off the top of my head, there was the man who wanted our help getting his son an internship with an American bank. And then there are the manufacturers of freestanding armoires who refuse to believe that most Americans have built-in closets. But the worst are the brochures. You wouldn't believe what's in some of the brochures. Some of these guys are too cheap to pay for a professional translation." He reached into his desk and pulled out an illustrated pamphlet. "I've kept this one just for laughs. This company makes metal fasteners. Just look at this: 'We can help you with your screwy problems!' Or this one: "Our tools can undo jammed nuts!' Well, I guess you get the idea."

"Who writes this stuff?"

"They all claim it was done by an expensive advertising agency, but it usually turns out that it was the handiwork of the company's export manager or, more likely, the owner's brother-in-law." Rolf slipped the pamphlet back in his desk. "Anyway, I think the best way for you to get oriented would be to familiarize yourself with the directories we use. But before you start on that, just a word to the wise about our office manager, Mrs. Bachhuber, who also doubles as Mr. Abt's secretary. She has an interesting background. Her best friend's husband was a big shot in the Nazi Party so she had a good time during the war. Despite having travelled in those circles, after the war she still somehow managed to get married to an American Army officer. The two of them live in some fancy town in Connecticut. Here's the important part. No one in this office knows more about what's going on around here than she does, which gives her a lot of power. My advice to you? Try to keep on good terms with her at all times."

"Thanks for the heads up. I'll do my best."

CHAPTER 42

The rest of the week flew by. After spending my workdays poring over the thick directories at the Chamber, I attended classes at Hunter in the evening, and then stayed up until the wee hours reading textbooks. By Friday, bursting with news about my job, I was ready for an evening out with Victoria.

When we met at our favorite dance club just off of Bleecker Street in Greenwich Village, the curvy African-American vocalist who was belting out her rendition of 'Leaving on a Jet Plane' waved at us in recognition. We had barely sat down when I began to bombard Victoria with a detailed report about my first four days at the Chamber.

"And once I learn the ropes I'll be meeting German and American businessmen and giving them advice," I boasted after talking uninterruptedly for ten minutes.

"Uh huh," Victoria replied without enthusiasm.

"Maybe even get to travel."

"Sounds nice." Her voice was flat.

I stopped talking and reached over to take both of her hands in mine. "Hey, did I do something to upset you? You're not yourself this evening. What's bothering you?"

"I was thinking about the words of the song. Boy, what I wouldn't give to leave this town on a jet plane myself."

"Because?"

"Listen, you know the neighborhood where I've been living isn't the best. So a few days ago I started looking for a new apartment in the West Village over by Sheridan Square. Each time I've called a phone number listed in an ad, they tell me to come by, but when I meet them in person it's always the same story. 'You're a few minutes too late. We just rented the place.' "

"And you think it's . . ."

"I don't THINK it, I KNOW it. What else can it be except for my skin color?"

"Well, there is a way to find out for sure," I said after giving the matter some thought. "When the Sunday *Times* real estate section hits the newsstands tomorrow night let's go over the listings together. If you find a place that you like and they reject you when you get there, I'll come by a few minutes later and see if they give me the same runaround. What do you say?"

"It just sounds crazy enough to work. Count me in!" Then, after a pause, she grinned and added, "Now tell me again about your week. I was only half listening before."

****

"Now *this* is exactly what I've been dreaming about." Victoria circled a listing and handed me the real estate section. "Can you imagine me living in a studio apartment in one of those hundred-year-old brick row houses on Gay Street? I'm going to call the number right now to make an appointment."

209

Gay Street, located between Christopher Street and Waverly Place in the heart of the West Village, was only one block long and unusually narrow. As planned, I stationed myself next to a nearby pay phone while Victoria found the address and rang the bell. Five minutes later, she was back. "Same story. It's already rented," she reported.

"Then I guess it's time for Plan B." I dropped in my dime and dialed the number. "Imagine that!" I said when I hung up the receiver. "I'm to come right over and have a look at the place."

A middle-aged white woman showed me the large, unfurnished ground-floor studio apartment with two windows facing a small backyard. Then she and I walked together to the front entrance of the building. "So," the landlady said when we reached the wrought-iron front steps. "I've told you the price and the terms. Would you like to take it?"

I waved to Victoria, who had stationed herself across the street and yelled, "Come on in! It was a misunderstanding. The place is yours!" Then I turned to the landlady, who was blushing from ear to ear. "Isn't that so, ma'am?"

"Sure. Sure. Just a small misunderstanding," she reluctantly agreed and, by then, Victoria had joined us and reached over to shake the lady's hand and seal the deal.

****

As I was helping Victoria move in the following Saturday, a neighbor from one of the upstairs apartments introduced himself. Tom was wearing tight jeans and a pink satin button-down shirt.

"Nice having you both in the building!"

"Oh, Victoria's the only one moving in," I explained. "I live on the Upper West Side."

"Well then, Victoria, I just wanted to let you know that I sing opera. If it ever bothers you when I practice my scales, please let me know. I'm assuming, of course, that you don't also sing?"

"I wish! I'm a Head Start teacher and Gunter works for a German company uptown."

"Well, give a holler if you need anything," Tom said before he headed back upstairs.

Once we were alone, Victoria rolled her eyes. "I know the Village is full of gay men, even though you can't always tell who they are. But with him? Not a doubt in my mind."

"I think it's kind of refreshing that someone like Tom is comfortable letting people know. People aren't so tolerant in Germany. In fact, Paragraph 175 of the German penal code makes homosexuality or, to be more precise, makes sex between two men, a crime. People are put in jail for it."

"That must be an idea left over from the Nazi times. Right?"

"Actually, you're off by more than sixty years. The law goes all the way back to Bismarck in 1871, if I'm not mistaken. Pretty much everyone in the Chamber knows that the manager of the Trade Fair Department is gay, for example. But if he were working in Germany I'm willing to bet he'd do everything in his power to keep that fact a secret."

"Well, I'm not so sure it's really all that different here when it comes to accepting people like Tom," Victoria said as she reached for another box to unpack. "Except in Greenwich Village of course. Anyway, I assume that there are plenty of American states with laws like your Paragraph 175 on the books. It's hard to get things changed, even when they're wrong. For instance, wasn't it just two years ago that the Supreme Court ruled that interracial marriage was okay?" She paused to wait for my reaction and then, since I didn't say anything and she already knew how I felt about getting married, she let the subject drop.

CHAPTER 43

*A*fter my first few weeks at the Chamber, Mr. Ledermann would occasionally call me into his office to talk over a particularly unusual request from a German company. Monday, May 19th was one of those days. At 9 a.m. that morning Mr. Ledermann had asked me to stop by in about an hour. At the appointed time, armed with a yellow pad and a pen, I was approaching his office when Mrs. Bachhuber held up her hand. "Wait just a minute; Mr. Abt is in there right now."

From the open door to Mr. Ledermann's office I could hear Mr. Abt screaming. "Mr. Campanelli! How could you submit a $45 invoice for three hours of legal advice? Do you realize that the American attorneys we recommend charge between $100 and $200 dollars an hour? You've made a fool of yourself and you've embarrassed me! The German company that received your ridiculous bill must think we're all nuts!"

"But Mr. Abt, I'm not an American attorney. I can't charge those rates!"

"Let's get this straight, Mr. Campanelli. You may be admitted to practice law in Germany, but you're not admitted in New York. What's more, you may know about German commercial law, but you're sadly lacking in common sense. Give legal advice regarding German

Commercial Law if you have to, but don't charge for it. Is that clear, Mr. Campanelli? IS THAT CLEAR?"

Mr. Abt stormed out of Mr. Ledermann's office and went into his office, leaving the door wide open, as was his custom. When Mr. Campanelli left Mr. Ledermann's office a few seconds later, he slammed the door to his own office with such force that I thought the ceiling would come down.

Mrs. Bachhuber smiled. "You may go into Mr. Ledermann's office now," she said.

"Sorry to keep you waiting," Mr. Ledermann said. "I hope you didn't overhear too much. But let me get right to the point. Tell me, Mr. Nitsch, have you ever been to Harlem?"

"Yes, Mr. Ledermann. Actually I've been up there several times."

"Really? That's not the answer I'd expected. You're a surprising young man." He looked for a moment as though he wasn't quite sure he believed me. Then he handed me a letter from the file on top of his desk. "The reason I'm asking is that we received an inquiry from a German bicycle manufacturer. A company in Harlem wrote to them about importing a large number of their bikes. They've sent us a copy of the letter they received and asked us to look into it. The letterhead looks a bit amateurish, wouldn't you say?"

"Well, they could certainly use a new typewriter," I agreed after a quick glance at the text.

"The problem is, I need to know if this is a bona fide outfit before we write back to the manufacturer. I've tried the phone number but no one answers. So, if you don't mind, please go up there and see what you can find out."

"Yes sir, I'll take the subway and report to you later."

"You can also take a taxi. Just get a receipt and Mrs. Bachhuber will reimburse you."

"Thanks. See you later Mr. Ledermann."

Despite the suggestion that I go by taxi, I decided to economize by taking the Lexington Avenue subway up to 125th Street. As the train sped along underground I thought again about how stunned Mr. Ledermann had been when I told him I'd been to Harlem before. *Perhaps*, I thought, *that was more than he needed to know*. After all, I had soon noticed that there wasn't a single person of color on the Chamber staff and I wanted desperately to fit in. What would the reaction be if the people in the office knew that I was dating an African-American woman? I had already decided it would be too risky to bring Victoria up to see my new office and it weighed on my conscience. I loved her. I was proud of her and the work she did. And yet I feared for my newfound job. To make matters worse, I had to wonder what the reaction at the Chamber would have been had they known that Victoria's opera-singing upstairs neighbor, Tom, was an anti-war activist. That just two days earlier we had been to a 'good-bye' party he had organized in the East Village for a young man who was leaving for Canada on his wedding night. I ardently hoped that the two different worlds in which I was living would never meet. And it made me ashamed.

****

"Oink! Oink!" several men raised their fists and shouted after me as I clutched my briefcase and quickly headed west across 125th Street from the Lexington Avenue subway station. Other men simply glared as I passed by. For the next fifteen very long minutes I had ample opportunity to regret having turned down Mr. Ledermann's generous offer of a taxi.

The address on the letterhead was a shabby brownstone building in the shadow of the thirteen-story Theresa Hotel. When I walked up the steep flight of steps to the front door and rang the doorbell, I secretly hoped no one would be at home.

After several minutes, an unusually tall, skeletally thin man in a full-length, dark-brown robe, a knitted white skullcap, and thick, round, tortoiseshell eyeglasses came to the door. As I somewhat nervously stood on the top step in my business suit, he looked me up and down as if I were the one who was oddly dressed.

"Good morning, sir! I'm Gunter Nitsch from the German American Chamber of Commerce." I reached into my briefcase to retrieve the letter. "Are you the person who wrote this?"

"That's me," he said, "and thanks for coming by, young man. How very kind of you. But unfortunately today's a bad day to conduct business because my friends and I are celebrating Ho Chi Minh's birthday."

"Excuse me, sir, did you say *Ho Chi Minh?*"

"Yes, I did. He turned seventy-nine years old today. Long may he live! I'm really sorry, young fellow. But would you mind coming back at a more convenient time?"

I bit my lip to force myself to keep a straight face. "I don't know about that, sir. I'd have to ask my boss." I started to leave, but couldn't resist asking one more question. "I was just wondering if there is anything wrong with your phone. We tried to call before I came up here."

"Just a little dispute I'm having with Ma Bell, that's all. A question about a bill. That sort of thing. It should be worked out in a day or so."

"I'll be sure to make a note of it," I said. "Have a nice day! It was a pleasure meeting you."

Then, rather than risk taking the long walk back to the subway, I stationed myself in front of the nearby Theresa Hotel, quickly hailed a cab, and headed back downtown to make my report to Mr. Ledermann.

****

"Welcome back, Mr. Nitsch. I'm glad you made it back safe and sound," Mr. Ledermann greeted me when I stepped into his office. "So, what's the good word? Is it a legitimate company?"

"Well, let me put it this way, sir, and then you can decide. The man who wrote the letter had no time for me because today is Ho Chi Minh's birthday."

"You must be joking!"

"Believe me, I couldn't make this up if I tried."

Mr. Ledermann burst out laughing. "Had I known," he finally said as he wiped the tears from his eyes. "I would have sent a birthday card."

"So, shall I write a report to the German bicycle company?"

"Yes, please. Just be sure to let me read it over before you send it."

****

That evening after my last class I found a pay phone and called Victoria. "I didn't want to ask anyone at the Chamber, but maybe you know. What does it mean when people glare at you and shout, 'Oink, oink'?"

"Where on earth did someone do that?"

"On 125th Street this morning. I had to see some guy who wanted to buy German bicycles."

"And the Chamber sent you up there in a business suit? To 125th Street? Then there's an easy explanation. They thought you were a cop. You know. A policeman. What protestors call 'a pig.'"

"I guess I wasn't winning any popularity contests up there."

"Listen, Gunter, it's nothing to joke about. You took a big risk walking along 125th Street in a suit. If your boss decides to send you up to Harlem again, just be sure to change into casual clothes first."

"I promise."

"I hope you at least accomplished what you went up there for."

"Maybe not in the way the Chamber expected. But it sure made for one hell of a good story. Now, before my three minutes run out, let me tell you why!"

CHAPTER 44

*O*n Friday, June 27th, I rushed home after class, changed into white tennis shorts, a navy blue tee shirt and Adidas running shoes and headed for the 96th Street subway station. My mouth was already watering at the thought of the home-cooked chicken dinner with sweet potatoes Victoria was preparing. Half a block from my building, I noticed an African-American man, impeccably dressed in a business suit, a white shirt and a tie, who was trying to hail a northbound cab on Broadway. It made my blood boil as I watched one empty cab after another speed up and zoom past him.

Once I got within earshot I said, "Here, let me give it a try." Ten yards further down the block, I raised my hand and, within seconds, a taxi screeched to a stop. "Where to, bud?" the white cabbie asked.

I opened the back door and leaned in to speak to the driver. "Just a minute please. My friend will be going with you." Then I waved the businessman over, being sure to hold onto the door until he was safely inside.

My blood was still boiling as I rode the local train downtown. How outrageous! It had taken a mere two seconds for a cab to stop for me, dressed as I was in my jogging clothes. Meanwhile that well-dressed man had been waiting on the curb for who knew how long. The more I thought it over, the more I wondered if he had appreciated my help or if what I had done was just one more humiliation for him. After all, all things being equal, which they clearly were not, he should have easily gotten himself a cab on his own.

To let off steam, I decided to go the rest of the way on foot. Leaving the subway before Victoria's stop I set out at a brisk pace, only slowing down a bit as I approached the crosswalk at the end of a one-way street. A pasty-faced, overweight taxi driver, apparently misinterpreting my reason for slowing down, pulled up next to me. "Need a ride?" he asked hopefully.

When I shook my head, he shrugged his shoulders, stepped on the gas, and pulled up so far over the crosswalk that an elderly lady with a walker had to hobble in a wide circle in front of his cab in order to get across. This was the last straw for me. All of my pent up rage towards thoughtless New York City cab drivers was now focused on that bright yellow Ford Crown Victoria cab. It was now or never to get my revenge. Taking a flying leap, I ran directly across the hood of the cab and, when I jumped off on the other side, I yelled, "That's for blocking the crosswalk!"

The driver reached for the door handle, shouting, "I'm gonna kill you, you sonofabitch!"

Not a chance, I thought smugly as I jogged off at a fast pace against the direction of traffic. But, to my horror, the taxi had suddenly gone into reverse and was rapidly backing up on that narrow one-way street. I tried to reassure myself that, by the time the driver stopped and got out of his cab, I would easily outrun him. But what if he had a weapon? What if he drove right up onto the sidewalk? Would I still have a chance?

Just then another Ford Crown Victoria, this time a New York City police car with sirens blaring, came tearing down the street blocking the cab's path. When the police officer got out of the squad car and swaggered over to talk to the driver, I couldn't resist the urge to get in a parting shot. From a safe distance on the sidewalk I waved at the pudgy driver and yelled, "Enjoy your day, sir!" before continuing on my way with a self-satisfied grin.

****

Victoria had listened to my account of the evening's events without saying a word. She was also unusually quiet all through dinner. Finally, as we were doing the dishes together, she put down her dishtowel and sighed. "Listen, Gunter, I know you see yourself as a hero for jumping on the hood of that cab, but you could've gotten yourself killed. So the man blocked the crosswalk. Big deal. Was that really worth the risk you took? I wish you'd come to your senses and stop trying to single-handedly right all the wrongs in the world."

"I can't promise, but I'll try."

"Good. Because I don't want to worry about you." She hesitated for a second. "There's one more thing. Are you sure you have to go home this evening? I was hoping you'd decide to stay over."

"I wish. But it's getting late and Peter Vollmann is meeting me on the tennis court up near Riverside Church at 5:30 a.m."

"He didn't even show up the last time you arranged for tennis so what makes you think he will this time?"

"Sorry, I really have to go. A promise is a promise. I'll come back down after we play."

I walked along Gay Street and started to turn left onto Christopher Street when a large crowd of young men running in my direction stormed past as dozens of policemen, their nightsticks raised, came charging after them. "The pigs are going to kill us all!" one young man with a bloodied head shouted at me. "Run for your life!" yelled another.

That was enough for me. Turning back onto Gay Street, I ran as fast as I could back to Victoria's house, rushed into the small vestibule, and pounded on her door. "Victoria! It's me, Gunter!" I rushed inside the minute she opened the door.

"What changed your mind?" she asked in astonishment as I struggled to catch my breath.

"I decided not to be a hero," I finally said and, after I told her what had happened, I gladly took up her renewed offer to stay the night.

Over the next few days Victoria and I read everything we could about the nearby Stonewall Inn where that night's riot had started. The gay club was, after all, only a two-minute walk from Victoria's apartment. In the two years since it had opened, the police had raided the place on a regular basis. But this had been the first time the gay men had decided to fight back.

Victoria shook her head after we'd watched the latest report on TV. "You were certainly in the wrong place at the wrong time. The way you were dressed. Those short shorts! And your Adidas shoes!" She could barely talk she was laughing so hard. "I really shouldn't laugh about it. You were damn lucky you didn't get your skull cracked open in that gay mob."

Of course, I couldn't deny it. I had been in the wrong place at the wrong time. Even so, history had been made that night and it was exciting to have been smack dab in the middle of it.

CHAPTER 45

"I'm tired of being the poster boy for the SS," I griped to Victoria in the middle of July.

She snuggled closer to me. "You? C'mon. You're the last person I would think of."

"That's easy for you to say. This evening it happened again. My political science professor was lecturing on the Third Reich and, no sooner had he described the ideal SS candidate, than first one student turned around to look at me, then another, then another, until the whole class was observing me like some kind of bizarre specimen in a bottle. Doesn't that idiot realize that Germans come in all sizes and hair colors just like everybody else?"

"Did you protest?"

"What good would that have done? I would have just called more attention to myself if I had."

"Poor baby," Victoria cooed. "Having to deal with being stereotyped like that."

"I guess you already know what that feels like."

"Since we're on the subject of your summer courses, how's that other professor coming along? You know, the one you told me was in love with his cat?"

"Professor Katzenberg? I still find it distracting that he wears those blousy silk shirts, a filigree gold chain, and an earring. And the way he sashays back and forth in front of the blackboard I can imagine him in a leotard and toe shoes. But his lectures on psychology really hold my interest. This evening he was talking about bad parenting skills and I realized that my father practiced every single one of them. Did I ever mention that my father hardly ever encouraged my brother and me? Or that he constantly found ways to let us know we didn't live up to his expectations, especially Hubert. Not that I didn't get my share. I'm willing to bet no one else in that class was laid flat by a punch from his father when he was twenty-one."

"But what about his cat? Does he still mention her every day?"

"Yeah. He still shares a West Side apartment with his cat and his mother. According to him, the three of them are one happy family."

"Well," Victoria teased, "if that's his idea of a happy family, maybe you should have just bought your father a cat!"

Later that month tears were streaming down Professor Katzenberg's face when he arrived for class. "God help me!" he wailed. "My darling cat passed away last night," and then he collapsed into his chair sobbing uncontrollably. After a few minutes, pulling himself together as best he could, he blew his nose, wiped his eyes, and in a voice choked with emotion confided, "I've been in analysis since high school, but this time my analyst can't help me."

Unfortunately for Professor Katzenberg, following the death of his beloved cat the health of his mother began to fail. Our class was subjected to daily bulletins on her medical condition until she died only a week after the loss of the cat. All things considered, despite being an overall emotional wreck, Professor Katzenberg took her loss better than expected. In fact, I was sure he had shed many more tears for his pet than for her. After attending Professor Katzenberg's psychology class I secretly vowed never to seek the advice of a psychologist, even if my life depended on it.

****

My summer semester classes ended in mid-August and on Sunday, the 17th, Victoria joined me on the Upper West Side for a long stroll, starting at the tennis courts in Riverside Park where I played with Peter Vollmann and ending up at the Fairway Market on Broadway and 74th Street. Taking advantage of the low prices, we stocked up on the basics: noodles, tuna fish, several pounds of apples and plums, two containers of orange juice, two cartons of milk, a loaf of bread, Philadelphia cream cheese, a pound of American cheese, and a pound of salami. Carrying two bulging bags of groceries each, we were grateful to get seats near the door of the local downtown subway on our way to Greenwich Village.

When the train stopped at Times Square, seven bedraggled teenagers with mud-caked clothes, squishy-wet shoes, and bulging backpacks stormed inside. We stared at them in amazement. They, in turn, stared at our Fairway Market shopping bags. "FOOD! Look people! There's FOOD!" several of them shouted at once. After a moment's hesitation, one of the girls stepped forward. "Can you make me a sandwich, miss?" she pleaded. I haven't eaten anything in days."

"Where on earth have you been?" Victoria asked her. "You all look like drowned rats!"

"Woodstock!" all seven of them replied in unison.

"What do you think?" Victoria asked me. "Shall we do it?"

Without another word, I ripped open the package of bread and held a slice in my hand while Victoria topped it with two slices of cheese and a slice of salami. I slapped a second slice of bread on top and handed the sandwich to the girl along with a half-gallon container of milk. By the time we reached our stop at Christopher Street, we had fixed six more sandwiches.

"So much for saving a few dollars at the Fairway Market," I joked as we stopped at a local market in Greenwich Village to replenish our supply of milk, bread, and cold cuts. "Seriously though, I know from my own childhood under the Russians what it means to be hungry so I'm glad we had a chance to help."

"Want to know what I'm glad about?" Victoria replied. "After seeing those kids, I'm really glad we weren't with them at Woodstock!"

CHAPTER 46

*L*ater that same month, the staff of the German American Chamber of Commerce received shocking news. Our boss, Mr. Abt, had suffered a stroke on the flight back from the opening of our new branch office in San Francisco. He died the following day. Mr. Ledermann immediately took over as the General Manager in New York leaving the Deputy position vacant.

Of the four department heads who applied for the position, Mr. Campanelli, who came from a politically well-connected German family, was the odds on favorite. When Mr. Ledermann passed over Mr. Campanelli in favor of Fred Jacobson, the editor of the *German American Trade News*, Mr. Campanelli was so incensed that he quit in a huff and returned with his wife to Germany. The selection process had generated a great deal of gossip around the water cooler. Even so, as a relative newcomer to the Chamber, I hadn't paid that much attention to it.

A few weeks later, Mrs. Bachhuber, who was now Mr. Ledermann's secretary, called out to me from the open door of her office. "Mr. Nitsch, come in for a moment. I have a message for you. Before he left on his latest business trip, Mr. Ledermann asked me to tell you that, from now on, whenever we have a big luncheon for our members and friends in the Union Club, or the Plaza Hotel or wherever, he wants you to come along. The idea is to circulate and meet as many new contacts as possible, not to hang around the people you already know from the Chamber."

"I understand, Mrs. Bachhuber."

Mrs. Bachhuber suddenly lowered her voice. "Tell me, Mr. Nitsch. Is it true, what Mr. Ledermann says? That you worked for a Jewish firm before you came here?"

Uncertain where this odd line of questioning was headed, I took a deep breath. "The owners were Jewish," I finally replied after some hesitation.

"Close the door please," Mrs. Bachhuber commanded. I meekly obeyed. "Do you want to know what I think? To be frank, it's gotten to be almost the same way around here."

"Sorry, I don't follow you," I responded.

She smirked. "I'll spell it out for you. Mr. Ledermann is a 'half Jew' and his new handpicked Deputy is a Jew from Lüneburg. I know from his file that Fred Jacobson came to the States in the 1930's and worked as an interrogation officer for the U.S. Army in Germany after the war. Oh, and did I mention that Mr. Ledermann's wife is also a 'half Jew'?"

I shifted awkwardly from foot to foot. "Not that it matters one way or the other," I said, "but when Mr. Ledermann found out that I had lived under Russian occupation as a child, he told me he had served in the Wehrmacht and was held in a Russian POW camp for several years."

"So what if he did? His father, a Jew, died very early and his mother did everything in her power to hide her son's Jewish blood. I see that I've shocked you. I thought I would." She tilted her head to one side and waited for my reaction.

What did she expect me to say? The best I could come up with was, "Thanks again for putting me on that list for the luncheons," before I beat a hasty retreat from Mrs. Bachhuber's office.

When I got back to our office, Rolf was just hanging up the phone. "What kept you so long? There were several calls for you." He handed me a slip of paper with the phone numbers. "So, where were you?"

"In Mrs. Bachhuber's office and . . . ."

He raised his hand. "Oh, then I know. No explanation necessary. Once that lady starts talking there's no stopping her. The other day she told me for what must have been the umpteenth time how wonderful her life had been during the Third Reich. Just between us, she still doesn't have anything good to say about the Jews. You really have to be on your guard around that woman. She's dangerous. Whatever you say she'll blab to everyone in the office. Like I said, it's best just to let her talk without revealing anything about yourself if you can help it."

I had intended to tell Rolf what had happened but now I thought better of it.

CHAPTER 47

I registered for three classes when the fall semester started in September 1969, among them a course in geology to fulfill the first part of my science requirement. Within a short time my head was spinning as I tried to memorize the meanings of exotic terms like alluvium, fluorapatite, lithify, and techtonics. A fellow student, Morayo Adesina, who was a diplomat with the Nigerian delegation to the United Nations, would often meet with me in the college cafeteria after class so that the two of us could quiz each other in preparation for upcoming tests. A short, stocky man with very dark skin and an easy smile, Morayo's appearance could not have been less like mine.

To my bewilderment, one day in early January 1970, our geology teacher, Professor Edelstein, invited Morayo and me for a beer at a bar on Lexington Avenue. After we had been served our beers and had exchanged some innocuous small talk, Professor Edelstein finally let us know what was on his mind. "I've been observing the two of you for a while now," he said, "Granted New York is supposed to be a melting pot but, even so, I can't for the life of me figure out how the two of you, coming from such different backgrounds, became friends. Mind telling me what brought you both together?"

Morayo grinned. "The answer is very simple, Professor Edelstein. You did! We study geology terms together to try to get good grades in your class."

"That's it?" Clearly he had expected some kind of kumbaya moment—a sharing of goals for world peace and harmony. That sort of thing. With evident disappointment, he finally asked, "Are those geology terms really so difficult for you? I thought I was bringing the subject down to the most basic level."

"Well, sir, you have to realize that Gunter and I are both older than most of your other students. We both work full time during the day. Besides, I have the responsibility of a wife and three children. So we have to make an extra effort to succeed in class."

Professor Edelstein turned to me, "Are you also married?"

"No, I'm not."

"Do you have a girlfriend?"

"Yes, sir."

"I imagine she's a tall, blond German girl?"

"Not exactly. She's African-American."

He set his glass down on the bar so hard that the beer sloshed over the top. "You're putting me on!"

"No, sir. I'm not."

"What's the world coming to? Of all things . . ." Professor Edelstein muttered.

"Let's just forget I said that," he finally said in the silence that followed. "It's really none of my business." He ordered another round of beers, tapped his fingers nervously on the table, and asked, "Did I ever tell you about the time I nearly got shot for trespassing when I was on a geology field trip in Colorado?"

"I think you may have mentioned it," Morayo said as he took another sip of beer. Actually, we had already heard that story at least three times in class. "But, if you don't mind, I have a question for you that has nothing to do with geology. Here's what I want to know. When an educated Nigerian hears the word Germany, where my friend Gunter comes from, he thinks of firms like Siemens, Bosch, BASF, Mercedes, and BMW. After all, Germany is one of Nigeria's largest trading partners. But here at Hunter, whenever the word Germany comes up, it's always linked to Nazis and the Holocaust. Can you explain why that is?"

Here we go again, I thought, while Professor Edelstein considered how best to reply. "Well," he finally said, "a large percent of our faculty is Jewish." This came as no surprise. Our professors constantly reminded us of that fact. "And, of course, we can't forget that the Germans killed six million of my people."

"Oh, I've heard all about that," Morayo countered, "but what about the tens of millions of victims of Stalin and of Mao Tse Tung? And why doesn't anyone talk about all the Africans who were murdered by the Europeans?"

"No one really knows those statistics," Professor Edelstein replied somewhat defensively.

"I'm no historian," Morayo insisted, "but I can assure you that the numbers have been very well documented by the largest African universities. Just in the Belgian Congo alone between nine and ten million Africans died. And for what? For diamonds and rubber to enrich the greedy Belgians! And don't forget the slave trade. No telling how many millions more died on those ships!"

Professor Edelstein nervously gulped down the last of his beer and paid the bill. "You've given us both some food for thought, Mr. Adesina. Wouldn't you agree, Mr. Nitsch?" I just nodded. When it came to the subject of the Holocaust, I always found it best to keep quiet. "Well," our Professor said somewhat lamely, "it was nice chatting with you. See you in class!" and, with that, we all left the bar and headed home in three different directions.

****

Now that Morayo knew about my African-American girlfriend, he was curious to meet her. A few days after our conversation with Professor Edelstein, Morayo invited Victoria and me to dinner in his high-rise East Side apartment.

"Wow!" Victoria exclaimed as we approached the doorman, an elderly, corpulent white man in a bright white uniform with golden shoulder tassels that would have made an admiral proud. "We're not in Kansas anymore!"

Ignoring the disdainful way the man was sizing the two of us up, I smiled and said, "We're guests of Mr. Adesina. My name is Gunter Nitsch."

He plugged into his switchboard and dialed. "Is that you, Mr. Adesina? The Gunter Nitsches are here!" With a curt gesture, he directed us to the correct bank of elevators.

Victoria teased me on our way up. "So when will it really be 'the Nitsches', if ever?"

"C'mon, Victoria. I've told you I'm not the marrying kind!"

Victoria sighed. "I know. You don't have to remind me," she said.

When the elevator doors opened Morayo was waiting in the doorway to his apartment to wave us inside. Fearsome African masks and a bright red hand-woven rug complemented the dark teak modern furniture in the spacious living room overlooking the East River. "How do you like my home?" Morayo asked.

Just then a short woman in an ankle-length dress came out of the kitchen and meekly approached us. Turning to her Morayo snapped,

"Don't be shy. They won't bite. Come meet Mr. Nitsch and his friend, Miss Hoyt." Wiping her hands on her apron, she gave each of us a limp handshake without making eye contact. "My wife," Morayo said by way of curt explanation as she hurried back to the kitchen. "Now let me show you our children's room."

A young woman was looking after the three little girls who were playing with their dolls in the adjoining room. Victoria bent down to the oldest child, who was perhaps five years old. "And what is your name?" she asked in a cheery voice.

But Morayo held up his hand. "Please, Miss Hoyt! I think it's better to leave the children alone; otherwise they may get too excited."

"If you say so," Victoria replied. As she straightened back up she glanced over at me. Her look said, "Is this man crazy?"

The two of us followed Morayo to the dining room where the three of us sat down on high-backed leather armchairs. "So, Gunter tells me you're a teacher," Morayo said to Victoria.

"Yes, pre-school. Children who are the ages of your daughters," she added pointedly. She then proceeded to briefly explain how the Head Start program works.

Morayo tapped his fingers impatiently. He had clearly asked Victoria about her job just to be polite. Suddenly he interrupted her. "Tell me, have you ever been to Africa?"

"No, not yet. Maybe, one of these days I will. But I have been to Italy and France with my . . ."

"There's no place like Africa," Morayo interjected, brusquely cutting off Victoria in mid-sentence. I didn't dare meet her eyes.

Just then Morayo's wife served each of us a small bowl of vegetable soup followed, a few minutes later, by a second course, a mixture of fish and kale. "I'll bring the lamb right out," she said in a barely audible voice before hurrying back to the kitchen.

Victoria glanced at me uneasily and I shrugged my shoulders as if to say, "*What do you want me to do about it?*"

But Victoria, never shy, put down her fork and confronted Morayo. "Pardon me for asking, but isn't your wife joining us for dinner?"

"My wife? Oh, no. But please, let's enjoy our food!"

"May I ask why not?" Victoria persisted.

Morayo gave a nervous laugh. "To be frank, my wife's not very educated. She really couldn't contribute anything to our conversation. Believe me, it's better this way." After that, Victoria didn't say another word until it was time to leave.

At the end of the evening, Morayo, obviously oblivious to Victoria's reaction, reached over to shake her hand. "It was nice meeting you, Miss Hoyt, and I hope to see you again," to which she mumbled under her breath, "Not in this lifetime."

All of her pent up anger exploded once the elevator door closed behind us. "Well, in case you didn't hear me, I don't ever want to see that man again. You saw it. He treats his wife like chattel! And those poor children! Imagine! Don't get them all excited! Give me a break! I'm willing to bet it would be different if they were boys."

"Maybe that's just the way they do things in Nigeria," I suggested. "His wife may not find his behavior the least bit strange."

We had been walking towards the Lexington Avenue subway but now Victoria stopped in her tracks. "It doesn't matter what she thinks," she said, "it still doesn't make it right." I couldn't argue with that.

CHAPTER 48

When the new term started at Hunter in mid-January, 1970, I was especially looking forward to taking another course with Professor Jaworskyj, the flamboyant Russian émigré who, just a few years earlier, had made such a good impression on my female classmates in his dark blue suits, white dress shirts with French cuffs, and expensive silk ties. But when I walked into his Political Philosophy class the change in Professor Jaworskyj left me flabbergasted. There he stood in a black tee shirt and faded blue jeans ripped at the knees. His hair now reached well below his shoulders and both of his elbows poked out through holes in his dark sweater.

Instead of the expected lecture on philosophy he perched on the edge of his desk and launched into a diatribe against Jacqueline Wexler, the ex-nun who had recently been appointed President of Hunter. "Administration must change policies!" he ranted. "College needs more black and Puerto Rican students!" Then, just when I thought things couldn't get any stranger, he extended an invitation to the entire class to come to his apartment for a party. "Let's share some wine and music at my place!" he announced. "Whatever's mine is yours!" It was to be the first of many such invitations, none of which, out of an uncharacteristic sense of caution, I accepted.

Except for Prof. Jaworskyj's shocking transformation, everything went smoothly until the end of February when, inspired by student rebellions at other City University campuses, the students at Hunter formed several protest groups all acting independently of one another. One group opposed the Vietnam War; another raged about the unjust treatment of minorities; a third demanded more student participation in college government. Week after week the number of groups proliferated so fast that it was as impossible to keep track of what any of them were for as it was to know what they were against. I wondered if they even knew themselves.

When I arrived at the multi-story classroom building in early March the elevators had been shut off. So, briefcase in hand, I trudged up seven flights of stairs only to find a notice on the door that Professor Jaworskyj's class had been cancelled. No reason was given.

On my way back downstairs, John Callahan, a fellow classmate and a Vietnam veteran, caught up with me on the third floor landing. He put his hand on my shoulder. "Hey, Gunter, I'm glad I ran into you! Want to join us? We're all going over to Wexler's office."

"President Wexler? What on earth for?"

"To air our grievances. We're demanding open admissions."

I followed John into the reception area of the President's ground floor office where, amid a buzz of angry voices, at least one hundred restless students, many of them wearing tie-dyed shirts, torn jeans, and beaded headbands, were already waiting. Since I was the only one in that entire crowd wearing a business suit, conversation stopped as all eyes turned in my direction.

"Hey you! Yes, YOU! You work for Wexler?" one young man with a scruffy beard yelled at me accusingly.

John hurried to reassure everyone. "Hey, cool it man! Trust me. Gunter's one of us!"

"Yeah, right!" someone yelled. His contempt was unmistakable.

"He's a spy!" shouted another.

Just then an administrator emerged from the inner office to announce that President Wexler would be coming out soon. But I had already seen enough. With everyone's attention no longer on me, I quietly slipped away.

Victoria was pretty shaken up when I told her what had happened. "Gunter, are you out of your mind? You may be thirty-two years old but you certainly don't act your age sometimes. Tell me this. Do you want to get kicked out of Hunter College? And what if you got arrested? Did you even consider that?"

"I guess you're right," I said sheepishly. "I just wanted to see for myself what was going on. The whole thing will probably blow over in a week or two anyway."

****

But it didn't blow over. It escalated. Within a few weeks radical students dead set on changing the way things were done at Hunter blocked the entrances to the classroom building leaving hundreds of disgruntled and frustrated students, with nowhere else to go, to mill around in the small courtyard outside the main entrance. Only faculty members and students who were leaving the building were allowed through the doors.

I walked around the entire building but, after finding every door blocked, I rejoined the crowd in the East 68th Street courtyard. In the meantime, tempers had been rising. Most of us gathered there worked full-time during the day and studied at night, and we could ill afford to lose even one precious hour of our education. In frustration, we began to chant to be let inside. But the agitators blocking the door raised their fists and drowned us out with shouts of "Shut it down!" "No more war!" "Equality in admissions!" "End the draft!" "Legalize pot!" and countless other demands.

Into that chaotic situation came Dr. Rosenthal, the feisty, pint-sized professor who was teaching my geology class that semester. We all stepped aside to give him room to pass through the crowd. When Professor Rosenthal reached the door he confronted the agitators, all of whom towered over him. "I have to go inside to get a file from my office. Please let me through!" he demanded.

"That's bullshit man! You just want to teach your class," one of the students blocking the door snarled.

"You have no right to keep me out!" Professor Rosenthal replied as he tried to get past the group blocking the door.

Then the incomprehensible happened. A bearded protestor grabbed Dr. Rosenthal's shoulders and violently shoved him away from the entrance. This was too much for me. I dropped my briefcase and rushed forward until the bearded bully and I were eye to eye. "Are you nuts?" I yelled. "Pick on someone your own size!"

"Mind your own damn business!" he retorted and he punched me in the chest with a hard right. Without thinking about the consequences, I took one long step backwards and then I slugged him as hard as I could in the face. Blood spurted from his mouth as he crumpled to his knees. To my astonishment I received shouts of support from the crowd behind me. "Right on, brother!" one man yelled. "Serves the bastard right!" agreed another.

Now four policemen hurried towards us as my bloodied opponent struggled to his feet. "All right!" one officer snapped. "What's the story here?"

To my relief, Professor Rosenthal stepped forward. "This young man came to my defense, officer," he explained. "I was just trying to get a file from my office when that other man assaulted me."

The police officer turned to me. "So you walloped him one, did you?"

"Only after he hit me first. I've got at least a hundred witnesses."

"Well," the officer said somewhat reluctantly, "unless one of you wants to press charges, you're all free to go. And as for you," he said to my bearded attacker, "you'd better get yourself over to the emergency room."

As they headed for their squad car, the youngest policeman patted me on the shoulder. "Nicely done, sir," he whispered. "Very nicely done."

I retrieved my briefcase and walked slowly to the crosstown bus, glancing every so often over my shoulder to be sure I wasn't being followed. It was only when I got back to my room that my nerves gave out. I tried to read a textbook but couldn't concentrate. *Would those thugs be lying in wait for me the next time I got to the campus?* I could fend them off one at a time, but if they were to gang up on me, I wouldn't stand a chance. I feared I was a marked man.

When classes resumed a few days later some students sought me out and said, "We heard what happened. Good job!" Others, perhaps fearful that I might explode at any moment, made a wide circle to avoid me when they saw me coming. Even so, I continued to watch my back.

One evening as I was waiting in our geology classroom for Dr. Rosenthal to arrive, two husky male students dressed in black suits, white dress shirts, and wide-brimmed black hats peeked inside. One of them strode over to me. "You're the guy who protected Dr. Rosenthal?" he asked. I swallowed hard and nodded. He reached over to shake my hand. "My name is Allan Schwartz. I'm so glad we finally found you. After what you did, we were wondering if you'd like to join the JDL."

"The JDL?"

"The Jewish Defense League. We were hoping you'd decide to join us." He and his companion waited expectantly for my reply. The other members of my class also leaned forward to hear what I would say.

"I'm going to have to turn you down," I said. "I work full time during the day and my courses at Hunter College keep me more than busy. Besides I'm not Jewish."

Allan Schwartz smiled. "We understand. But please give it some thought. We need people like you. Here's my phone number in case you change your mind."

As soon as the two of them left the room my friend, John Callahan, convulsed with laughter. When he finally caught his breath he exclaimed, "You're being recruited by the Jewish Defense League. Imagine that! No one could make this stuff up!"

"Laugh if you want to," I said. "But if anyone had to seek me out, I would sure as hell prefer it to be them."

CHAPTER *49*

*C*lasses were held sporadically over the next few months before being cancelled entirely for the semester. Since I never knew whether or not any particular class would be in session, I continued to show up at school in the evenings after work. Hunter was like a war zone. Directly challenging the helmeted police officers patrolling the campus, protest groups with bullhorns blasted their competing demands from behind picket lines and hastily erected blockades. Professor Luis Rodriguez-Abad, who only a few years earlier had warned us that revolution would come to Hunter, was denied reappointment. On April 30th, despite having tenure, Professor Michael Jaworskyj was suspended "for conduct unbecoming a member of the staff." It was rumored that he had pushed a fellow faculty member out of the elevator, blocked a door, and spat on the dean of the math department.

To my relief, I still received credit for all three of my classes. Dr. Rosenthal gave each of us a P for 'passing.' Both my economics professor and Professor Jaworskyj gave me unexpected and, under the circumstances, clearly undeserved A's. Word had it that Professor Jaworskyj gave everyone an A just to spite the administration.

Whatever his reason for it, I didn't care. It looked good on my transcript.

Before classes were scheduled to resume for the summer session, I took a two-week vacation from the Chamber and flew down via Mexico City to Mérida on the Yucatán Peninsula. Lounging by the pool at the Hotel Flamingo in the shade of swaying palm trees, touring the Mayan ruins at Chichen Itza and Uxmal with newfound German-speaking friends, and snorkeling in the crystal-clear waters off the coast of the Isla de Mujeres, I quickly recuperated from the stresses of the past few months.

This brief time away also gave me the opportunity to think about my relationship with Victoria. We had been together for nearly three years, the longest I had ever dated anyone in my life; so long, in fact, that Victoria often told me she considered us "married without the ring." But what would *really* being married to Victoria actually mean?

All too often when we were out together, I came dangerously close to slugging someone who made a disparaging racial remark. Could I control my temper over a lifetime of such comments? And what of our children, if we had any? Wouldn't they be ostracized, belonging neither to black nor white? Even setting racial issues aside, could I see myself married to someone who ran up exorbitant credit card charges without a thought of the consequences? Or who continued to take incompletes or to drop nearly every course for which she registered?

On the other hand, I had never met anyone I cared for as much as Victoria. She could make me laugh no matter what had happened that day. When I was with her, I couldn't take myself too seriously. And she made me proud. In my opinion her work at Head Start would be more worthwhile in the long run than whatever help I provided to German businessmen at the Chamber. What she did certainly required more courage and more dedication than I knew I was capable of.

But there were also my own flaws and self-doubts, not the least of which was wondering whether I would be capable of being true to one woman for the rest of my life. My father's infidelity had nearly destroyed my parents' own marriage. The fear that I might turn out like him had, more than anything else, long since convinced me that I was not the marrying kind. And yet, in a way, Victoria was right. We were like a married couple. In all the time we had been together I had not so much as looked at another woman. But then, what was the point of remaining single? This question would soon be put to the test.

****

The day I got back from my Mexican vacation I rushed home from the airport to drop off my suitcase and change before hurrying downtown to Hunter College to attend my summer school classes. While I was gulping down a quick snack in the cafeteria, a longhaired blond girl in a full-length tie-dyed dress and matching headband came over to where I was sitting.

"Hi! I'm Edie. Do you have a moment?" Without waiting for a reply she settled into the chair next to mine. "A friend of mine from your *Faust* class told me about you," she went on. "You work at the German Chamber of Commerce, right? Nice tan, by the way!"

"Thanks, I was on vacation in Mexico. And, yes, I work at the German American Chamber of Commerce. Is there some way I can be of help?"

"Actually I was wondering if you could find out for me what they charge in Germany for a bassoon?"

"A bassoon?"

"Yes. I'm majoring in music and I want to buy one, but they're outrageously expensive in the U.S."

"Well, sure. I'll see what I can find out for you." I was about to ask her for her contact information, when she reached over and tore a page out of my notebook.

"Here. Let me give you my phone number," she said as she jotted it down. Then she looked up at me and smiled. "You live close to me don't you? My building is on 104th Street just off Riverside Drive. I'm sure I've seen you in the neighborhood." *Wait a minute!* I thought to myself. *What does this girl really want from me?* "So," Edie went on before I could collect my thoughts, "I'm also working full-time which keeps me very busy. But if you want, we could meet for a walk on Saturday morning around 9 a.m."

By now her intentions were clear. "Sure, I'd love to," I blurted in reply, though I knew I was playing with fire.

That Saturday morning Edie and I took a long walk together and then we had brunch in an old fashioned diner on Broadway. Afterwards we went over to her small studio apartment where she sat on the edge of her bed and sang "California Dreaming" and "Monday, Monday." If I closed my eyes, I could imagine that Mama Cass herself was serenading me. Then, after putting down her guitar, Edie held out her hand for me to join her. By the time I left for home later that afternoon I had deep scratches in my back where her fingernails had clawed me, and my conscience was weighing me down. After I had showered and changed my clothes, I tried to study my textbooks, but the words were a meaningless blur. It was the first time I had cheated on Victoria and I knew that later I would spend the night with her.

However, once I had Victoria in my arms I felt a kind of guilty pleasure. I had behaved badly and gotten away with it. And, besides, what she didn't know couldn't hurt her, right? But then, without thinking, I took off my shirt and Victoria gasped.

"My God! What happened to your back?"

"What do you mean?"

"It's all bloody!" She led me into the bathroom, turned my back to the mirror, and pointed at the deep scratches. Meanwhile I was desperately trying to think up a plausible explanation. A barbed wire fence? A neighbor's cat? A crazed woman on Broadway? Nothing I could think of was convincing, even to me.

"I see what you mean," I finally said, trying my best to act surprised. "And, to be honest, I really can't say how that happened." Which was, of course, true. I really couldn't say.

With a sigh Victoria reached into the medicine cabinet for a bottle of alcohol and some Band-Aids. "You're sure you have no idea?" I bit my lip as she dabbed the alcohol onto my open wounds. Then, as she sloshed some more alcohol on a piece of cotton, she added, "I find that very strange," and left it at that.

CHAPTER 50

Victoria's stoic reaction unnerved me. She must have guessed what I had done. Yet there were no accusations; there were no tears. Everything went on as if nothing had happened which, in a way, was the worst punishment of all. I had already made up my mind never to see Edie again when I ran into her a week or so later in the Hunter cafeteria. She was wearing the same tie-dyed dress, five strands of multi-colored glass beads, a silver ring on every finger, and a bright-green feather in her hair.

"Listen, Gunter," she said before I had a chance to make my own excuses, "I really had a good time with you, but I can't see you any more. My boyfriend from California got back into town last night. I hope that's okay?"

"Sure, sure," I replied, much relieved. "I understand."

"Oh, and never mind about that bassoon. I don't need it any more. See you around." And she left for her class.

****

To avoid the crowds Victoria and I waited for a rainy Saturday in July to ride the subway out to Rockaway Beach where we held hands as we took a long walk along the edge of the sand, letting the chilly water lap against our bare feet. To my great relief, no one, white or black, was around to yell derogatory remarks at the two of us.

"It's nice to have the place to ourselves, don't you think?" Victoria asked me after a while and, when I didn't answer her right away, she added, "A penny for your thoughts!"

"It's just," I began, "that I sometimes wonder if it's worth putting up with all the crap we take by being together. Or doesn't it bother you the way it does me?"

"Oh, that? I've been dealing with it all my life. Just let it roll right off your back. That's what I do."

"Easier said than done."

"It's really not that hard. Here, let me give you an example. When my sister Eve and I were in Italy we met very few people who spoke English, but when the men, regardless whether they were young or old, found out that we were Americans, they all knew the same sentence."

"And that was?"

She laughed out loud. "I want to sleep with a Negress."

"So how did the two of you react?"

"Eve blew her stack, but I just laughed it off."

"I wish I had your sense of humor."

"Anyway, in answer to your question, it's definitely worth it for me. Like I always say, 'Give people time and they'll come around eventually,' and, in the meantime, we have each other, so who cares? Right?"

I gave her a hug. "You're right," I said. "It shouldn't matter what anyone else thinks." I vowed to myself to try to follow her example, but I knew damn well that it wouldn't be easy.

****

"You know," I said to Victoria when we got back to Greenwich Village. "I've been thinking about our conversation at the beach. There's a German expression that goes, *'Wennschon, dennschon,'* that roughly translates as, 'If you're going to do something, you might as well go whole hog.'"

"Fair enough," Victoria replied. "But what's that got to do with us?"

I pulled her over to a nearby newsstand. "Just look at this cover picture of Angela Davis! I'd love it if you got an Afro like hers."

"Whoa. Hold your horses. Slow down. Let's not go overboard with this 'in your face' stuff. You really want me to look like someone who's on the FBI's most wanted list?"

"Never mind that! You'd look great with an Afro. At least think about it!"

"And I suppose you're going to get yourself a Fidel Castro-style green military cap and grow a long beard?"

"I'm serious, Victoria. You'd look great with an Afro."

It took quite a bit of convincing but, by the following Saturday morning, Victoria finally relented. Right after breakfast we took the subway up to a unisex hairdressing salon on 125th Street. The minute we walked inside, all conversation stopped as the dozen or so customers and staff turned to stare at us through a thick haze of cigarette and cigar smoke. I hesitated a moment in the doorway, but Victoria pulled me forward. *"Wennschon, dennschon,"* she reminded me as we approached the front counter. Victoria took a deep breath and cleared her throat. "I'd like to have an Afro please."

"Sandra!" the cashier called out to one of the beauticians. "Give this lady a shampoo. She's getting an Afro." Then she eyed me quizzically. "And for you?"

"No, I'm fine, ma'am. I'll just wait for my girlfriend if you don't mind." I took a seat and idly flipped through the pages of an outdated copy of *Ebony* magazine. Years earlier, when I first discovered *Ebony* at the Amerika-Haus in Cologne, I could never have imagined that I would read it one day in a beauty parlor in Harlem. Yet, here I was.

While Victoria was getting her hair shaped, a young, heavily perfumed barber with dyed blond streaks in his hair, gold necklaces and bracelets, and more then half a dozen cheap rings on his fingers came over to me. "Excuth me thir, but I would love to give you a nithe haircut." I could see Victoria's face in the mirror. She was suppressing a laughing fit.

I tried to wave the man away. "No thanks. I just had one two weeks ago."

"Well, then what do you think about a nithe shampoo? I would love the chanth to work with your hair."

By now Victoria was giggling so hard that her hairdresser switched off her trimmer and snapped, "Sanford, I can't work this way. Leave that poor man alone."

"Thorry!" the crestfallen barber said and, as he busied himself straightening up a shelf full of beauty supplies, Victoria regained her self-control and her hair stylist got back to work. As I had predicted, the Afro made Victoria even more beautiful. As she somewhat uncertainly studied herself in the mirror once the beautician had finished, I came over to run my fingers gently through her soft, sweet-smelling hair.

Clutching a small bag with her newly acquired hair pick on our way back downtown, Victoria suddenly turned to me. "I shouldn't have laughed when that barber was so persistent. It's hard enough to be black. I can't even imagine what it must be like to be both gay AND black."

"Never mind him," I replied, squeezing her hand. "Have you noticed the admiring looks you're getting from the other women on the train? Just like I told you. If you've got it, flaunt it!" By Monday morning, when the mothers at her Head Start program showered her with compliments, any reservations Victoria may have had about her new hair style quickly vanished.

But, for my part, if I had actually thought it through, it should have been clear that Victoria's Afro would make things worse for me, not better. Now, when the two of us went for a stroll in Greenwich Village many of the black men who saw us were even more hostile than before. Perhaps if I had been short and dark complexioned, it would have been different. But, of course, I was just the opposite. I would be lying if I said it didn't matter to me. It shouldn't have, but it did.

****

"I have a surprise for you," Victoria announced the following weekend. "You're still uneasy when people stare at us, right? Well, now that I have an Afro, I've decided it's because the two of us don't match." She reached into a dresser drawer, pulled out a soft, flat package wrapped in bright silver paper, and handed it to me. Inside was a brightly colored dashiki. "Do you like it? I bought the material up on 125th Street and sewed it myself." I slipped on the loose-fitting top and started to tuck it into my trousers. "Don't be so German!" Victoria teased. "You have to wear it outside your pants."

"I know. *Wennschon, dennschon*," I said as I walked into the bathroom to admire myself in the mirror. The dashiki had a square neckline and long baggy raglan sleeves. The patchwork pattern on the thick cotton cloth was made up of multicolored triangles, some with a dark-red background, others with a white. I had to admit that it looked good on me.

"I think I've discovered the English equivalent to your *'wennschon, dennschon'*," Victoria said as she came up behind me. "It's 'If you can't beat 'em, join 'em.' And that's what we're going to do from now on. What do you say to that?"

Filled with new determination, I turned around and gave Victoria a hug. "Let's go for a walk in the Village!" I replied. "I'm ready to take on all comers!"

CHAPTER 51

*W*hen my fall semester classes started at Hunter, Victoria was also back in school. But, this time, she vowed to stick it out. After having had to drop course after course at City College due to her poor attendance, she had enrolled in an independent study program offered by Goddard College in Plainfield, Vermont. She and her fellow students studied at home using a curriculum each of them designed for themselves. Victoria had chosen to focus on Early Childhood Education in Head Start in Harlem, a subject near and dear to her heart. To satisfy her course requirements, every three weeks she had to mail essays to her assigned professor in Vermont. Twice during the school year, she was required to spend eight days in Plainfield attending lectures during the day and working in study groups with her fellow students and her professor in the evening.

Early on a Friday morning in the middle of October, Victoria left for Plainfield, having taken a week off from work. On the following Saturday, at the crack of dawn, I hopped aboard a bus and headed up to Vermont to visit her.

Tiffany, Victoria's flaxen blond roommate, had arranged to stay over with a fellow student that night so that Victoria and I could have the small dorm room to ourselves. The two of them were waiting to greet me in front of their dorm when I arrived in the early afternoon.

"So nice to meet you, Gunter," Tiffany gushed after we were introduced. "My great-grandparents from both my mother's and my father's side came from Germany, but I don't remember the name of the town."

"With your coloring, they were probably from somewhere in the north like me," I said as the three of us headed upstairs. "That's where most of the blondes come from." I set my overnight bag down in the corner of the dorm room and turned to Victoria. "I feel pretty sweaty after that bus ride. Any chance I could take a quick shower?"

Tiffany and Victoria exchanged glances and grinned. "Sure you can," Victoria replied, "but this might not be the best time. How about waiting for, say, half an hour?" Tiffany put her hand over her mouth and giggled.

"Why not now?"

"It's just that our showers are coed and this time of day there's always someone in there." Another giggle from Tiffany.

"That's okay. I'm a tolerant person."

Victoria shrugged. "Okay, suit yourself. Here's a towel."

Following Victoria's instructions, and dressed only in a pair of boxer shorts and the towel, I found my way down the long corridor to the showers. To my amazement, none of the shower stalls had doors so that, on entering the room, I came face to face with a six-foot-tall woman, her three hundred pounds of rolling pink flesh lathered in soap from head to toe. She had been belting out a Mama Cass song but she stopped just long enough to greet me: "Well, HELLO there, handsome. Where did YOU come from?" If I'd had dentures, I would have lost them on the spot. I hopped into the stall farthest away from hers and, while I took the fastest shower in my life, that big mama kept right on singing as if she were alone. When, still dripping wet, I escaped back down the hall, the words to the song drifted after me: ". . . it's getting better, growing stronger, warm and wilder . . ."

Victoria was barely able to blurt out, "So, how was your shower?" before she and Tiffany doubled over with laughter. When she finally composed herself, Victoria added, "Don't say I didn't warn you!"

"Fair enough," I agreed. "So before I take a walk around the campus to let you two ladies do some studying, is there anything else I need to know?"

"You should be just fine," Victoria reassured me. "You've already seen the worst of it."

****

For the rest of Saturday afternoon I kept out of the way as much as possible while Tiffany and Victoria attended study groups. But, at 10 a.m. on Sunday morning, I was invited to participate with them in a project that was supposed to teach the importance of teamwork. Together with seventeen other students, all but four of them women, we gathered along the bank of a deep, fast-flowing creek and waited for instructions from the professor, a young man with a scraggly beard and a receding hairline.

"Good morning, everyone," he announced. "Today's task is to slow down this creek by piling up enough stones to form a dam. So, unless you have any questions, I'll leave you to it." He then climbed up the embankment to monitor our progress.

While some students scavenged for good-sized stones, others formed a human chain, passing the stones from hand to hand until the last person tossed them into the water at the designated spot. Our enthusiasm soon flagged as it became apparent that it would take many more stones, and much more time than we had thought to achieve the desired effect.

Just then a middle-aged woman with dark hair separated herself from the group and stood to one side like a field marshal, barking out orders. "You there! More to the left! C'mon you slackers, you can do better than that!" Shirtless and soaked with sweat I had just dropped a heavy boulder into the water when she pointed to me and yelled, "You! Yes you! For God's sake, you should've dropped that thing a foot further over!"

"One more word from her like that and I'll let her have it," Victoria muttered under her breath.

Still huffing and puffing I turned to her and asked, "Who is she anyway? Is she a professor?"

"She's a student just like us, but what can you expect from a typical pushy Jew. Never working. Always taking charge and telling other people what to do. She wouldn't dream of getting her hands dirty. Oh, no. Not her."

I had never heard Victoria talk that way and was taken aback by her comment. Hours after the dam had been built, good-byes were said, and we were seated together on a bus back to New York City, I was still puzzled by it, but I hesitated to bring the subject up.

"You know," Victoria said as we rolled south through Vermont, "You may not have noticed that I was the only African-American student on campus. Still, everyone was nice to me, especially the faculty members. They practically fell all over themselves to prove how unbiased they were. I have to wonder how sincere some of them actually were, or whether some of them were ever aware of being patronizing."

"Patronizing? How so?"

"Well, there was this one professor who complimented me several times for speaking Standard English. That was beyond patronizing; that was downright offensive. But I'm sure he didn't see it that way!"

"Is it possible that many of the students and professors weren't used to interacting with an African-American? Maybe they came from places where there weren't any?"

"Yeah, right. As if *that* would explain it. Anyway, let's change the subject. You must have noticed all the admiring looks you were getting from the girls."

"Apart from Mama Cass in the shower? No, I didn't notice," I fibbed, although I had daydreamed that, had I been there on my own, I would have hit on Manuela, a pretty Mexican woman from Chicago, who had a nice tan and long black hair! "Now let me change the subject. Did you have more contact with that Jewish woman from this morning? Your reaction seemed totally out of proportion. You have Jewish friends in New York who aren't anything like her."

"That loudmouth? We were in several study groups together and she always had to have the last word. It's the same with some of the Jewish teachers at Head Start. They're always the organizers. Never the workers."

As I considered how best to reply, Victoria dozed off, her head resting on my shoulder. *How ironic*, I thought, *that, in one breath, Victoria could complain about being stereotyped while, in the next, she didn't realize she was doing it herself.* Our minds can play tricks on us. We can like and accept the people we know personally yet still harbor deep-seated prejudices against the groups from which they come. How often do we hear people say, "I met a nice Negro once (or a nice Jew, or a nice German)," as though this excuses their otherwise hateful remarks? Are any of us really immune from this self-deception? Was I? After all, I could smugly broadcast the message: *See how unprejudiced*

I am. I've got a black girlfriend. And yet, at the same time, despise the black men who resented our being together.

On that long ride back to New York, I thought again about my relationship with Victoria. We had gotten used to each other, in spite of the outside pressure, but somehow the hum was gone. What had begun as a romance was now more like a convenient arrangement for both of us. And, yes, I *had* noticed how the other girls had looked at me. Was it time to find myself a new girlfriend?

CHAPTER 52

*D*uring the first week of November, Rolf Klingenberg and I were comparing notes at the German American Chamber of Commerce. We had each spent the past two weeks visiting importers, wholesalers, department stores, and supermarkets. Our market study about German cookies and candies in the New York metropolitan area was due in just three days and we had been working overtime to meet the deadline.

With so much else on my plate, I hadn't had the time nor the energy to look for a new girlfriend and I was actually looking forward to a relaxing weekend with Victoria as an escape from the stress I was under at the office.

Then the telephone rang.

"Where'd you say?" Rolf asked. "An abandoned warehouse? They WHAT? Are you pulling my leg? No, I'm going to pass, but if my colleague would like to go, I'll call you right back." Rolf put down the receiver and grinned. "So, here's the thing. Do you want to go to a bottle party in the Village on Friday night?"

"Who's hosting it?"

"Some guy from N.Y.U."

I could wait until Saturday to see Victoria, I thought. *Maybe this was finally my chance to find someone new.* "Sure, why not."

Rolf wrote down an address on a scrap of paper and handed it to me. "There's just one small catch. You can either go in costume or buck naked!"

"You're not serious?"

"I kid you not. That's what the man said. So, still want to go?"

"What the heck. Sure! If nothing else, it'll be a break in the routine."

****

On Friday night I was wearing a pair of jeans, a checkered shirt, and a red bandanna under my warm overcoat. It was the best cowboy outfit I could put together without actually investing in a ten-gallon hat. I had lied to Victoria, saying that I had to work late and, as I walked through her West Village neighborhood on my way to the party, there was a slight chance I might run into her. But, rather than feel guilty, I had an odd sense of exhilaration. She and I were not married, after all. So why should she have any hold on me? I was a thirty-two-year-old confirmed bachelor and I might as well enjoy myself.

The entrance to the building was on the second floor, up a steep flight of narrow metal stairs. Just inside the door a young man in polka dot pajamas, fuzzy slippers and a bright orange fright wig was sitting behind a table made from a wooden shipping crate. After I had handed him a bottle of Moselle wine and he had checked off my name on the guest list, I hung up my coat on the metal coat rack and stepped inside to take a look around the cavernous party room. To my right, four floor-to-ceiling windows overlooked the street below. On the opposite wall were four open doors leading into small, dimly lit rooms. And, nearly fifty feet away, at the far end of the room, next to an improvised bar made from a folding card table, a young man who had set up a portable phonograph on a rickety metal stand was sitting cross-legged on the floor sorting through a pile of records. Three beanbag chairs, red, green and blue, made up the only other furniture in that vast, empty space.

Even though I had arrived more than half an hour late, there were only six other guests. In the bright-red beanbag a man in mud-stained overalls, a sleeveless white undershirt, and a plastic hard hat was embracing a petite brunette in a fluffy pink tutu. A few feet away a redheaded girl with iridescent butterfly wings cuddled on Superman's lap. The only other guests were a beer-guzzling, middle-aged cowboy and an overweight cowgirl both of whom were wearing tight-fitting black denim trousers and matching black shirts with long white fringes.

This was it? The big, bad Greenwich Village bottle party? An evening with Victoria would have been more fun! But there was no way I could show up now at her apartment dressed as a cowboy. How would I explain it? I had already made up my mind to go home when, as if on cue, three new arrivals slipped out of their ankle-length coats at the same time. And there before us, in all their pasty-skinned pallor, stood two shapely young women clad only in high-heeled shoes and a completely naked young man. Now the party was getting interesting!

Within minutes, several dozen more guests arrived, most of them in costume, a few dressed only in their birthday suits. The disc jockey put the Temptations' "I can't get next to you" on the turntable and turned up the volume full blast. Taking up the challenge, two nude women were the first to dance, melting together skin on skin. Soon others joined them on the dance floor. After surveying the scene I finally chose as a partner an unusually tall Asian girl who was wearing a tight-fitting flapper-style silver dress and a black cloche hat with a green plume. She had wrapped a fluffy green feather boa around her neck and was clenching a cigarette in a six-inch-long cigarette holder between her teeth. We had to shout at each other to be heard over the music.

"My name's Suki. I suppose from your accent that you're German, am I right?" she said after a few minutes. I had been trying to make small talk but this was the first time she had spoken. Her voice was slurred and her breath smelled of liquor. "I like Germany. I visited there several times when I lived in Paris."

When the music stopped, Suki and I exchanged phone numbers and then she wandered off to get herself another drink. Once she was gone, I took the opportunity to find a new dance partner. There weren't many good choices. Sprawled in a circle along the wall by the windows a group of longhaired hippies were sharing a joint. Other couples had slipped away into the adjacent rooms where mattresses were spread out on the floor. Nearly everyone else was clustered around the bartender.

But then I noticed a young woman standing hesitantly in the doorway. She had dimples in her cheeks, pearly white, slightly bucked teeth, and long brown hair that framed her narrow face. She was wearing a white blouse and a long skirt made up of dozens of colorful pleated panels. The red bandanna in her hair matched the triangular scarf tied in a sash around her waist. I asked her for the next dance. And the next. And the next.

Her name was Irene Cardinal and, dancing with her, I blocked out everything else in the room. When, after a short pause, the disc jockey put on the Tom Jones hit "I'll Never Fall in Love Again" I turned to Irene and asked, "Is that your motto too?"

She laughed as she replied, "That all depends!"

"We should really take a break," I suggested the next time the disc jockey changed records. "Let me get you a glass of wine before it's all gone."

"No, please don't. Listen! I don't know about you, but this whole scene is grossing me out. Would you like to go over to my place and have a glass of wine there? I live on 12th Street just off of Fifth Avenue." I didn't need any convincing.

As Irene and I walked arm in arm over to her place, I tried not to let my bad conscience nag me. After all, going to that crazy party wasn't really my idea, right? If Rolf Klingenberg hadn't gotten a phone call, I would be with Victoria right now. So why should I feel guilty? When it got right down to it, no matter how it had come about, now that I had met Irene I wasn't going to let anything spoil the moment.

Irene lived in an elegant, turn-of-the century building with a spacious lobby and a uniformed doorman. The elevator brought us to the fifth floor. Just inside the door to her apartment, hundreds of yellowed, musty-smelling books were crammed, two-deep into built-in bookshelves on both sides of a long hallway. The entry hall led to a large living room furnished with mahogany cabinets, a huge leather couch, and two matching leather armchairs; even more jam-packed bookcases lined two walls. A wide archway in the back of the living room led into a dining room and the nearby kitchen.

While Irene was hanging up our coats, I walked over to study the titles of some of the books. As best as I could tell, every single one of them dealt with psychology. "You really live alone in this huge place?" I asked when Irene rejoined me. "You aren't married, are you? Or maybe you're a psychologist?"

She shook her head. "No, you're wrong on both counts. I inherited this place from my parents when they passed away more than a year ago, but I've just been too busy to get rid of all their books. We can talk about them some other time. Right now let's get ourselves some wine. I don't have any that's chilled, so maybe red would be best. Come to the kitchen and you can take your pick."

From the nearly two-dozen bottles in her wine rack, I randomly selected a bottle of Château Beychevelle Bordeaux. Irene clearly approved. "You have good taste in wine!" she murmured as she rummaged through a kitchen drawer looking for a corkscrew. I thought it best not to admit that the wines I was most familiar with were the ones I occasionally picked up on sale for $1.99 at my neighborhood liquor store on the Upper West Side.

We brought our wine glasses into the living room and sat down together on the couch. Irene, as it turned out, was taking courses at NYU, which is how she had learned about the party. "And you? Didn't you say you're going to Hunter College? So, what's your connection to NYU?" she asked.

"A friend of a friend goes there," I said and I left it at that. I had never actually found out the name of the person who had called Rolf about the party.

We talked about our shared love of travel and I told her about my hitchhiking trips in Germany, Austria, Belgium, the Netherlands, Great Britain and France. I had always imagined that I was well travelled but it turned out that she had been to many more foreign countries than I had. Her favorites were Greece and France.

When Irene went into the kitchen to refill our wine glasses, I got up to study her large collection of LP's, many of them by French artists.

"Who are your favorites?" Irene inquired when she rejoined me.

"Piaf, Juliette Greco, George Brassens and, before I left Germany, the big rage was Françoise Hardy. Would you mind putting on the one by Juliette Greco?"

She smiled, "No, let's not play a record now. I've got a better idea. If you'll excuse me," and she disappeared into another room, returning a minute later with a guitar. "It's been a while," she apologized. "Bear with me while I tune it."

As I watched Irene turn the pegs to adjust the strings, I was reminded of Edie, who had so charmed me with her rendition of a Mama Cass song that I had cheated on Victoria for the very first time. But when Irene began to accompany herself on the guitar while she sang "Sous le ciel de Paris" all thoughts of Edie were gone. Irene's voice was magical, her mastery of the guitar astonishing. She was Edie times ten. And, as I listened, I could look out the window and see the brightly lit top of the Empire State Building barely a mile away. *This is heaven* I said to myself.

After singing about fifteen lines of the *chanson*, Irene suddenly stopped. "Sorry. That's all I know by heart." But with a bit of encouragement on my part, she then went on to sing other songs in French, in English, and in Greek. *Don't insist on staying over*, I kept reminding myself. *This shouldn't turn into a one-night-stand. I want to see her again.*

As it turned out, I did spend the night with Irene, but we spent it talking. Talking about our travels, our jobs, our studies, about just about everything and anything. Somehow the topic of her parents' books never did come up. We talked and talked until Irene suddenly said, "Do you realize it's almost 6 a.m.? Time to have some breakfast. Come help me fix it."

After breakfast Irene and I arranged to meet again later for dinner and then I left for home. Throughout the day I knew I should phone Victoria to make my excuses, but somehow I never got around to it.

CHAPTER 53

*L*ater that Saturday evening when I picked Irene up at her apartment she suggested that we dine at Monte's Trattoria on MacDougal Street instead of going to the midtown French restaurant I had had in mind. "Monte's isn't too far to walk if we cut through Washington Square Park," she explained. "And their food is delicious."

The unctuous Maitre D' at Monte's Trattoria rushed over to Irene. "Good evening, Miss Cardinal," he said while trying to inspect me surreptitiously from head to toe. "What an unexpected pleasure! Will that be a table for two? Or will there be others in your party?"

"No, it's just the two of us this time!" Irene replied. The strong whiff of garlic that hung in the air as we were led to our table had whetted our appetites and we both pored over the menu. "I'd like the veal pizzaiola, if it's all right with you," Irene said.

"Have whatever your heart desires," I grandly replied, determined to impress her. "Let's go for all four courses!"

"I gather you're a regular here," I commented after the waiter had taken our order.

"I've sometimes been here with friends but mostly with clients."

Over dinner I learned that Irene had a B.A. in English from Boston University. Shortly after graduation she had landed a demanding job as an executive with a cruise line based in lower Manhattan, for which she put in long working hours and made frequent business trips throughout the United States, Europe, and the Caribbean. All in all quite an achievement, considering she was not yet thirty, and I complimented her on her success.

"Thanks. I sometimes can't believe it myself," Irene said with a smile. Then she reached over and took my hand. "You know, Gunter, I know you haven't asked for my advice, but I'm going to give it to you anyway. Once you get your B.A. from Hunter, you should really go for an MBA. It doesn't take all that long to get one. That's my plan, too, but right now I don't have time for more than the one course at NYU." She paused for a second. "And here's an even better piece of advice. Don't pass up the chance to try the *tiramisu*. It's out of this world!"

When we savored our desserts, I mentioned that my parents owned a café in a small town near Cologne. "By café do you mean an American-style coffee shop or what the French call a *patisserie?*"

"Oh! Definitely a *patisserie*; it's what the Germans call a *Konditerei*. In any case, it's a pity that my father doesn't make *tiramisu*. He could earn a fortune with it. Honestly, this is one of the best desserts I've ever tasted."

"Do you know what *tiramisu* means?"

"No, I thought that it was just an Italian name, but I guess I'm wrong."

Irene smiled. "*Tiramisu* literally means 'pull me up' but it could also mean 'cheer me up'! Why don't we go back to my apartment so you can *tiramisu!*" Her suggestion was the one I had been hoping for; I was only too happy to comply.

While Irene made a batch of French toast the next morning, I told her some details about my strange childhood in Russian-occupied East Prussia after the war. How, for three-and-a-half years I had lived as a starving street urchin, begging for bread in the daytime and then lying awake at night worrying when my mother slipped away to steal potatoes. Irene's reaction surprised me.

"That must have been very tough for you but at least your mother must have loved you!" she said, her voice bitter.

"Of course she did. I don't know how many times she risked her life for my brother and me. I wouldn't be here if it hadn't been for her. But, enough about me. Let's talk about your childhood. Do you really mean to tell me that your mother didn't love you?"

To my amazement, Irene started to sob. "They didn't have time for me, neither one of them, but my mother was the worst! The maid brought me up, not her." She took a deep breath before continuing. "And do you know what the maid confided in me one day? That rather than breastfeed me, my mother had her give me goat milk to drink! Goat milk from Haiti! Can you believe it?"

"But surely they must have done something right. Look how well you turned out," I suggested somewhat feebly.

"No thanks to them. Listen! My father was a psychiatrist. My mother was a psychologist. They spent their lives solving everyone's problems but mine. Sometimes I wonder why they even bothered to have me. So, no, I can't say my mother loved me."

I was at a loss. What does one say to all that? "C'mon Irene," I finally said, "It's too bad that you went through that, but all in all you must have had a comfortable life here in this apartment, in this neighborhood, with good food and a good school. I would have given a lot to have had the same when I was a child."

"That might be so, but don't you get it? There was no love and that's the one thing I needed more than anything else." She threw her arms around me as tears again ran down her cheeks.

As I held her tight, my mind was racing. The way things were going, the whole weekend would end in disaster, which was the last thing I wanted to happen. "You know what," I said soothingly, "there must be too many bad memories for you in this place right now, so how about this idea? After we have brunch, let's go up to Central Park and take a long walk. That always makes me feel better." To my relief, she readily agreed.

CHAPTER 54

The weather was perfect for a walk, sunny and cool. Irene's mood brightened as soon as we hopped aboard the Madison Avenue bus that brought us to midtown. We entered the Park at 60th Street and strolled in the direction of the boat basin, about a mile to the north. The air was filled with the pungent odor of rotting leaves, the last vestige of autumn. Young mothers pushed toddlers in strollers on their way to the zoo. A couple nestled together in a tight embrace on a metal bench. A small boy clutched the bright-red model sailboat he was going to launch in the sailboat pond. Fellow strollers, bicycle riders and teenagers on roller skates passed us right and left as fluffy gray squirrels scampered out of their way. Some people smiled at us and we smiled back. No one shot us a hostile glance, as had so often happened when I was out with Victoria.

I had my Voigtländer camera with me and was looking for someone who could take a picture of Irene and me when I spotted the two young lawyers who were working as interns at the German American Chamber of Commerce. We walked over to them and, after I made the introductions, one of them snapped several photos. Since, as it turned out, both he and Irene were avid photographers the two of them got into a conversation about f-stops and zoom lenses. While they talked the other young lawyer came over to me and whispered, "Pardon me, Mr. Nitsch, but does your girlfriend speak German?"

"No, just French and Greek. Why do you ask?"

His voice so soft that I had to strain to hear him, he spoke to me in German. "I've only been working at the Chamber for a couple of weeks, but you can't imagine the awful gossip. You know Hans Teetz from the Trade Fair Department? Several people have confided in me that he's got a Negro boyfriend and that you, I hate the say this, that *you* have a Negro girlfriend."

"Really? You don't say? Who told you that?"

"I really shouldn't tell."

I shrugged. "Well, it just goes to show that you can't believe everything you hear," I replied. Then, as if to prove my point, I gave Irene a big hug before we continued on our walk.

****

Before I left for home that evening, Irene hesitated a moment and then said, "It's kind of awkward to ask you this, since I've known you for such a short time, but do you think you could help me get rid of most of these psychology and psychiatry books?"

"Sure, I'd be glad to help. How about this coming weekend? But wouldn't you be better off donating them to a library?"

"No, I don't want to bother with that. Anyway I can't imagine anyone wanting them considering that they're crumbling to pieces and most of them have scribbled notes in the margins."

"Fair enough. So when should I come by?"

"How about coming next Friday at 7 p.m. That way we'll be ready to start first thing Saturday morning. And be sure to dress casual and bring a couple of extra tee shirts. There's years' worth of dust on those things."

****

We set to work right after breakfast on Saturday, first putting sturdy corrugated cartons together with masking tape and then, after setting aside the nearly one hundred volumes of fiction that Irene wanted to keep, packing up the rest of the books. I had lugged several dozen cartons full of yellowing psychiatry and psychology books into the basement and was busy arranging them in six-foot high stacks along the wall when the elevator door opened and I was no longer alone.

The angry man who stood before me was at least my height but double my weight. I had no doubt that most of his weight was made up of pure muscle. "Hey, mister, who the hell do you think you are?" he snapped. "You can't bring down any more of them cartons! Where's all this junk coming from anyhow?"

When I found my voice and said, "From Irene Cardinal's apartment," he changed his tone.

"Oh, well, why dincha say so? Nice folks the Cardinals was and generous, too. Lived here a long time." He scratched his head, deep in thought. "Tell you what. You tell Miss Cardinal I'll let you bring down five, maybe six, more of them boxes, but that'll be it for today. Any more cartons'll have to wait for a coupla days, if you get my drift."

"Oh, so you've met our janitor, I see," Irene said when I came back upstairs. "Actually, the man's quite harmless, despite the way he looks. But let's try not to pull his chain. How about just four more boxes? And then I guess we'll have to continue next weekend, if you don't mind."

"I'd be happy to. Count me in."

As we were talking Irene retrieved a book from the last box we'd packed. "This is the one I've been looking for. I've shown you some of those nutty marginal notes like 'The road to hell is paved with good intentions.'" She leafed through some pages. "But this one really takes the cake." Irene held out the book for me to see. "What do you make of that?" Scrawled in the margin were the words, 'You can't unscramble eggs.' As I put the book back in the carton and sealed up the box with tape, she choked back tears. "That's my mother's handwriting. What made her write those words, do you think? 'You can't unscramble eggs.' It has nothing to do with the text. So I wonder, I've been wondering for a long time, whether she actually meant *me?*"

"Come now, you're imagining things," I soothed. "I'm sure she didn't mean anything of the kind." But, to myself, I couldn't understand how such a smart, successful businesswoman could also be so insecure. Had she really had such a rough childhood? Looking around that spacious apartment it was hard to imagine. And yet if her parents really *did* abandon her like that, I resolved not to do the same. I was determined to make this relationship last.

****

By the following weekend, when we had disposed of the rest of the books, we both stood back and took a look around. To my untrained eye, all of the character had been drained out of the living room. I was the first to speak. "So, what are you going to do to fill up all these empty shelves?"

"That's easy. I'm going to hire an interior decorator to help me make this place over the way I'd like it to be. And if that means tearing out every single one of the bookcases, so be it. I'm tired of living in my parents' shadow." The whole idea sounded rather extravagant to me, but I bit my tongue. "Oh, and before I forget," Irene went on, "just so you know, I'll be away over Christmas. I'm flying to London for three days to visit some old friends!"

Just for three days? There must be a really good reason for such a waste of money and effort. "Do you have a boyfriend in London?" I couldn't help asking.

"No, don't be silly. My best girlfriend from college married an Englishman. They invited me ages ago. Maybe the next time I visit them you can come along."

Somewhere in the back of my mind I remembered my old mentor Quincy's rule: *Never travel with a woman or she'll think you're ready to settle down.* But maybe I was ready this time. Maybe Irene was "the one."

"That would be great!" I said. "I'd really like that."

CHAPTER 55

*I*t had been several weeks since I had picked up the phone to call Victoria. Whenever she had called me during that time, I had come up with lame excuses about overtime and business trips. It only seemed right to tell her that I had met someone new. On Thursday, December 3rd, my thirty-third birthday, I invited Victoria out to dinner at Nirvana, a recently opened Indian restaurant located in a 15th floor penthouse at 30 Central Park South just off of Fifth Avenue. Since I was coming directly from the Chamber, we arranged to meet in front of the building at 6 p.m.

I had arrived ten minutes early and was looking up and down the block for Victoria when I spotted Hans Teetz, the manager of the Trade Fair Department, walking towards me. He was carrying on an animated conversation with a distinguished-looking black man and only noticed me at the last minute. "Well, what a coincidence!" Hans Teetz said. "I saw you at the Chamber no more than a half an hour ago and we both turn up here." He turned to his companion. "Gene, this is one of my colleagues, Gunter Nitsch."

"Nice to meet you," the man said as he reached over to shake my hand. "I'm Gene Hovis. Hans and I go back a long way together."

Just then Victoria arrived and exclaimed, "How's the birthday boy?" as she flung her arms around my neck.

"Looks like it's time for more introductions," I said. "Hans Teetz and Gene Hovis, please meet Victoria Hoyt."

"Gunter's taking me to dinner at Nirvana," Victoria added, making it clear that we were more than just casual acquaintances, in case there had been any doubt.

"Well, we shouldn't keep you then," Hans Teetz said. "Enjoy your meal!"

Then, under his breath, he muttered to me in German, "*Na das war ja eine Überraschung!*" ("That was a surprise!") It was clear that he had no more believed the rumors circulating at the Chamber about me, than I had believed the rumors about him.

On the way up in the elevator Victoria smiled. "They seem very happy together, wouldn't you say?" I nodded in agreement. "And I'm glad to have finally met someone from your office, even if it was purely by chance. You've never brought me up there, you know." It was a point well taken. I hadn't dared.

I had reserved a window table and, from that height, the streetlights along the paths in Central Park and the glow of lamps from high-rise buildings on nearby Fifth Avenue gave the evening a festive look. Victoria was beaming as though nothing in our relationship had changed.

"So how's the birthday boy?" she asked again as she lifted her wine glass to toast me." Then, as I struggled to find just the right words to say what I had to say, she tilted her head to one side and, still smiling, asked, "You're seeing somebody else, aren't you?"

"Kind of," I lamely replied. Her question had thrown me off balance. How had I lost control of the situation so quickly?

"For heavens sake! What kind of an answer is that? Tell me all about her! Is she younger than I am? Do you know her from Hunter College? Is she well off? And, I hate to ask this. She's white, isn't she?" I blushed. "I thought so," Victoria said.

"Well, if you must know," I began, "she's an executive with a big cruise line company. She's fluent in French and Greek, and she lives not too far from you in the Village."

"And?" Victoria paused. "How much younger is she?"

"Oh, that? Just a few years, give or take. But her age has nothing to do with it."

"Well, it's good to know about the competition," Victoria said. "Listen, Gunter, I have no idea how long this infatuation of yours will last, but I'm sure of this. You'll be back. Trust me! No matter what you may think now, the two of us are meant for each other." Then she relaxed her grip and leaned back in her chair. "But as long as we're here, let's change the subject and enjoy this wonderful food. It's your birthday after all!"

We lingered over dinner for the next two hours, reminiscing about our past adventures together and catching up on recent events at Head Start and at the Chamber. By the time the waiter served our dessert, we had finished an entire bottle of Sauvignon Blanc. When I brought Victoria back downtown on the subway, I had intended to give her a friendly kiss goodnight and go home, but when we reached her door and she gave me a hug, I lost my resolve and stayed the night.

CHAPTER 56

*I*rene and I spent the weekend together before her flight to London. I knew I was going to miss her and, as we lay in bed together, I held her close. But then, quite out of the blue, she pulled away from me and sat up. "Gunter, promise you won't get me pregnant. That's the last thing in the world I need right now."

At that moment Quincy's words on the subject flashed through my mind: "*The way I look at it,*" he had declared, "*that'd be her problem, not mine. A woman should be smart enough to protect herself.*" But, as much as I always had tried to adhere to Quincy's rules, I felt it was finally time to steer a different course. In the short time we had known each other I had fallen hard for Irene and I did not want to risk losing her.

Even so, I surprised myself by blurting out, "Look, Irene, there's no need to worry about that. I love you and, in the unlikely event that you become pregnant, I would just marry you sooner than I had already planned to." Then I beamed at her and held out my arms for the expected embrace.

To my utter astonishment she leaned back against the headboard, clasped her hands behind her head, and laughed out loud. "Was that strange offer meant to be a marriage proposal? Because, if so, I'm sorry, but I could never marry you!"

Stunned, I looked at her in disbelief. "Why not?" I realized I had made a muddle of things and my choice of words had clearly not been the best, but surely she could see that my heart was in the right place.

"All right then. Let's face facts. There are at least four good reasons. Do I need to spell them out? You don't make much money. You're still working on your education. You have a foreign accent and you don't even own a car!" Then, just to irritate me, she lit a cigarette.

I felt crushed, especially since everything she had criticized me for was true. Even worse, I had exposed my true feelings and received nothing but rejection in return. Not knowing what to reply, I got up and got dressed. "To be frank, I've never been in a situation like this before," I finally said. "I don't know what possessed me to be so honest with you. But, if that's the way you feel, I guess I'll just wish you a nice trip and be on my way."

I reached over to shake hands with her and was about to leave when she pulled me back. "Come on, this isn't what I had in mind. Don't blow things all out of proportion. All I said was that I wouldn't marry you. Not that we should stop seeing each other. I'm flying home on the 27th of December and have to be back at work on the 28th so I'll need a few days to get over my jet lag. Actually, I was hoping the two of us could celebrate New Year's Eve together. What do you say?" and then she gave me a hug.

If I had wanted to preserve whatever dignity I had left, I should have walked out right then and there. But her invitation intrigued me. Maybe there was still hope for a future with Irene after all. "Did you have anything special in mind?" My voice was barely a whisper.

"Actually, yes. I've already made a reservation for 8 p.m. at Monte Trattoria. I figured that, after dinner, we could come back here, have some wine, and wait for Guy Lombardo to bring in 1971 on TV. Can I count on you to join me?"

And, with that, I threw away my last shred of self-respect "Sure. Why not?" I said. "I'll see you then."

****

As if I weren't feeling bad enough, when I got back home I found a long Christmas letter from my mother full of terrible news. Two months earlier my brother had lost control of his car while driving my father back from the ANUGA Food Fair in Cologne. During the five weeks my father had spent in the hospital recovering from multiple bone fractures, Café Nitsch had been closed. And now, since my father was no longer physically able to put in the twelve to fourteen hours a day, six and a half days a week, necessary to keep the Café running, my parents had been forced to sell at a substantial loss the business they had so proudly owned and run since 1956.

"But that's not the worst part," Mutti's letter went on. "When we move to the one-bedroom apartment we've bought in Cologne-Nippes in a few days, your father will try to find a job with more normal hours so, hopefully, we should be fine on that account. The real problem is that your father and Hubert are once again not on speaking terms, which makes life extremely difficult for me. As a wife and a mother, I really can't take sides. Sometimes I wonder whether, if you were here, you would be in a better position to mediate between those two stubborn men. Anyway, I hope you have a very Merry Christmas. Love, Mutti."

First thing Monday morning I called my mother from my office. "Have things gotten any better in the meantime?" I asked her. I was pretty sure I already knew the answer.

"He's not here right now so I can speak freely. If anything, things have gotten worse. Your father still gets so angry with Hubert that I hope he finds a job soon and gets out of the house. His constant complaining about your brother is driving me crazy."

"I can imagine. On the other hand maybe it's a good thing that he'll no longer be working ninety to a hundred hours a week. Have you reminded him that he had a stroke when he was forty?"

"Of course I have, but he just can't deal with the loss of the café. Anyway, as long as I have you on the phone, here's a piece of good news. Hubert is going to marry his girlfriend Irmgard."

"That should make Vati happy."

"It might if he knew about it but Hubert doesn't want me to tell him just yet. It's been that tense. But enough about my problems! How're things with you and Victoria? You haven't sent us any new photos of her recently."

"Pretty much the same," I replied. "We had dinner together on my birthday."

"Oh, how nice. Well, thanks for calling! I'll write again soon," and she hung up.

So Hubert, who was short, grossly overweight, and five years my junior, was getting married? Yet my somewhat bungled offer of marriage to Irene had been flat-out rejected. It didn't seem quite fair. At least I could thank my lucky stars that I hadn't already sent Mutti any pictures of Irene. If she had asked me how things stood with her, I wouldn't have known what to say.

CHAPTER 57

*B*y the time New Year's Eve arrived, I had long since regretted having made plans with Irene. Still, I was determined to make the best of things. I put on my dark blue suit, a white dress shirt with French cuffs, and the red tie with tiny black and white woven checks that Charlotte had given to me years before in Cologne. For some strange reason, I was convinced that the tie brought me luck, and I would certainly need luck that night.

The doorman in Irene's building had called ahead from downstairs and Irene was holding her coat and waiting for me outside the door to her apartment. She looked stunning in a long woolen skirt and a matching black, long-sleeved, form fitting turtleneck sweater. She flashed me a radiant smile. "You're right on time. Punctual as always," she said and she turned to lock the door behind her. "If it's okay with you, let's leave now to beat the crowds." Her mouth tasted of stale cigarettes when I gave her a kiss before helping her on with her coat.

"So tell me all about your trip to London," I said once the waiter at Monte's Trattoria had taken our order.

"Well, I finally met Sally's husband. He's an investment banker and he's absolutely gorgeous. Tall, fine features, dark-brown wavy hair. They have a brand-new Jaguar, season tickets to the opera, and most of their friends are upper class Brits."

Clearly he had everything I lacked: money, connections, and a car. "Well," I interjected. "What else could a girl want? Good for her!"

Irene bit her lip. "Yes, I guess so. But here's the thing. Please don't misunderstand me. My girlfriend's a great person, but it's beyond me how she could get someone like that to marry her."

For a moment I was tempted to say, *"Perhaps, one day your prince will come,"'* but I restrained myself. "Some people have all the luck," I replied with more than just a touch of irony.

No sooner had I said the word 'luck,' than Irene suddenly reached over and touched my tie. "How could you wear this awful thing on such a special occasion? It's all frayed at the edges!"

I had no intention of telling her about Charlotte, so I simply said, "It's been my 'good luck tie' but, you're right, it's definitely seen better days." *Certainly*, I thought to myself, *much better days than this one!*

We had eaten our salads and our main courses arrived, Tuscan grilled chicken for Irene and a New York cut sirloin steak for me.

"He didn't bring you a steak knife," Irene commented as I struggled to cut my meat.

"I can manage."

"Why are you so stubborn? Just ask for a steak knife! The waiter should have brought you one in the first place."

"I'm fine," I insisted. "It just takes a bit more effort," and then it happened. The blunt knife slipped in my right hand and its flat side smacked down into the brown gravy splattering a long string of greasy spots onto Irene's thin black sweater. At that moment I wished I could crawl under the table and disappear.

"You idiot!" Irene shrieked. "I told you to get a steak knife. Now, look what you've done! Just look at my beautiful sweater!"

I dipped my napkin in my water glass and reached over to try to clean up the mess but she pushed away my hand. "Just leave me alone," she snapped before rushing to the powder room.

There were tearstains on her cheeks and wet splotches on her sweater when she came back.

"Let's finish our meal," she said through clenched teeth. From then on every effort I made to start a conversation failed, no matter how hard I tried. After I paid the bill, I walked Irene back to her building, but not hand in hand or arm in arm as usual. The night doorman tipped his hat at us as we approached.

"You're certainly not coming upstairs. I'm going to leave you right here," Irene said. "Since we're clearly not meant for each other, I never want to see you again." She turned away to walk into her lobby.

"Fine with me!" I called after her. Then, just before she disappeared inside, I added, "Happy New Year!"

It was quite a distance but I walked all the way back to 42nd Street where a vast crowd of happy couples had gathered to watch the ball drop at midnight. But, rather than stick around to celebrate, I headed for the subway to take me home. As I waited for the train on the platform I took off my 'good-luck tie' and dropped it into the trash.

CHAPTER 58

After the disaster with Irene, I was too humiliated to call Victoria and admit that things hadn't worked out. Instead, to take my mind off things, I bought the books for my second semester classes and tried to get a head start on the reading. Then, just by chance, I came across the crumpled slip of paper in my winter coat pocket on which I'd jotted down Suki's telephone number. She was the young Japanese woman I had met at the crazy party the same night I met Irene. Even though I doubted she would remember me, I picked up the phone and made the call.

"Of course I know who you are!" she said when I gave her my name. "You were the tall German cowboy!"

"That's me all right. Hey, I was wondering whether you'd like to go out with me next Saturday."

"Sure, I'd be glad to."

"I could come down to the Village to pick you up at your place around six o'clock. Just let me write down the address."

"How about this?" Suki replied. And, instead of giving me her home address, she gave me the address of a bar on MacDougal Street just down the block from the Village Gate nightclub.

****

I arrived at the bar at ten minutes to six. As expected, the place was nearly empty at that early hour. A tall woman with long jet-black hair, an ankle-length black overcoat, and black stiletto boots was sitting alone at the bar.

"Suki, is that you?" When I had approached her, she spun around on the bar stool to face me. She was holding a half-empty glass. "I wanted to be the first to arrive so I wouldn't keep you waiting."

"Don't worry. I haven't been here all that long," she assured me.

"Oh, then I don't feel so bad. I've made an 8 p.m. dinner reservation at the Alpine Cellar on 34th Street. Have you ever been there? It's a German-style restaurant with a dance floor in the basement of the McAlpin Hotel."

She shook her head. "No I don't think so. But that's a great idea. I like German food."

"But as long as we're here," I continued, "let's have a drink together before we head uptown. I'm going to have a glass of wine. Would you like another one of whatever it is you're drinking?"

"Yes, please. A gin and tonic if you don't mind."

When we had finished our drinks and the bartender brought the check I was stunned to read the amount and to learn that, aside from my inexpensive glass of white wine, I would be paying, not for two gin and tonics, but for four. I was tempted to ask Suki again just how long she had been waiting for me; but it didn't seem polite, so I held my peace, sucked it up, and paid the bill.

****

Suki was a little unsteady on her feet as we walked to the McAlpin Hotel. Her eyes lit up when I led her downstairs to the Alpine Cellar, a huge Bavarian-themed restaurant with a vaulted ceiling where the lederhosen-clad members of a five-piece band were playing lively oompah music.

I helped Suki out of her long black coat and could see, for the first time, what she was wearing: a white taffeta blouse and an ankle-length black woolen skirt cinched around her narrow waist with a wide belt made of large silver coins held together with leather straps. As we were shown to our table she got admiring glances from everyone we passed.

A buxom waitress in a Bavarian dirndl handed us the menu and asked, "What can I get you to drink?"

Even though, all around us, couples were drinking beer from one-liter steins, in an effort to impress Suki I decided to take a more elegant approach. "Can you recommend a red wine? I think that would go better with our food."

"Our German Spätburgunder is very popular with our guests who don't want to fill up on beer," the waitress replied.

"Should we have a bottle of German red wine with our dinner?" I asked Suki.

"Yes, please! I developed a taste for red wine when I was living in Paris, but I've never tried German red wine."

Minutes later the waitress uncorked a bottle of Spätburgunder wine for us and poured some in my glass. After I took a sip and signaled my approval, she filled both of our glasses.

"Here's to a wonderful evening!" I said, lifting my glass in a toast and taking another sip. Suki nodded in agreement. Then she leaned back and gulped down the entire glassful before taking a breath. Rather than lingering over our wine, I decided to order the main course before Suki had anything else to drink. "Can I interest you in the house specialty? It's a Bavarian *Schlachtplatte*, a combination of smoked pork loin, blood sausage, liver sausage, and sauerkraut." She crinkled up her nose in disgust and so we ordered Wiener schnitzel for her and a Bavarian *Schlachtplatte* for me. While I took a few more sips of wine, Suki reached for the bottle and poured herself another glass. By the time our food came the bottle was empty.

"I'm thirsty, aren't you?" Suki not so subtly hinted once the waitress had walked away.

Before she drank me under the table I decided it was time to switch to a less expensive drink. I called the waitress over and ordered two beers. By now I was no longer surprised when Suki, who was merely picking at her food, managed to guzzle down first one stein of beer and then another before I had gotten through my first. What did puzzle me was that she never once went to the powder room. *Where was she putting it all* I wondered. *She probably weighs fifty pounds less than me!*

If I'd been sure she would get home safely, I would have abandoned Suki in front of the hotel after dinner. However, considering how much she had to drink, it didn't seem right to leave her there at the curb. So I hailed a cab and we both climbed inside. She gave the driver directions and then cuddled up to me in the back seat for the ride back down to Greenwich Village. But the adventure wasn't over yet. The address she had given the driver was not her home. It was a cocktail lounge. When the cabbie dropped us off there she steered me inside. "I need another drink before we go upstairs," she explained.

It goes without saying that the bartender recognized her right away. "The usual for you, miss?" he inquired before turning to me. "And for the gentleman?"

"Just a Budweiser, thanks."

One Budweiser and two guzzled gin and tonics later, Suki turned to me and smiled. "Now let's go up to my apartment."

I took her arm to steady her as she wobbled along on her stiletto heels. A block from the cocktail lounge she turned onto a street full of rundown warehouses and stopped in front of a building, which had a long iron staircase leading up to the second floor, just like the building where the bottle party had taken place.

"This is where you live?" I asked in astonishment.

"Oh! Did I forget to mention that I'm an artist? So this is pretty much all I can afford. Follow me and I'll show you around."

There were no lights on in any of the windows; all of the surrounding buildings were dark. Clinging tightly to the railing, I cautiously felt my way, tread by tread, all the while imagining how I would defend the two of us from attack if someone were to spring out of the shadows with a club or a gun.

Suki fumbled in her purse before finding the keys to the double locks on the heavy wooden door. Once inside, she flicked a switch and two naked light bulbs, one at each end of that cavernous, high-ceilinged loft, cast an eerie glow. In the far left corner, reaching nearly to the ceiling, empty Chianti bottles were skillfully stacked in a broad-based pyramid. Other than the pyramid and the neatly made double bed, a small table and two chairs at the opposite end of the loft, that vast floor space was bare of furnishings.

The same wasn't true of the walls, however. They were lined at eye-level with hundreds of 8"x10" photographs of nudes, some of young men whose hands were positioned to hide their private parts, but mostly of young Asian women (including some of Suki), who boldly faced the camera without a touch of shame. While I studied the photographs, Suki poured Chianti into two tall water glasses. She put one glass on the small table for me and gulped down the contents of the other. Then after pulling off her boots, she sat down on her bed and assumed the Lotus position.

I should have gotten up and left but, just as I was about to make my excuses, Suki smiled and said, "I guess I haven't told you very much about myself and you've been too much of a gentleman to ask. But I'd like to tell you now, if you don't mind." Intrigued, I sat down on one of the chairs in front of her bed, stretched my legs out in front of me, and prepared to listen to her story.

Suki's family had sent her to an expensive girls' boarding school in Tokyo where, at the age of sixteen, she had become the mistress of a junior diplomat from the French Embassy, who had assured her for two long years that he would get a divorce and marry her. When he and his family were transferred back to Paris, Suki borrowed money from relatives and wheedled money from her parents in order to follow him. Once there, she had thrown herself at him, again becoming his mistress.

"That whole next year I supported myself by working as a model and a photographer while he kept promising and promising."

"So, did he finally get a divorce?" I asked as Suki handed me her glass for a refill.

Her eyes filled with tears. "Yes, he did, but then he went and married someone else, a strawberry blond French woman about my age. That's when I packed my things and moved to New York." She lifted her glass and drank it down. "And that's also why I drink. You can understand that, right?" When I didn't answer her right away, she flashed me a smile. "Enough of my sad story. Come join me on my bed," she said as she patted the pillow.

"Sorry, Suki," I hastened to say as I put on my coat, "but I can't stay. I'm very tired and I'm going home."

I had really made a mess of things. First the disaster with Irene and now this. On the long subway ride back to the Upper West Side, I wondered if I should give Victoria a call. Perhaps she and I were made for each other after all.

CHAPTER 59

*B*ut any plans to call Victoria had to be deferred because, just then, orders for several time-consuming market studies came in to the German American Chamber of Commerce. Rolf Klingenberg and I were out of the office for days on end, interviewing importers, wholesalers, and supermarket managers in New York City about how best to improve the sales of German cookies and candies, German pickles and sauerkraut, and German cheese. The most difficult part of the job was scheduling appointments, especially with the importers who often insisted on meeting with us as early as 6 a.m. On those days, I had to drag myself out of bed no later than 4:30 in the morning even though I had left work late the previous evening.

In connection with the market study, I accompanied Rolf to Chicago on my very first business trip. While there, we spent several grueling days doing interviews during the day and writing memos in our hotel rooms after supper. Long before I had left Germany, I had dreamed about exploring the jazz scene in Chicago. So, one evening, when Rolf took off early to visit an old army buddy, I headed for Mr. Kelly's nightclub at 1028 North Rush Street to see Roberta Flack perform. I had seen many jazz performers before, from a great distance away on stage at the Apollo Theater in Harlem. Mr. Kelly's was a far more intimate setting and when, during intermission, Roberta Flack came out front to mingle with the audience, I boldly walked right up to her, introduced myself, and told her I was a big fan.

"You're German?" she asked. "I studied German when I was getting my music degree at Howard University. Sorry if I'm a little rusty. *Leider habe ich sehr viel vergessen!*" And, with that, she switched back to English. Despite her fame as a singer of jazz, blues, and folk music, she confessed that her favorite composers were Bach, Mozart, Beethoven, Schubert and Brahms, names she pronounced like a native German speaker. "And actually," she confided, "two of the best singers I know are Fischer-Dieskau and Hermann Prey. When they sing German lieder, I'm in heaven!"

"Maybe you should sing some lieder for us?" I suggested, half in jest.

"In my next life perhaps," she replied with a smile before shaking my hand and excusing herself to go back on stage.

****

On our return to the office a few days later, Rolf and I set to work combining our notes into a written summary of our New York and Chicago findings. That way we would have a standard of reference when we embarked on the next stage of our research in California at the end of the month.

Most of the time when Rolf got a phone call it was a distracting interruption for us both. But, every so often, the ringing of the phone brought a welcome break in the routine. This was one of those days.

"*Hallo?*" Rolf answered. I could hear a female voice at the other end of the line. After listening to the caller for a minute or two,

Rolf suddenly interrupted her. That was when the phone call really got my attention. "*Entschuldigung Fräulein*, I think you have the wrong number. Like I said, this is the German American Chamber of Commerce, not a dance studio."

He paused and covered the receiver with his right hand. Rolling his eyes toward the ceiling he whispered to me, "This one really takes the cake!" and then he returned to the conversation. "So, let me get this straight. You're looking for a young man who knows how to do the Viennese waltz to take you to the Quadrille this Saturday?"

Rolf listened to the woman again and then said, "No I don't know anyone like that. Me? No, I'm not at all interested and I don't think we can help you." I tapped Rolf on the arm, grinned, and pointed to myself. "Just a moment please," he said to the woman on the other end of the line. With his hand over the receiver he turned to me. "She claims she's a doctor and she would pay for the whole thing. It sounds a little fishy to me, but if you'd really like to go . . ."

"Sure, let me talk to her," I said as I reached for the phone. Her name was Amalia Sonnenburg. She lived in Bedford, an upscale suburb in Westchester County, and was a physician at the Sloan-Kettering cancer hospital. After telling me a little about herself, she proceeded to interview me to see whether I qualified to be her escort. "I'm thirty-three years old and 6'2" tall," I replied in answer to her questions. "And, no, of course I don't mind that you're nine years older. Why should that matter?" At this point Rolf walked to the other side of our small office so she wouldn't hear him laughing.

"One more thing," she said after we'd arranged to meet just outside the Americana Hotel grand ballroom on Saturday at 7:45 p.m. "Everyone comes to the quadrille in full evening dress. You'd have to wear white tie and tails."

"No problem. I'll rent some," I assured her. "How will I recognize you?"

"I'll be wearing a light green evening gown and carrying a small black beaded handbag. I look forward to meeting you in person."

The minute I hung up, Rolf came over to me and slapped me on the back. "Is there nothing you won't try? Anyway, congratulations. You've just become an archaeologist!"

"What do you mean?"

"You know exactly what I mean. Archaeologists go digging for old things, and, let's face it, she's practically old enough to be your mother!"

"Nonsense! She's only nine years older. But if we could be serious for a moment, have you ever rented a white tie and tails?"

"Who me? I don't travel in those social circles," he said as he sat back down at his desk. "Now, if you don't mind, Mr. High Society, let's get back to writing the sauerkraut report!"

CHAPTER 60

With little time to spare before I was to meet Dr. Sonnenburg, I rented a white tie outfit from a small shop in the garment district not far from where I had once worked for Brewster, Leeds. When the elderly clerk with a yarmulke handed me the box, he posed what seemed like an insulting question. "So, young man," he began, "since you mentioned that you've never worn a suit like this before, are you sure you know how to put it on?"

"I'll manage," I replied, somewhat annoyed. Did he think I was stupid?

"Well, then" the clerk called after me as I turned to leave, "wear it in good health!"

I foolishly waited until shortly after six o'clock on Saturday evening to open the box and, as I laid out the contents on my bed, I felt a growing sense of panic. Inside were a pair of black trousers with vertical satin stripes, a matching black jacket that was much longer in the back than in the front, a wing-tip collar dress shirt, a vest, white button-on suspenders, a clip-on white bow tie, a pair of white kid leather gloves, a pair of shiny black shoes, and a small bag containing mother-of-pearl cuff links and assorted studs. If only I had let the friendly store clerk show me how!

In desperation, I decided to turn to Frau Winter as my only hope. Since she was from Vienna, I figured that, if anyone on the Upper West Side of Manhattan could help me put on that strange suit, it would be her. Wearing just a tee shirt, the suit trousers, the suspenders, and my slippers, I padded down the hallway and knocked on her door.

When she opened the door and saw how I was dressed, she shook her head in disbelief. "Just where do you think you're going in that outfit, Mr. Nitsch?" she inquired. Her cheeks were rosier than usual and I could smell the whiskey on her breath when she spoke.

"I hate to bother you, Frau Winter, but I'm going to a German ball and I can't for the life of me figure out how to put all this stuff on, so I was hoping . . ."

"No need to explain further," she said, holding up her hand. "Back in the day I always helped my husband get into his penguin suit, that's what we called it, so you can count on me. Please put all the pieces except the jacket back in the box and bring them to me while I go and pour myself another drink. I'll have you ready in no time flat."

When I returned, Frau Winter was telling Frau Apfel all about my predicament in Viennese-accented German. Within minutes the two of them set to work, unfolding and tucking and adding tiny buttons and studs exactly where they belonged, until the only things left in the box were the patent leather shoes. Frau Winter reached in and held them up.

"Here's a word to the wise," she said. "I hope you'll take the advice of an old lady and forget about the shoes! They'll only make you suffer. My husband never wore the damn things. Put on a comfortable pair of your own black shoes instead, provided, of course, that they have leather soles." She dropped the shoes back into the box and handed it to me. "So, off you go to put on your own shoes and the jacket, and be sure to come back so that Frau Apfel and I can admire you before you leave."

Frau Winter and Frau Apfel made such a fuss over me on my way out that I was afraid I'd be late to the Quadrille after all. "*Jesses, Maria, Josef!*" Frau Winter exclaimed. "Don't you look dashing! You remind me of the young men I used to dance with at the Vienna Opera Balls in my younger days." For at least the third time, she asked me to turn around slowly so that she could make sure everything was in place. "You know, Mr. Nitsch, there's a striking similarity between you and my late husband."

"I appreciate the compliment, Frau Winter," I said, "and, more importantly, thanks to you both for your help."

"Now go!" Frau Winter commanded. "Go and enjoy yourself!"

"And don't miss a single Viennese Waltz!" Frau Apfel added as I put on my overcoat and headed for the door.

****

All dressed up in my penguin suit, I decided to splurge and take a taxi to the hotel. After checking my winter coat, I spotted Dr. Sonnenburg standing near the ballroom entrance. The tight fitting, light green evening gown she was wearing showed off her shapely figure and her small waist. Granted her hairstyle, smooth on top and permed at the sides, was a bit outmoded, but all in all she wasn't bad-looking for a lady nine years my senior. Not that it mattered, of course, since she was only going to be my dance partner, not my girlfriend.

I walked over to her and bowed. "Dr. Amalia Sonnenburg?"

She smiled and shook my hand. "Oh! You must be Gunter Nitsch. And you needn't be so formal. Please call me Amalia, all right?"

After Amalia presented her tickets, the two of us joined the receiving line and waited our turn to be greeted by several prominent politicians and diplomats from Bonn and from Washington. Then, surrounded by a glittering crowd of elegant women in gorgeous gowns and men in white tie wearing medals on colorful sashes, we helped ourselves to glasses of champagne from the open bar.

"I know you're a physician," I said, "but do you have any particular specialty?"

"Childhood leukemia, but let's not talk about that tonight. It can be too depressing." Then she went on to tell me that her hobbies were the opera, downhill skiing, and hiking. "Do you have family here in New York?" she asked me.

"They're all in Germany. How about you?"

"Just my mother," she said. "She and I live together in Bedford." Then she looked around for a moment. "I have the feeling that those men over there are staring at us. Do you recognize them?"

The men Amalia pointed out were several elderly German-American lawyers I had met at the Chamber. When I nodded at them and smiled they each gave me a friendly wave. I could just imagine the comments they were making to their wives: "*See that tall guy over there? The one with the lady in the light green gown? He just started at the Chamber a short time ago. How in earth did he manage to get in here?*" It was a good thing Amalia couldn't read my thoughts.

"Oh you mean them?" I replied and then, trying to impress Amalia, I added, "They're just some attorneys I know from work."

When the four-course dinner was served we were seated at a round table together with four married couples. I tried several times to strike up a conversation with some of our neighbors but I soon noticed that Amalia, by speaking so softly that only I could hear her, wanted me all to herself. Once the music started and she led me onto the dance floor, she confirmed my suspicion.

"You really shouldn't bother with those people," she chastened. "We'll never see them again anyway." As it turned out, there wasn't much time after that to socialize, even if I had wanted to, because the two of us scarcely missed a dance for the rest of the evening.

An hour after midnight, even though the Quadrille was still in full swing, Amalia told me that she had rented a room at the hotel because she didn't want to risk driving home to Westchester County after having had wine with dinner.

"Very sensible," I agreed. To myself, I wondered just where she was going with this.

Then it came. "It's a little presumptuous of me, but I hope you don't mind escorting me up to my room." Once inside Amalia's large suite, she kicked off her shoes with a sigh of relief. Then she poured each of us a glass of champagne from the chilled bottle in the ice bucket on the coffee table. "Cheers!" she said as we clinked glasses. "I've had a really wonderful time tonight, and I would like to see you again. I'll be leaving for a ten-day ski trip to Aspen next week, but the Viennese Opera Ball will be held at the end of February. Can I count on you to come as my guest to that event as well?"

Having tasted the highlife I didn't hesitate a second. "It would be my pleasure!"

"Wonderful. But now I'm ready to go to bed." She grinned and added, "But not with you. At least not this time. I've had a long, hard day and I'm on call at the hospital tomorrow afternoon as well."

That settled that. Since I was no longer welcome, we exchanged business cards after scribbling our private phone numbers on the back and I went home.

CHAPTER 61

*T*hrough someone I had met while playing tennis on the public courts up near Riverside Church, I learned that an affordable studio apartment in a solid building on West End Avenue near 104th Street was available for rent. In addition to being only a short walk from Riverside Drive, the studio had two large windows, a private bathroom, a huge closet, a bed, a desk, and two chairs. It even had the wiring for its own private telephone line. Since I had recently gotten a raise at the office, I decided it was time to have a place of my own.

"Are you really moving to 104th Street?" Frau Winter gave me a sly wink. "Or are you moving in with that doctor in Bedford?"

"No, I'm really staying right here in the neighborhood so I'm sure we'll run into each other. I've left my new contact information on the table in the hall." Then I grasped her hands in mine. "Frau Winter, I have to make a confession. If you were forty-five years younger, I would have asked you for a date a long time ago!"

She laughed. "Guess what, Mr. Nitsch. If you had asked, I would have gladly accepted," and she gave me a motherly hug.

****

Even though I moved into my new apartment on Saturday, January 23, 1971, I still insisted on paying Frau Winter through the end of the month. I hadn't missed a single weekly rent payment in all the time I had lived in her apartment and I didn't want to spoil my record now.

The following Saturday, Rolf Klingenberg and I flew out to San Francisco where we spent a hectic week doing interviews for our market study. It was the first time I had been back there since I had been the guest of Bob Proctor's family in Marin County nearly seven years earlier. But, since I still hadn't forgiven Bob for the way he had reacted when he met Victoria in New York, I decided not to call him.

Once we had completed our work in San Francisco, we moved on to Los Angeles. After checking in to the Biltmore Hotel around noon on that Saturday, we spent the rest of the weekend in supermarkets, copying down information about the prices of German imported food products. That way, we were ready on Monday to begin meeting with supermarket managers, food wholesalers, and importers to compile the necessary statistics. By Monday night, with barely half of our Los Angeles assignments completed, Rolf and I sat down together in the lobby to look over the schedule of people we were each planning to see on Tuesday. Then, after we both put in requests for 7:00 a.m. wake up calls, we went up to our rooms. Rolf's was on the 9th floor; mine was on the 10th.

I quickly undressed, brushed my teeth, and took a long look out the window at the twinkling lights of the city down below before stretching out, totally exhausted, on the king size bed and falling fast asleep.

It was still dark at 6:00 a.m. on Tuesday morning, February 9th, when, exactly an hour before my expected wake up call, I fell out of bed. As the floor shook beneath me I could hear guests screaming in nearby rooms as a man outside my door kept yelling, over and over, "Keep calm! Don't use the elevator! Take the stairs!" My heart pounded wildly as I tried to collect my thoughts. Was I having a bad dream? No, that couldn't be it. And I hadn't been drinking, so I certainly wasn't drunk. In the few seconds it took me to grab on to the edge of the bed and stagger to my feet, the shaking suddenly stopped. In a panic, I considered the possibility that a bomb had landed somewhere in the city. Unsteadily making my way over to the window, I peered down at the street but at least at that moment, everything was quiet down below. It was then that I realized what had happened. I had just experienced an earthquake!

I put on blue jeans over my boxer shorts, shoved my wallet into my pocket, and went out into the hallway where other terrified guests, some fully dressed, others clad only in nightgowns or pajamas, were rushing out of their rooms. Frantic that the building would collapse at any moment, I raced down the ten flights of stairs. Hundreds of hysterically babbling people were already gathered in the lobby, with many more pouring out the stairwells every minute. No one, it seemed, was in charge.

I needed some fresh air so I walked outside to survey the damage. The sun was just coming up and the weather was crisp. All around the hotel huge sandstone ornaments from the roof, some as much as a foot high, had crashed onto the pavement below. *How fortunate*, I thought, *that the earthquake had not struck an hour or two later when the sidewalk would have been crowded with people on their way to work.*

Looking over the debris, I could see shattered wine and liquor bottles lying in pools of liquid in the window of one of the hotel shops. At the curb a dozen people were pushing and shoving each other, desperately trying to be first in line to hail a cab should one miraculously appear. Did they really imagine that the earthquake had only struck the area around the Biltmore Hotel? In contrast to them, I was sure it had affected the entire metropolitan area of Los Angeles and way beyond.

Feeling cold and still shaken up I went back inside and sat down on a stool at the hotel coffee shop counter to order a cup of coffee. Just as I lifted the cup to my lips, the hanging lamps at the ceiling began to sway.

"Miss! Miss!" I called out in terror to the waitress behind the counter. "Do you see that? Is it starting again?"

She laughed. "Oh don't worry about that. It's only some aftershocks. There'll be many more so you may as well relax and get used to it!"

Just then Rolf came up behind me. "Well, that was a surprise! Have you ever been in an earthquake before?"

"No! You?"

"It's a first for me, too. Let's have some breakfast and get to work. But I have a gut feeling that we won't get much accomplished today."

As it turned out, we couldn't get anything done. All of our appointments for both Tuesday and Wednesday had been cancelled. From each business we called, the explanations were all more or less the same. "We don't have any time." "Everything fell off the shelves." "The place is a mess." "Half our staff hasn't shown up for work today." "We'll need at least a week to clean up."

It wasn't until late Tuesday afternoon that we found out the earthquake, which had measured 6.6 on the Richter scale, had caused sections of two hospitals to collapse. Highways had cracked and buckled. Sixty-two people had lost their lives. Many more were injured. Compared to all that, our inability to gather statistics about the sales of German pickles and cookies seemed relatively unimportant.

I didn't sleep well that night. Every time I dozed off, the slightest noise made me jump. When I met Rolf for breakfast before dawn on Wednesday morning I was totally exhausted. We both agreed that it was fruitless to try to reschedule the interviews. At precisely 6 a.m. local time, when we knew the Chamber would be open in New York, Rolf put in a call to the office.

"Oh!" Mr. Ledermann said. "I'm so relieved to hear from you. We tried all day yesterday to reach you at the hotel but couldn't get a line through. Are you both all right?" Rolf briefly explained the situation. "That's what I suspected," Mr. Ledermann continued. "Forget about the rest of the interviews. There's no sense wasting any more time out there. I want you both to try to get a flight back to New York either today or tomorrow. If you have to pay more to come back early, do it. The Chamber will reimburse you."

"Let's pack!" Rolf said when he hung up the phone. "If we're lucky we might get a flight out of here today. And if we don't? Well, quite frankly, I'd rather spend a night on a bench at the airport than another night in this hotel."

As luck would have it, we got seats on a half-empty, mid-morning direct flight to New York. Rolf chose a window seat on the left side toward the back of the cabin; I found four free seats in the center section where I lay down to take a well-needed nap once we were in the air. Three hours into the flight, I woke up feeling rested, relaxed, and ready for lunch. A tall stewardess hurried past me. She had a long ponytail and she bore a striking resemblance to the film star Claudia Cardinale. I moved to an aisle seat on the left side of the plane hoping to get her attention so that I could ask her when food would be served.

When my efforts failed, I closed my eyes and began to daydream about how I would have loved to have swept the pretty stewardess into my arms and rescued her from the falling blocks of sandstone. Just then, someone tapped me on the shoulder. I opened my eyes, and there she was, bending down over me, her dark-brown ponytail brushing against my cheek.

"Sir," she whispered. "I'd like to talk to you in private. Will you follow me, please?"

"Of course," I stammered. My heart began to pump faster and my mind was racing as I followed her towards the back of the cabin. *Was she going to ask me for a date? But why me? She didn't know anything about me. Was it my height? My blond hair? She looked Mediterranean. Was she of Italian, or perhaps Lebanese descent?* I could hardly wait to find out more about her. Rolf smirked as I passed by his seat.

When the stewardess and I reached the far end of the plane, she pointed to two empty seats in the very last row. "'Won't you please take the window seat so that I can sit down next to you?"

My mouth was so dry that I could only nod as I squeezed into the narrow space, angling my long legs toward the aisle to make them fit; her knees touched mine as she sat down beside me. She reached over to gently put her hand on my arm and spoke so softly that I could barely hear her over the sound of the engine. But these were hardly the words I had hoped to hear.

"Look, I need to level with you. The captain is pretty sure we've lost the hydraulic fluid we need to release the landing gear. So it's very likely the wheels won't come down when we get to JFK. When the captain makes an announcement minutes before we land we expect that passengers will storm the exit door behind you in their haste to leave the aircraft. Are you with me so far?"

"Yes, miss," I murmured, completely crestfallen.

"Now, since you're a big strapping fellow, I want you to get up the minute we land, plant yourself in the middle of the aisle, and hold the passengers back when they come charging towards you. Some people may get violent. Feel free to use force if necessary, whatever it takes. Can you do that for us?"

I could feel the color draining from my face and I had to swallow hard. "I'll do my best."

She smiled. "I knew I could count on you. Oh! One more thing before I forget! If anyone asks why you're sitting back here, just tell them you like it here. Not a word about our conversation, all right? Thanks for your cooperation." She patted me on the arm and left me there all alone.

Rolf sauntered down the aisle toward me. "So? Did you two lovebirds make exciting plans?"

"Not really."

"C'mon. You can't just leave me hanging like that. Every red-blooded man at this end of the plane is jealous of you."

"It's really no big deal. I'd rather talk about it some other time, if you don't mind." This was no way to talk to my boss, but what choice did I have?

The harm was done. "Well, pardon me for asking," Rolf snapped as he turned away and returned to his seat.

I stared blankly ahead, brooding about the challenge I would soon face. The pilot announced that we were passing over Philadelphia and would soon start our descent to JFK. A short time later the plane made a sharp turn. The pilot's voice once again came over the intercom. "May I have your attention, please? We have not yet been cleared for landing. We appreciate your patience."

A few passengers grumbled about the unexpected delay; others continued to doze or read. I clutched the sides of my seat in sheer panic. It felt like an eternity before we again approached New York. And then it came. "This is your captain speaking! We're having a small problem with the landing gear and might have to make an emergency landing. Please remain calm, buckle your seatbelts, and be sure to review the instructions on the plastic card in the seat pocket in front of you." All conversation stopped abruptly as passengers turned to look for the quickest way out.

Well, I thought to myself, as we made our final approach, *if I'm trampled to death, at least Rolf would understand why I brushed him off the way I did.* But, just then, as I was girding myself up to ward off my fellow passengers, we heard the familiar thump of the landing gear falling into place and everyone cheered. Minutes later the plane taxied past eight fire engines, four on each side, that had been awaiting our arrival at the edge of the runway.

I made my way back to my original seat to retrieve my briefcase from the overhead bin and then walked to the exit at the front of the plane. The beautiful brunette stewardess was saying good-bye to the departing passengers. When my turn finally came, she smiled at me without the least glimmer of recognition and intoned, "Thank you for flying with us! We hope you enjoyed your flight."

CHAPTER 62

At first it felt good to be back in my cozy new apartment. Here at last was a safe haven where I could drift off to sleep without worrying about aftershocks or plane crashes. And yet it was quiet, so very quiet. There was no one to welcome me back; no one around to talk to about my recent brushes with death. Worst of all, not a single one of my friends knew my new telephone number. After staring at the walls for a few more minutes, I impulsively picked up the phone and dialed Victoria's number.

"Oh, what a relief to hear from you! It's been such a while and I haven't been able to reach you."

"Sorry," I said. "I just got back tonight from a business trip to California. By the way, I've moved to my own place so I have a new phone number."

"That's great! So that's why I couldn't reach you. Are you still on the Upper West Side?"

"104th."

"You don't say! Well I've got big news of my own!"

"Do you have a new boyfriend?" I said half jokingly.

"Is that what you're hoping for?"

"It's what I kind of expected after all this time," I admitted.

"No, you're still the only boyfriend I need. But, guess what? We're neighbors! A few days ago I moved into a studio on West 104th Street just off of Riverside Drive. It's a great place and when I found out about it, I rushed to take it before someone else could."

"You're pulling my leg. That's practically next door to my new studio!"

"I kid you not. Listen! I know you must be jet lagged but I'd love to know what you've been up to. Do you have the energy to stop by for an hour or so and have a glass of wine so we can catch up in person? How about it?"

My brain screamed, *don't do it! She's like a spider, luring you back into her web.* It was so much safer to talk things over on the phone. But, after all I had been through—the rejection by Irene, the drunken evening with Suki, the disastrous trip to Los Angeles—who better than Victoria to take me in her arms with soothing reassurance? Suddenly wide awake and without giving a further thought to the consequences, I said, "All right, I'll be over in a few minutes."

Victoria's apartment was only half a block away. It was located on the ground floor slightly below street level. Curved iron bars covered the two tall windows. *Wait a minute! The place looked familiar.* In an uncanny twist of fate, Victoria had rented the very same apartment where I had had my one-night stand with Edie, the Finnish music major from Hunter College. The door to the small lobby was open as it had been the first time I'd gone there. When I knocked, Victoria flung open her door and exclaimed, "I'm so glad to see you!" before embracing me. "So, how do you like my new place?"

There was a double bed along the wall to the left of the windows. *Was it the same bed?* I wondered. No doubt it had been passed along from tenant to tenant. It was definitely the same refrigerator to the left of the door. And the same armchairs. And the couch. Only the small table and the three stools were new.

For a fraction of a second I was tempted to blurt out, *it hasn't changed much*, but I caught myself in time. "It's great, but I suppose you'll have to keep the curtains closed all the time to keep people from peeping inside. It must be nice to have a much shorter commute to Head Start."

I sat down on one of the armchairs and told her briefly about my business trips to Chicago and to California ending with an account of the last twenty-four rather harrowing hours.

"You must be exhausted," Victoria said when I finally stopped talking. "And yet, I was still the first person you called when you got back, wasn't I? That means a lot to me." She paused. "Listen, I know there's a lot you haven't told me. I'm sure there have been other women in your life in the meantime. But I'm willing to let bygones be bygones. Are you?"

I lifted my glass in a toast and, before long, we were back together like old times. When I finally left Victoria's apartment the next morning, I had barely enough time to go home, change, and get to work.

CHAPTER 63

"**W**elcome back!" Mr. Ledermann greeted us when Rolf and I sat down in his office that Thursday morning to report on our trip. "When my wife and I saw the TV reports about the earthquake, we couldn't believe the devastation. I'm glad to have you both back here safe and sound."

"Thank you, sir," Rolf replied. "But of course, for obvious reasons, we couldn't get all of our research done. However, we do have very complete data from San Francisco."

"Yes, I know, but I imagine the figures for Los Angeles should be similar so just extrapolate that information from what you have. A lot is riding on these reports, as you well know. According to headquarters in Bonn, if these market studies result in improved American sales for German food companies, we may get orders to update the market trends and the statistics on an annual basis. That would be a real feather in our cap here in New York."

"You can count on us," Rolf assured him.

Still, as the weeks went on, Rolf's enthusiasm for the project seemed to wane. As I ate a sandwich at my desk while I labored over the reports, he would disappear for two-hour lunches. With ever more of the work falling onto my shoulders, I was no longer sure we would be able to complete the studies by April 23rd so that they would reach Bonn by the April 30th deadline. In the late evening, when I finally dragged myself home from the office, I got into the habit of drinking a bottle of white wine before going to bed to calm my jangled nerves and to help me get to sleep.

On the 22nd of March, with the deadline barely a month away, Rolf closed the door to our office, cleared his throat, and confessed the truth. "Listen Gunter, I might as well tell you now before I go in to see Ledermann. I've found a better paying job with a German building parts manufacturer in New Jersey. So March 31st will be my last day at the Chamber. I'm really sorry to leave you alone with all of this, but I'll do all I can to help before I leave."

"I sure hope so," I said, "because I've been swamped around here as it is."

****

Mr. Ledermann called me into his office on April 1st. "I sympathize with your situation, Mr. Nitsch," he said. "With Mr. Klingenberg gone, I know you'll be under tremendous pressure to complete the market studies before the deadline on your own. Since your secretary, Miss Block, can't stay beyond 5 p.m., I'll arrange to have someone else available to work with you until 10 p.m. whenever you need to stay late. And I will definitely try to hire an assistant for you."

"I'll do my best sir," I said although I knew that, if I were to have any chance of success, I would have to cut classes at Hunter, and give up tennis with Peter Vollmann as well as my early-morning jogs in Riverside Park.

Mr. Ledermann smiled. "Cheer up, Mr. Nitsch. It's not all bad news. As of today you've become our new Manager of Market Development, which brings with it a fifty percent increase in salary. Congratulations!"

****

On Saturday afternoon, I took a short break from the work I'd brought home from the office to stock up on cheap white wine. As I approached my favorite liquor store on 107th Street just east of Broadway, I wondered what Mr. Ledermann would think if he could see the neighborhood where his new department manager was living. Near the entrance to the liquor store, three stocky Puerto Rican men had set up a shell game on an overturned cardboard box. As a small crowd of black and Puerto Rican men gathered around to place bets with his two associates, the third man shuffled the three plastic cups; a tiny pea was hidden under one of them. Leaning against a nearby wall, a giant of a young black man in a dashiki casually chewed on a toothpick and watched.

After a moment's hesitation, I elbowed my way through the crowd and into the store. *"¡Hola, mi amigo!"* the Cuban proprietor greeted me with the honor due to one of his best customers. Then, with an occasional wary glance at the scene outside, he waited at the cash register while I selected five bottles of his cheapest French white wine and two bottles of inexpensive California Pinot Grigio. I peeled off the bills from my wallet to pay for the wine and was about to leave the shop when the tall black man suddenly reached under his dashiki and drew out a steel gray revolver. In his left hand, he held up a badge. The liquor store proprietor ducked down behind the counter. I was frozen in place near the door.

"POLICE!" the undercover policeman shouted. "Hands up! You're all under arrest!"

The three principals, who were clearly used to the routine, surrendered immediately. But several of their 'customers,' acting as if they were only innocent bystanders, tried to slip away. Then, out of nowhere, nearly a dozen uniformed officers swooped onto the scene, guns drawn and handcuffs at the ready. Minutes later the gamblers and their customers were hauled away in the paddy wagons that screeched down the one-way street in both directions.

After waiting a few minutes, I cautiously stepped out onto the sidewalk and was startled when someone came up behind me. "Well, Gunner, I reckon you saw the whole thing go down. I could tell from half way down the block that the dude in the dashiki was the fuzz." It was Charlie, my old friend from the bar who had saved my life on the day that Dr. Martin Luther King got shot.

"I had the same thought. He looked out of place somehow."

Charlie peeked into my shopping bag. "You got some real good stuff in there. You givin' a party?"

"No, I drink it at night so that I can get to sleep!"

"That too bad, man. That too bad."

"Well, I don't need them all," I said as I handed Charlie a bottle of the French wine. "Here's one you can enjoy with your friends."

"Thanks, brother!" he said. Then we shook hands and went our separate ways.

****

Despite the tremendous pressure I was under at the office, I accompanied Amalia, first to the Hungarian Ball and then to the Viennese Opera Ball and, each time, I had to rent another white tie outfit. It had been fun to put on that ridiculous getup when Frau Winter and Frau Apfel were fussing over me. But now that I was on my own, it felt more like getting into a uniform and going off to work. Compared to Victoria, with whom I had been spending what little free time I could spare, Amalia was a real sad sack. At each of these glittering events, Amalia could never manage to leave her work behind. As other couples chatted about the weather or the stock market or their most recent cruise, she told me one story after another about the precious young leukemia patients who, despite her best efforts, had died in her arms. I admired the work she did and I pitied her whenever tragedy struck, but her sorrowful reports put a damper on the evening for both of us.

It was at the Viennese Opera Ball that Amalia invited me to come up to Bedford to see where she lived and to meet her mother. We arranged for a visit some time in May when the food marketing studies on which I was still slaving away were completed. It seemed to me like a long time off and I soon forgot all about the invitation.

****

"You know," Victoria admonished me when I returned to her apartment the following day, "you may have a deadline to meet, but if you keep drinking like a fish you're going to turn into an alcoholic."

"Don't be ridiculous!" I protested, despite the telltale bottle of Chardonnay in my hand. I put the bottle back down. "No, you're right. I have to pace myself better and cut down on the alcohol."

"Let's get some fresh air," Victoria suggested. "A long walk in the park is better than any sleeping pill in my opinion." Bundled up against the cold, we headed outside to brave the elements, eventually stopping to eat at a Cuban restaurant on Amsterdam Avenue. "Since you're getting your BA in Economics from Hunter in June," Victoria said after we had thawed out a bit, "have you given any thought to going on to graduate school?"

"Well, now that you mention it, Rolf Klingenberg made the same suggestion shortly before he left the Chamber. He thought I should get an MBA. That's what he did."

"And you're hesitating because . . . ?"

"Look, it was just a fluke that I got into Hunter. I didn't even get to go to high school in Germany. Do you really think . . ."?

"There's one way to find out," Victoria said. "Sign up to take the Graduate Record Exam, buy yourself a review book, and take the test. I'm willing to bet you'll get in."

CHAPTER 64

By pushing myself almost to the breaking point at the office, I finally met the deadline set by headquarters. The Chamber got a substantial fee; I received a pat on the back from Mr. Ledermann. With that project behind me, I rushed to catch up on my coursework for Hunter College while, at the same time, gradually resuming my normal routine of early-morning jogging and playing tennis with Peter Vollmann in Riverside Park. Victoria was back in my life and, now that we were neighbors we saw each other often.

Then, one evening two weeks after the reports had been completed, Amalia phoned. "I hope you haven't forgotten your promise to come visit my mother and me in Bedford," she said.

"Of course not," I fibbed as I desperately tried to think of a way to beg off. I had no desire to see Amalia again. Besides her being way too old for me, I clearly didn't belong to the circles she traveled in. Convinced that I was the only man at the Quadrille who had to *rent* his white tie and tails, I imagined that every other man there had closets full of formal clothes appropriate for any occasion.

But I didn't react in time. "How about this coming Saturday?" It was more of a command than a question. "Take the train from Grand

Central that gets to Bedford at 2:40 p.m. You can wear a sports jacket and you don't need a tie. Oh, and if you'd like to stay over until Sunday, don't forget to bring your toothbrush. We have guest rooms."

Well, that was blunt, I thought to myself, and now my curiosity got the better of me. "Fine," I agreed. "I'll see you then."

****

Rather than the fancy BMW I expected she would be driving, Amalia was waiting for me at the Bedford station in a dark-green Buick with dented fenders and a deep scratch on the passenger side door. "It must be nice to own a car," I said to hide my surprise as I climbed inside.

"You mean this old heap? I'm stingy about things like this. That way I don't feel guilty when I fly down to Bermuda to spend a weekend at my beach club."

We drove past landscaped estates with ornate gates, leafy trees, and brightly-colored flower beds, all leading to huge homes set back far from the road. Amalia turned into a long brick-paved driveway. "Here we are."

Shaded by four giant oak trees, the large house stood on a hill overlooking a well-trimmed expanse of green lawn. The first floor level was of red brick; above that, dark-brown wooden beams crisscrossed a façade of white stucco under a sharply sloping roof.

"Wow! You never told me you lived in a mansion!" was all I could say.

"I wouldn't call it a mansion exactly. My father bought it for a song during the Depression when we moved here from Nicaragua where I were born."

"In Nicaragua? I thought your father was Austrian and your mother is German."

"That's true. But my father was an executive with an American bank in Nicaragua so my brother and I grew up learning German, English, and Spanish."

A tall lady opened the front door and called to us. "I've been watching the two of you for a while. Are you going to stay in the car forever?"

"Sorry, Mother. We were just talking," Amalia said as I reached over to the back seat to retrieve my overnight bag before following Amalia up the front walk.

"Nice to meet you, Mrs. Sonnenburg," I said, giving a little bow.

"Welcome to Bedford, Mr. Nitsch," she replied. "I'm sure you've heard this before, but you look like a typical northern German!"

I had indeed heard that remark before and, as always, I resented being stereotyped. Still, I presumed she intended it as a compliment and I thanked her.

While Mrs. Sonnenburg went to the kitchen to brew a pot of coffee and prepare a delicious snack of pound cake covered in strawberries and whipped cream, Amalia led me to the back of the house to show me their 15-meter-long swimming pool and the adjoining cabin where guests could shower and change into their swimsuits.

A table had already been set on the flagstone terrace between the house and the pool and, a few minutes later, Mrs. Sonnenburg joined us there.

"I hadn't known until today that your family had once lived in Nicaragua," I said when we had all taken our seats.

"Ah, Nicaragua! The good old days!" Amalia's mother replied. Then she leaned forward and lowered her voice conspiratorially even though there were just the three of us there. "You won't believe what

I'm going to tell you, Mr. Nitsch, but it's the truth. For most of the time we lived in Nicaragua, my husband and I were the only married couple among all the expatriates. Whenever a single young man was sent down there on business, it didn't take him long before he shacked up with a young girl, one of the locals, you know. But if any of those girls got into trouble, a sewing machine did the trick."

"Oh mother, not that old chestnut again," Amalia protested.

"I'm sorry," I said. "I don't follow."

"Now don't interrupt me, Amalia," Mrs. Sonnenburg said, "Mr. Nitsch wants to hear the rest of the story. So, as I was saying, when one of those ignorant peasant girls got pregnant, all the young man had to do was buy her off with a sewing machine. That way he didn't have to marry her and she had the means to make a good living. It worked out well for both sides, don't you think?" She chuckled and then waited for my reaction. Since I didn't see the humor in the situation, I just smiled politely.

"Come!" Amalia said when we'd finished our coffee and cake. "Let me show you around the house." She took me first to the dining room. Eight gold brocaded armchairs fit comfortably around the large table. Completing the décor were several Tiffany wall lamps, an enormous crystal chandelier, a massive glass cabinet filled with wine and liqueur glasses and cut glass crystal bowls, and a Persian carpet, which covered almost the entire room.

From the dining room, Amalia walked me through the kitchen, the living room, the music room with its grand piano and its vast collection of classical records, and the library where the shelves were filled with hundreds, if not thousands, of leather-bound hardcover books in English, German and Spanish.

"And there are four bedrooms upstairs," Amalia mentioned almost as an afterthought. "One for me, one for my mother, and two for guests."

Towards dinnertime a tall, heavyset gentleman with a head full of snow-white hair arrived in a big, old Mercedes. This 'acquaintance of my mother,' as Amalia had called him when she had mentioned that he would join us that evening, had trouble walking, even with the support of his cane. Mr. Carstensen had being living for the last decade in affluent retirement ever since selling his import-export company at an enormous profit. He spoke German with a Hamburg accent.

"It's about time I met you in person. I've heard so much about you!" he said in a booming voice as he gave me such a crushing handshake, I thought I wouldn't be able to play tennis for weeks.

The four of us sat down to a German-style supper of open sandwiches topped with cold cuts and French cheeses (which we ate with knives and forks, just like in the old country), washed down with frosty bottles of Beck's Beer. Since Mr. Carstensen was hard of hearing, our conversation was lively but loud and, to my surprise, entirely in German.

The next morning right after an early breakfast Amalia and I drove to the nearby Arthur W. Butler Memorial Sanctuary where we took a long hike while her mother was at church.

"I don't know about you," Amalia confided, "but except on Christmas Eve, I never go to church. Maybe it has to do with my work. I often ask myself, if God really existed, how could He stand by and watch so many little children die from terminal cancer? But here, in the forest, I find the peace I need."

"But your mother . . . ?"

"She doesn't just go to church; she provides enough funds to keep the congregation going. It's her money and she can do with it what she likes, I suppose. But basically she's just supporting the young pastor and his tiny flock of old ladies. There can't be more than thirty of them in that church on any given Sunday. I can think of better ways to spend it."

"It's different in Germany," I told her. "Over there, if you say you're Catholic or Lutheran, a percentage of your tax dollars goes to support your church, or your synagogue for that matter. Clergy are salaried like government employees. They even get a pension when they retire. You won't hear any fund-raising pitches in the sermons in German churches."

"That's about as far from separation of Church and State as you can get, but I kind of like the idea." We walked a while in silence, following the trail markers. "Music," Amalia suddenly remarked. "Music is also like a religion to me. I have a subscription to the Metropolitan Opera, you know? Have you been?"

"To be honest, I've only seen one opera in my entire life, a production of *Fidelio* when I was still living in Cologne. Frankly, I prefer operettas and jazz."

Amalia stopped walking and stared at me in amazement. "I don't know how anyone could dislike opera," she said. "Let me play one of my opera LP's for you when we get back to the house and maybe I can change your mind."

From then on I usually spent one or two weekends each month throughout the summer and the fall with Amalia in Bedford, sometimes from Saturday afternoon to Sunday morning and sometimes from Friday evening to Sunday night. When the weather was good, we swam in the pool or we took long walks in the nature sanctuary. On rainy days I gritted my teeth as we listened to recordings of gloomy Wagnerian operas in the music room.

Very often, Mrs. Sonnenburg invited her friends, including some who were closer to my age, over to the house for afternoon barbeque parties on the terrace or for dinner in the evening. Yet, for some inexplicable reason, I never met any of Amalia's friends, and I started to wonder whether she had any. Was it because she didn't have the time to meet other people? Or was it the endless supply of heartbreaking stories that she brought home from work, which scared would-be friends away? Come to think of it, could even I call myself her friend? Or was I nothing more than the convenient companion she needed for appearance's sake? After all, when it came to our relationship, I was always at her beck and call. On the other hand, she had introduced me to an elegant world I could never have discovered on my own and for that I was grateful.

CHAPTER 65

Not that I stopped seeing Victoria, mind you. Most evenings during the week when I got home from work and on those weekends when I wasn't up in Bedford, Victoria and I were usually together, either dining in ethnic restaurants on the Upper West Side, or going to dinner parties at friends' apartments, or attending avant-garde off-off Broadway theatre performances, or enjoying jazz concerts in Greenwich Village, or going by subway to the beach. Sometimes, we would just spend a quiet evening at Victoria's apartment, where she would help me edit one of the term papers I had typed on my Smith-Corona portable typewriter. Or we would curl up together on the couch to watch Johnny Carson on TV.

Amalia was too wrapped up in her own work at the hospital to care much about mine. Victoria, on the other hand, loved to hear about the odd characters who sometimes showed up at my desk at the Chamber. There was, for example, the evening when I told her about the German businessman who wanted to incorporate a business in Manhattan and who insisted on speaking to me in faulty English. "The good man refused to take the list of German-speaking lawyers I offered him. 'Oh, no sank you, Mr. Nitsch,' he said. 'All I vant iz to know vare can I buy a book wiz za title, *How to Zet Up a Corporation Wizout a Lawyer*.'"

Victoria bit her lip to keep from laughing. "So what did you tell the poor man?"

"Go home!"

"You didn't!"

"I did. I told him he was wasting his time."

"Tell me again what the man said!" she insisted. "I love the way you imitate his accent!" I could always count on Victoria to cheer me up after a hard day at the office.

Still, despite the good times we shared together, on one or two weekends a month I would claim to have so much work that I couldn't spare the time to be with her. I doubt that Victoria ever believed my lame excuses but she never raised her voice in protest. At first I felt guilty, but before long it became a routine. The two worlds I lived in during my leisure time had very little to do with each other. I definitely had more in common with Victoria than with Amalia. Victoria understood me and I understood her. The only real bone of contention between us was her reckless extravagance. Amalia had more than enough money to spend; Victoria constantly spent more than she earned.

"Will you ever stop buying clothes? When are you going to wear all that stuff, anyway?" I would chide whenever Victoria opened the door to her overstuffed closet.

"It is a lot, isn't it? But if I try something on and I like how I look in the dressing room mirror, I just can't resist." Then she would ask, "Don't you like it when I look nice?" and I would give up and change the subject. It was hopeless.

****

327

I knew why Victoria wasn't married. She was patiently waiting for me to propose to her. But I was puzzled about Amalia, who at the age of forty-three was practically friendless, despite her demanding, high-paying job in a hospital with almost endless chances to meet other doctors. She wasn't exactly beautiful but, then again, she wasn't all that bad-looking either. Yet, with all her advantages, Amalia always dwelled on her failures and ignored her successes. For her the glass was always half empty. When we were together, she constantly poured her heart out to me about the injustices of God and the world.

I began to wonder if some long-lost love underlay her bitter sorrow and, one day I had the gall to raise the subject with her directly. "Amalia, I hope you don't mind my asking but, with everything you have to offer, how come you never got married?"

If looks could kill, I would have dropped dead on the spot. With an icy voice, she snarled, "How DARE you? That's none of your business. Don't you EVER raise that question again!" Then, forcing a thin smile, she added, "Come, let's go in and eat. Mother has fixed supper."

CHAPTER 66

I received my Bachelor's Degree in Economics from Hunter College in June 1971. At the same time I learned that I had been accepted into the Pace College evening MBA program for the upcoming fall semester. At least through the summer, my evenings were now free, however my days at the Chamber were as busy as ever. As Manager of Market Development I met with a steady stream of executives of German companies who wanted advice about marketing their products or services in the United States.

Besides dealing with marketing questions, I was also asked to create contacts with organizations such as State Development Agencies and the Underwriter's Laboratory as well as to recommend the services of law firms, CPA's, executive recruiters, and advertising agencies. As a result, almost overnight, I found myself suddenly popular with attorneys, CPA's and executive recruiters who began inviting me out to lunch on a regular basis. Whether the meal was at moderately priced restaurants such as the Top of the Sixes on the 41st floor of our office building, or at exorbitantly expensive places like La Réserve, La Grenouille, or The Four Seasons, the goal of my hosts was always the same: to leverage their way to the top of the referral list.

To keep from ballooning into a fat blimp, I quickly learned to forego the desserts at lunch and to limit myself to a light supper when I got home. My six-mile-long early-morning jogs in Riverside Park three times a week also helped me to cope with all that rich food.

Most of the German businessmen who contacted me were fluent in English. Still, when it came to legal issues, such as setting up a corporation, they understandably preferred to discuss such matters in German. As it turned out, more than a dozen law firms in Manhattan had been founded by German and Austrian immigrants who had had to flee Europe when Jews began to be persecuted during the early years of the Third Reich. After arranging meetings for me with the partners of these firms (all of whom claimed to be the best in town, if not the entire country), Mr. Ledermann cautioned me to be sure to recommend no fewer than three service firms, never just one. As he put it, "Let the German executive pick one of the service companies. That way, if there is a problem, the Chamber cannot be criticized."

****

Many of my German visitors were looking for importers. Others, who already had an American subsidiary, needed help with marketing or personnel problems. Mr. Ledermann soon introduced me to owners of import companies in the New York metropolitan area to whom I could turn for advice on technical questions if the necessary information wasn't in one of our standard directories. The importers, of course, were hoping for referrals of new German product lines in return for their help.

At least once a month, but more often twice a month, the Chamber organized a luncheon for approximately two hundred people at the University Club or at the Union Club or at a hotel ballroom. In attendance were the managers of American subsidiaries of German firms, executives of Fortune 500 companies with subsidiaries in Germany, and lawyers, CPAs, executive recruiters, international consultants and representatives of the State Development Agencies from New York, New Jersey and Connecticut. The affair always started with a cocktail reception where I could mingle, make contacts, and exchange business cards. During lunch a prominent business leader or an economist from the German or American government or a speaker from an international bank would give a thirty-minute talk. The whole affair usually lasted two hours and, within a few months, I made some good contacts that I could tap for marketing information. I also met experts to recommend to firms looking for specialists in certain fields.

At the suggestion of Mr. Ledermann I joined the Sales Executive Club of New York, which was run by Ed Flanagan, a former U.S. Air Force officer, who had been stationed in Germany, where he had met his wife. The Sales Executive Club luncheons for one hundred to one hundred fifty people took place each Friday at noon in the Waldorf Astoria Hotel. Since it was another source of useful contacts, I tried to attend the luncheons at least twice a month. At the cocktail reception preceding one such luncheon, a gentleman named Henry Cohen glanced at my nametag.

"With a first name like Gunter I presume you must be German?" was his opening line.

"That's right. I'm from Cologne."

"So, tell me," Mr. Cohen went on. "Did you serve in the German Army during the war?"

"No, I was only seven when the war was over. Why do you ask?"

He blushed. "Well, your hair is gray around the temples, so I thought . . ."

"I was born in December 1937," I added, thinking that would put an end to the matter.

Mr. Cohen paused for second, "So what about your father? Where did he fight?"

"He hardly saw any action at all. Most of the time he worked as a chef in military hospitals in Berlin, Paris and Vienna."

"Forgive me for asking so many personal questions," Mr. Cohen said. "It's just that I lost more than a dozen relatives in the Holocaust so I'm kind of wary whenever I meet a German."

"I'm truly sorry for your loss," I replied as I turned to leave. But Mr. Cohen put up his hand.

"Please don't run off. I shouldn't have assumed you had anything to do with all that. If it's okay with you, let me buy you a drink."

Two weeks later it was Mr. Shapiro's turn to ask, "You're German, I take it. So tell me, when did you leave Germany?"

"Seven years ago in April."

"So what do you know about the Holocaust?"

"Quite a bit, sir. I've read books about it and I've also met some Holocaust survivors."

Apparently satisfied with my answer, Mr. Shapiro handed me his business card and I gave him mine. "Well, it was certainly nice meeting you, Mr. Nitsch. If any of the German companies you meet with need a management consultant, feel free to give them my name. I'm always looking for new clients." Then he added, "Oh, in case it would help, I'm fluent in Yiddish so, even though I can't speak German, I can understand it."

"Thank you, sir. I'll keep that in mind!" I said.

Over the next few weeks, at least half a dozen other Jewish businessmen worked their way over to me during the cocktail hour and asked similar questions and, each time, I resented being singled out simply because of my first name or my accent. Eventually, as the word got around that I wasn't a former Nazi, the subject was dropped.

When I complained to Victoria about these incidents one evening over supper in a Cuban restaurant on Columbus Avenue, she said with a derisive smile, "So these old Jewish men (and I presume they're old) have the nerve to blame you for the Holocaust? Only a fool could think you were old enough to have participated in World War II. Even if you had, so what? I'm guessing the men who asked you were short and ugly. Maybe they were intimidated by your height."

"No, Mr. Shapiro is taller then I am."

"Well, whatever you've experienced is nothing. Can you imagine what would happen if I walked up to an old white man in Mississippi and asked, 'Pardon me sir, was your grandfather a slaveholder, because two or three generations ago my ancestors were owned by white men like you?'"

"You'd be hit with a barrage of verbal bullets, I suppose."

"Forget verbal bullets! That racist fool would shoot me dead on the spot. I was a Freedom Rider down there remember? So I know what I'm talking about. Listen, Gunter, if someone brings up the Holocaust with you again, don't be so defensive. You have nothing to apologize for, absolutely nothing. If I were you I'd tell those old curmudgeons from the tribe of the chosen people to go fly a kite!"

CHAPTER 67

By this time I had a staff of two working for me. In addition to Irma Block, my secretary, Mr. Ledermann had also provided me with an assistant. Ruth Haab was a young Swiss woman who was very efficient in searching our directories for information, which she gave out over the telephone, mailed off to enquiring parties, or provided to visitors who stopped by the Chamber in person. But one afternoon Mrs. Haab came to the door of my office and threw up her hands in desperation. "I hope I'm not disturbing you, Mr. Nitsch," she said, "but there's an elderly lady out front who wants the addresses of American musical instrument manufacturers. I could have helped her but she insists that she only wants to deal with a 'gentleman.' Here's her business card," and she grinned. That was how I ended up wasting fifteen precious minutes with "Annegret Fiedler, Composer's Widow, Wien, Austria."

Mrs. Fiedler wasn't the only oddball who sat down in my office for advice. One day Miss Block called me on the intercom. "There's a Baron von Protzhausen here to see you. He says you know him."

"I don't remember meeting anyone like that."

"Shall I send him in?"

"Sure. Now I'm nosy." A minute later an unusually short, bald young man with an irritating lisp joined me. I recognized him at once as plain old Felix Müller who had come to see me nearly two years earlier. It would have been rude to ask him how much he had paid for his title.

"Nice to see you again, Mr. Nitsch," the newly minted Baron said. "I'm back in business again but, this time, I expect to get the respect I deserve."

And there were others: the gentleman who wanted to sell liquor in bottles shaped like Elvis Presley; the purveyor of rainbow-colored prophylactics; the vendor of kitchen equipment whose catalogue recommended that you have a 'crispy joint' for your midday meal; the company president who was determined to hire a sales rep for each of the fifty United States; and the elderly gentleman who couldn't see why his business address in Dachau might be a bit off-putting to Americans, just to mention a few.

But there was also another, darker kind of oddball, like the German businessman in his late fifties who needed a German-speaking attorney to help him set up a sales office and a distribution center for his line of office equipment in the United States. He stared at the typed list I provided for a moment and then he shook his head. "Excuse me, Mr. Nitsch," he said as he handed the list back to me, "but these attorneys are all *Jews*. Don't you have a different list?"

I wasn't sure I'd heard him correctly. "Could you repeat that please?"

"I said," he replied impatiently, "I can't use this list. They're all Jews."

I got up from my chair, "I'm afraid I can't help you. That's not the way we do business here at the Chamber."

He turned red as a beet. "Believe me, Mr. Nitsch, I didn't mean it that way and . . ." but I interrupted him.

"Sir," I repeated, "I can't help you. If you want to complain about me, you can go to our manager, Mr. Ledermann, or you can write to our headquarters in Bonn! Have a good day!"

My job was never boring.

CHAPTER 68

On a crisp Saturday afternoon in late September after Peter Vollmann and I had played tennis, we went to the West End Bar on Broadway and 114th Street to eat hamburgers, drink a few beers, and listen to the sound of the cool jazz being played in the adjacent room. I felt like celebrating because I had beaten Peter in three sets. Over the second beer Peter informed me that he had recently met a beautiful Cuban woman at a business meeting.

Since Peter changed girlfriends almost as often as I changed shirts, I asked, "So when are you taking her out?"

"Well, there's a catch. She has an identical twin sister and she'll only go out with me if I bring a friend along to be her sister's date. So I told her about you and she liked the idea of my bringing you along." He put down his glass and leaned towards me. "Now don't get mad but, as a matter of fact, I've already said that you'd come. We're meeting the two of them next Friday at the Riverboat bar in the Empire State Building. Have you been there? It's a great place to pick up girls."

"C'mon Peter. My life's complicated enough as it is. I'm already involved with two different women. I sure don't need a third."

"I know that, but I really just need you to show up. The way I see it, we have a few drinks and dance a few times with the girls, and then you go home and I take over. Come on, be a good sport, Gunter. If you do this for me, I'll owe you one."

"Well, if you're sure that's all I'd have to do, I guess I'll come then."

"Great. I knew I could count on you. By the way, speaking of your multiple girlfriends, you've never told me much about that doctor you've been dating for the past couple of months." Peter picked up his beer glass and flashed me a sly smile. "Out with it. I'm all ears. How is she in the sack?"

"That's none of your damn business!" I shot back.

But he kept digging, "Well, she must be very special, seeing as you'd rather go to Bedford every other weekend than spend time with Victoria."

I sighed and had another sip of beer. Since this was a matter that had been bothering me for some time, Peter's question had struck a nerve. "Well, since you ask, the whole thing's rather odd, sort of like it's choreographed. Around 10:30 p.m. Amalia, her mother, and I say good night and then we each go off to our separate rooms on the second floor. Amalia's room is at one end of the hall opposite her mother's. The guestroom, where I sleep, is at the opposite end of the house."

"And then?" Peter asked.

"Bear with me. Amalia then insists that I wait a half an hour to be sure her mother's asleep before I sneak fully dressed down the long hallway. I could easily break my leg doing that 'cause there's no night-light. When I feel my way to Amalia's room, she smiles, puts down the book she's been reading, and puts her fingers to her lips to signal me to keep quiet. Then she turns off the light and we both get undressed in the pitch dark. And after that she jumps into bed and covers herself with a sheet. That's when I join her under the covers."

"Let me get this straight," Peter said. "You've never seen her undressed?"

"Not once. I can't see her, but I sure can feel how flabby she is. Oh, and I should mention, too, that her room smells of vinegar. It's a real turn off."

Peter sneered. "I've slept with many women, but never with a nutcase like that! You'd think she was a member of 19th century Austrian nobility. According to what I've read, back then married couples never saw each other naked, but they still managed to wind up with a dozen kids. Maybe that's why the husbands spent so much time in high-class brothels."

"Peter, you haven't heard anything yet."

"You mean there's more? Go on, I won't interrupt again."

"The whole time we're together she's, what's the best word to describe it? She's passive, unemotional. And when we're done, she tells me 'good night' and sends me back to my room!"

"Get out of here! You don't stay with her in bed?"

"No, she claims she can't sleep with another person in her bed and besides she needs her rest!"

"I'll be damned! I'd be frustrated as all hell. How do you cope?"

"It sounds crazy, but when I come home from a weekend with the doctor I rush over to Victoria's place and we spend the night together in bed like normal people."

"Well, without a doubt, your lovely doctor in Bedford has a few screws loose. But, tell me this, my friend. Why do you keep seeing her?"

"I really don't know myself. The whole thing doesn't make much sense, does it?"

****

On Friday evening I joined Peter at the bar in the Riverboat. All around us young men and young women in separate groups were carefully eyeballing one another. "What did I tell you?" Peter said when I sat down. "Is this a great place, or what?" Then he checked his watch. Let's hope our dates show up soon, so we can get a table."

Just then two tall men decked out in leather boots, blue jeans, Western shirts and ten-gallon hats, settled onto the bar stools next to us. "Howdy!" one of them greeted us while tipping his hat. "We reckon y'all are from around here. My friend and I are fixin' to get us some action. Is this a good place to meet the ladies?"

Peter raised his glass. "You've picked the right spot. One of the best I know. Where're you guys from?"

"Bandera, 'bout an hour's drive from San Antonio," the cowboy in the white hat drawled. "Hey, is that a German accent I hear?"

"You hear right. We're both from Cologne."

"My brother was stationed in Frankfurt for a coupla years so I know all 'bout them pretty frauleins and your good German beer." He was about to make another comment when his friend poked him in the ribs.

"Well, I'll be damned. Do you see what just walked in? Three plug-ugly Niggers with white girls on their arms!" The two of them gawked at the new arrivals.

"I guess you don't see that very often in Bandera," Peter said. "Tell me, what would happen if a black guy went out with a white girl where you come from?"

"That Nigger wouldn't live long. White folks just wouldn't tolerate it."

"Back home," his friend added, "New York doesn't have the best reputation what with all its crime and Jews and Niggers doin' whatever they please."

"It's really not that bad," Peter said. "Most people here just like to live and let live, that's all."

"Well, never mind that," one of the Texans replied. "But tell us, how're the two of you gonna to meet women, here at the bar or do you walk over to a table and ask a girl for a dance?"

Peter smirked and gave me a wink, "Neither one. Our dates are coming right now," and he waved wildly at two attractive young women with short Afros and big gold earrings who smiled at Peter and waved back at us as they slowly worked their way through the crowd.

Meanwhile the mouths of our newfound friends from Texas gaped wide open. "Fine Germans you are! You're the biggest hypocrites I've ever met," one of them said. "Letting us shoot our mouths off about Niggers like that."

"Like I said," Peter added, "around here we like to live and let live. Well, gentlemen, it's been nice chatting with you. Good luck meeting some ladies! My friend and I are going to meet our dates and get ourselves a table."

The Cuban twins were so similar in appearance that it was difficult to keep them apart. They were even more difficult to understand since, the more they had to drink, the more they drifted from limited English to rapid-fire Spanish. Around 10 p.m. with the three of them already pretty intoxicated and Peter no longer bothering to translate for me, I excused myself and went home.

341

A week later when Peter and I met again to play tennis I asked him, "So, what happened to your two Cuban sisters?"

"The twins? I did them both!"

"So, will you see them again?"

"No way. A thing like that only works once!"

CHAPTER 69

*W*henever Amalia and I took long hikes not far from her home in Bedford, she always suggested that we spend a weekend together at the Skytop Lodge in the Pocono Mountains of eastern Pennsylvania. "There are wonderful hiking trails there," she explained, "and, of course, it would be my treat." Adhering to Quincy's second rule, I had never travelled with a woman I was dating. But after weeks of persuasion, I finally gave in. It turned out that I had nothing to lose but my self-respect.

Amalia phoned me a few days ahead to explain the ground rules. "Please bring only casual clothes. Don't bring a suit and for heaven's sake leave your hideous blue and white striped pants at home. They're way too loud for Skytop."

I felt like saying, "Yes, mother!" but I bit my tongue.

"And, another thing," Amalia continued, "when we go to the dining room in the evening I want you to wear a plaid flannel shirt like all the other gentlemen."

"You can't be serious. You want me to dress like that at dinner? That sounds ludicrous."

"I'm completely serious. Skytop caters to well-to-do congenial people who like to relax by dressing like common folks and I certainly don't want you to embarrass me by looking out of place."

"Well, I know lots of common folks who don't run around in lumberjack shirts, but you're calling the shots, so okay."

"Good, that's settled then. The last thing I would want is to be accused of damaging Skytop's image."

****

I arrived at the Bedford train station at mid-afternoon on Saturday all decked out like 'common folks' apparently do, in blue jeans, the obligatory flannel shirt, thick gray woolen socks, and hiking boots. Instead of the large sports bag I usually brought with me, I had packed an assortment of casual clothes in a rucksack attached to which, as a final touch, I had hung an Army surplus canteen. Amalia, who was waiting for me by her car, inspected me approvingly.

During the two-hour drive to Skytop, Amalia did most of the talking. By the time we crossed the Pennsylvania line she had brought me up to date on all of the events that had occurred at the hospital over the past week. Then, just when I thought I would get a word in edgewise, she slapped her forehead. "I nearly forgot. I've been meaning to ask you if you know a Mr. George Perau? He's originally from Hamburg, like my mother, and he claims he knows you."

"Of course I do. He's the American representative for the Port of Bremen. We run into each other all the time at receptions. And you say he's a friend of your mother?"

"Not a friend, more like an acquaintance of my mother."

"You mean an 'acquaintance' like Mr. Carstensen who comes over so often for dinner?"

344

"No, not like that. Let me correct myself. Mr. Carstensen is my mother's boyfriend; Mr. Perau is merely her acquaintance. You do know that he's gay, don't you?"

"I never really thought about it either way."

"The old dear's a real chatterbox, and he's so well educated and widely travelled. Mother finds him delightful and, of course, he's perfectly harmless. He's the best kind of friend for her to have, wouldn't you say?"

****

Nestled in the forested foothills of the Pocono Mountains, Skytop Lodge was a palatial, four-story stone building with a wide, white-columned veranda, all in all a far cry from the rustic old hotel made of rough-hewn logs I had been expecting. "Most guests take the same parking space every time they come to avoid any little unpleasantries," Amalia explained as she pulled into a leafy spot in the shade. "This one's mine."

After we checked in an elderly bell cap reached down to carry our bags to our room. "No thank you, sir," I insisted. "I can manage."

Once we got upstairs Amalia scolded me. "Really, Gunter, you should have let that old man bring up our things. We're the guests here and his job is to serve us!" Then she muttered under her breath, "You've got a lot to learn."

"Excuse me?" I asked. "What did you say?"

"Oh never mind. We can talk about it later."

I set down the bags, hers on one of the twin beds and mine on the other. After we had unpacked, Amalia changed into a white blouse, a long black skirt, and a red neckerchief and then we headed downstairs to the wood beamed dining room. Candles flickered on every table, the only other light being provided by pairs of dim lamps bracketed onto the walls near the ceiling. Nearly all of the other diners were gray-haired couples in their sixties and seventies who, in sharp contrast to the high-pitched chatter I was used to in New York City, conversed with each other in the hushed tones of spies sharing state secrets.

"I feel at home whenever I'm at Skytop," Amalia confided after we were seated, "since I can always count on being among congenial people."

"You used that term once before, 'congenial.' So, tell me, what does it actually mean?" Her reply was surprisingly straightforward.

"It means getting along with each other because you all belong to the same group or class of people. For example, I've been coming here for years and I've never seen a Jew, at least not that I was aware of and, of course, never any coloreds, not a single one. That's what makes it so pleasant."

"In other words," I asked in an effort to pin her down, "'congenial' is really a codeword for 'restricted'?"

"No, I wouldn't say that. It's just that 'those people' would feel out of place here. Just like anyone else, they prefer the company of their own kind and so do we. It's as simple as that."

While Amalia was talking, I noticed that several of the elderly couples at nearby tables, who apparently had run out of things to say to each other after thirty or forty years of marriage, were no longer talking to each other. Instead they were trying their best to eavesdrop on our conversation.

"But Amalia, don't you have Jewish colleagues in your hospital?" I persisted, intentionally raising my voice.

"Of course I do," she whispered in reply. "Way too many of them as far as I'm concerned. It's not that they aren't competent; most of them are good at what they do. It's the ones that get all pushy and power-hungry I really can't stand." She paused while the waiter served our steaks. Once he was out of earshot she continued, her voice barely above a whisper, "Since we're on the subject, my brother dated one once, would you believe it? A Jew, I mean, not a colored person, which would have been even worse. I tried to talk him out of it but he wouldn't listen. And, one day, he actually dared to bring her up to Bedford to meet my parents. I mean, she couldn't help having a Brooklyn accent, or having dark, wavy hair and a prominent nose, but did she have to come in a tight, fire red dress and matching stilettos? She looked like a woman from the horizontal trade. It was only after my father threatened to disinherit him that my brother dropped her. Can you imagine the scandal if he'd actually married her?"

"You told me your brother is married. Is he happy?"

"I think so. He's a partner in a law firm in Charleston, South Carolina, and my sister-in-law comes from an old Southern family. They have three adorable children. So, everything turned out for the best."

"Well, that's nice," I said, "and all very congenial I suppose," I couldn't resist adding. "I assume you also have African-American colleagues at the hospital. How do you get along with them?"

"That's another sore subject. I'm convinced most of them wouldn't have gotten into medical school without affirmative action. Why should a Negro take the place of a qualified white applicant, that's what I'd like to know? And, you may not believe this, but there've been any number of times a colored mother has asked me to treat her child because she doesn't have confidence in the Negro doctor on the case. Everybody on the staff talks about the problem, but no one does anything about it. What do you say to that?"

After dinner a combo of three old men began to play a selection of slow tunes such as "The Tennessee Waltz" and some old Glen

347

Miller favorites. Since Amalia was wearing high heels, the two of us towered over the other guests as we danced but, aside from our height, we matched the rest of the crowd. All of the women wore long skirts, blouses, and kerchiefs; all of the men wore plaid flannel lumberjack shirts. And I noticed that not a single person in the room was the least bit overweight.

"I'm going to ask the band leader to play a Viennese Waltz," I said to Amalia as we drifted slowly to the music. "It would be nice to pick up the pace a bit."

"Please don't! It's just not done here. I could never live it down if you did."

How ironic, I thought. *Jeanine had said practically the same thing to me at the Haitian Ball more than four years earlier.* The only difference was, back then I got my waltz. This time, I didn't dare ask.

When the music stopped Amalia and I returned to our room and, after taking turns changing in the bathroom, we climbed into our separate twin beds and went to sleep. After a leisurely breakfast the following morning, we took a long hike. It had rained during the night and my leaky hiking boots squished in the mud as we walked. On the drive back to Bedford, it suddenly struck me that despite her frequent visits to Skytop, Amalia hadn't introduced me to a single friend, nor for that matter even to a casual acquaintance whom she knew there. She was, so far as I could tell, the most friendless person I had ever met.

Amalia dropped me off at the Bedford train station where I caught the next train back to Grand Central Station, which, to my great delight, was swarming with an assortment of non-congenial people. And, much to my relief, between Grand Central and my apartment on the upper West Side, I didn't see anyone else in a flannel lumberjack shirt.

When I walked into my apartment, the phone was ringing. It was Amalia. "Just checking to make sure you got home safely," she said.

This time I couldn't help myself. "Yes, Mother," I said. "You needn't have worried." I hung up the phone, unpacked, had a beer, got my clothes ready for the next morning, and then headed over to Victoria's apartment to spend the night.

CHAPTER 70

In the middle of October my mother wrote to let me know that my father had terminal liver cancer. With her letter in hand, I phoned her first thing the next morning from my office. "Mutti, how bad is it? Should I fly over for two weeks or so?" I asked.

"No, please don't. If you came now it would only make him suspicious. Come for Christmas instead! It's not that far off."

"I don't understand. You mean you told him he's going to live?"

"I couldn't bear to tell him the truth. You would've done the same if you'd seen how hopeful he was when he came out of the anesthesia. And he was so relieved when I said that the surgery had gone well. His doctor assured me I did the right thing."

"But what did his doctor actually tell you?"

Her voice choked up. "That Vati's only got a few months left at best."

If I were in his place, would I have preferred to hear the truth? I really couldn't be sure. "Well, I guess that's best for Vati," I finally said. "But it must make it twice as hard for you."

"Never mind about me," Mutti said. "I'm a tough old bird as you know."

While we were talking I was frantically checking my desk calendar. "Listen, Mutti, unless you need me to come sooner, I'll plan to get to Cologne on Wednesday, December 15th and stay until Sunday, January 2nd, so I can go back to work on that Monday. How does that sound?"

"Can you really arrange things that fast? That's wonderful. Your father will be thrilled when I tell him you're coming home for Christmas."

"Give him my best regards when you see him and say hello to Hubert for me! And please be sure to let me know if there's any way I can help in the meantime."

"Just knowing you'll be here that soon . . ." Her voice trailed off.

"I'll call you again in a few days," I said and I hung up.

I was pretty shaken up by our conversation and needed someone to talk to. From a medical point of view, Amalia would be the logical person, but the last thing I wanted was another dose of her gloom and doom. That left only one person I could depend on to cheer me up, Victoria. I went over to see her as soon as I got home from the Chamber.

"How old is your dad?" was her first question after I told her the bad news.

"He just turned sixty-two in September."

"That's all? He's pretty young to be facing death. On the other hand, have you considered that the doctor might be wrong? They do make mistakes you know."

"Thanks, you always know the right thing to say. And as long as we're on the subject, there's another thing that's got me really spooked. I'm almost embarrassed to tell you this, but the last time I saw my father was back in 1966. When I left for the airport he gave me a hug. He had never done that before, not even once that I can recall and I wasn't sure how to react. Do you suppose he had a premonition of what was going to happen? It was so unexpected, so out of character."

"This happened in 1966? That's already five years ago. No, I don't think so. I'd guess he was just sorry to see you go. But if that was really the only hug he ever gave you, I can't decide what I find more strange, that he only hugged you that one time, or that you couldn't just accept his hug for what it was."

"Which was?"

"It's simple. For the same reason anyone gives someone else a hug. He wanted you to know that he loves you. That shouldn't be so hard for you to understand, should it?"

"You really think he does?"

"I don't just *think* so." Victoria said. "I'm certain of it."

****

In the meantime the fall semester was well underway at Pace College where I had started my MBA program. Most of my all-male classmates were married men with responsible well-paying jobs at banks, brokerage houses, and investment firms. And even though I hated to foot the bill for my tuition from my own pocket while their employers were picking up the tab, I really couldn't complain. Aside from helping to take my mind off the problems back home, I was enjoying every minute of it. The best part was that my professors weren't just academics; they used their own real-life experiences in the business world to bring their lectures on Marketing Theory and Marketing Planning to life by providing practical examples that I could also use in my work at the Chamber. I hung on their every word.

****

I had once again booked an inexpensive flight on Icelandic Airlines, which, after a stopover in Reykjavik, Iceland, would take me to Luxembourg. From there I would need several more hours by train to reach Mutti in Cologne. The last time I had held an Icelandic ticket, I had backed out of the trip at the last minute, stranding Charlotte at the Luxembourg airport. This time, with my father's health failing rapidly, I couldn't get home fast enough.

When my plane landed in Luxembourg on the morning of Wednesday, December 15, 1971, I phoned Mutti from the airport only to learn that I was one day too late. While I had been in the air somewhere over the Atlantic Ocean, my father had quietly passed away in his sleep. And now, just like Charlotte years before, I had a long, sad train ride ahead of me before I got home. Actually, home wasn't quite the right word for it. When I had last visited my parents, they were still living in the familiar apartment over Café Nitsch in Bergheim some miles outside of Cologne. Now I was on my way to an apartment I had never seen.

When, several hours later, my taxi driver pulled up at the doorway to Freiherr-Vom-Stein-Strasse 5, Mutti was standing at the window waiting for me. She met me at the entrance to her building and wrapped me in her arms. "I'm so glad you're here," she kept repeating as both of us clung together. After a minute, Mutti stood back and wiped her eyes with her apron. "You must be tired and hungry," she said. "After you've washed up a bit, come join me for lunch. I've fixed stuffed cabbage, your favorite." She didn't have to tell me. I had recognized that familiar aroma the minute I walked in the door.

"So, to bring you up to date, first thing this morning Hubert and I arranged to have the funeral this coming Saturday," Mutti said when she and I sat down on the bench that curved around two sides of the wooden table in the corner of the kitchen. "And I've already phoned both Aunt Käte and Uncle Bruno. The hardest part was finding a pastor to officiate. We haven't been living in Cologne all that long and, besides, you know how your father felt about religion. But the funeral director is going to line someone up for us."

Right after lunch Mutti brought me into the living room and asked me to take a seat on the armchair across from the couch. Then she went into the bedroom, returning with an armful of my father's clothes. She laid out a suit, a jacket and half a dozen white dress shirts on the couch before returning to the bedroom to get a brand new dark blue sweat suit, a sheepskin coat, and the pair of binoculars that I had once given my father for his birthday. "Your father would have wanted you to have these binoculars," Mutti said, handing them to me. "As for the clothes, let me see you try everything on. Whatever fits I want you to bring back with you to New York."

The thought of putting on my father's things so soon after he had died gave me the creeps, especially since the smell of my father's sweat still clung to the jacket, but Mutti was insistent. "At least there's no reason to try on the shirts and the suit," I said. "I know already that the sleeves would be too short. But what about Hubert? Couldn't he use these things better than I could?"

"I wish," she said. "But he's put on so much weight, there's nothing that would fit."

"Exactly how much do you mean?"

"I'd guess a bit over 150 kilos." I did the math in my head: my brother was now a massive three hundred thirty pounds.

"Well, since it makes you happy, I'll take the sweat suit, the binoculars, and the sheepskin coat," I reluctantly agreed. "I really can't use the rest of it."

Towards suppertime Hubert came by with his wife Irmgard, whom I had previously only known from photos. An inch taller than Hubert but more than two hundred pounds lighter, she had close-cropped brunette hair and wore thick-framed glasses. Irmgard looked crisp and cool in contrast to my brother who was breathing heavily after carrying in a case of wine from his car. Mutti had tactfully put away the rest of my father's clothes before Hubert arrived. She was right. None of it would have fit.

****

Shortly before 11:30 a.m. on Saturday morning, our family members began to gather in the parking area next to Mutti's apartment house. First to arrive were my father's brother, Bruno, and his wife, followed by my father's sister, my Aunt Käte, her son, Siegfried, and his wife, Ruth. My Aunt Liesbeth and my cousin, Gerda, soon joined them. As we all prepared to drive over to the cemetery to join the forty or more friends and neighbors who were already in the chapel, it was arranged that I would ride in my cousin Siegfried's spacious Opel Kapitän. I would have preferred to ride in the same car with Mutti, but once Hubert, Irmgard, and Mutti had gotten into Hubert's tiny Citroën 2CV, there was no longer enough space for me.

Just as I was about to climb into Siegfried's car someone called out, "Günter, if you'd like you can also come with me." I turned around and there was my old flame Charlotte. She was now a married woman and the mother of a young son. It had been five years since I'd last seen her and she was more beautiful than ever. She wore a tight-fitting black business suit, with a matching cape open in the front, and a small black hat that barely covered her hair, which was pulled back in a loose chignon.

How could I resist? "Forgive me, Siegfried," I said, "but that's my former girlfriend and I'll be going with her."

Aunt Käte hissed, "Günter! How can you do this to us? Are you forgetting why we're here?"

"Oh, come on. Be reasonable, Mother," Siegfried chided. "Can't you see that the girl drove up in a huge BMW? Günter'd be a fool to pass up a ride in a car like that!"

"Sorry, Aunt Käte," I mumbled before rushing over to Charlotte. My words came tumbling out. "What a surprise! I hadn't expected to see you here. Thanks for coming. You look stunning." I gave her a hug and stepped back.

"I'm sorry it had to be under these circumstances," she said as she brushed a strand of her hair back in place.

"How'd you know that my father passed away?"

"Your mother called to tell me and I'm glad she did. Don't forget. I kind of belonged to your family for a while, didn't I?"

No, I thought, *I haven't forgotten!*

"Look! They're about to leave. Hop in so we can follow Hubert's car to the cemetery." Charlotte turned on the engine and joined the line of cars. With the windows rolled up, and even more pervasive than the new car smell of her huge BMW, was the unmistakable scent of *L'Air du Temps*. I studied the self-assured young woman next to me as she delighted in telling me about her son, Alexander, who had just celebrated his first birthday, and I realized just how much the tables had turned. Now I was the one who was confused and insecure. *What was I doing with my life? Why had I ever left Charlotte anyway? What were Victoria and Amalia and all the rest compared to her?* With Charlotte married and out of reach, she was more enticing to me than ever before.

When she stopped the car in the Nordfriedhof parking lot a few minutes later, Charlotte reached over and put her hand into mine. "We won't be able to talk during the funeral and, judging from the nasty looks Aunt Käte was giving you, don't you think it would be better if I just drop you off at your mother's apartment later and didn't come inside?"

"I guess so," I reluctantly agreed, already regretting that our time together would be so short.

****

Daylight streamed through the skylight in the small, dark-wood paneled cemetery chapel, casting an eerie glow on my father's open casket, which was surrounded by dozens of flickering candles and five beribboned funeral wreaths. By the time Charlotte and I came inside, nearly half of the eighty wooden chairs were filled. I gave Charlotte's hand a squeeze before joining Mutti, Hubert, and Irmgard in the front row.

Aunt Käte and Uncle Bruno walked up to the coffin and bent down to say a last good-bye to their brother. "Hubert, Irmgard, and I have already gone up there," Mutti whispered. "Don't you want to pay your respects before they put on the lid?"

As a young child in the years after World War II, I had seen more than my share of corpses—of soldiers and civilians, of babies and old ladies, of Russians and Germans. It still gave me the shivers to think of the lifeless shell my beloved grandfather had become when he died in Russian-occupied East Prussia in 1946. And how my sweet little cousin Dorchen had looked when she was laid out in our apartment after she died of TB the following year. I had no desire to see my father that way. So when Mutti asked me, I firmly shook my head and didn't budge from my chair.

Now it was time for the pastor to speak. Armed only with the few facts he had gleaned from Mutti beforehand, he droned on. "Dearly beloved," he began, "we come here today to honor the memory of our brother in Christ, um," (a pause to check his notes) "Willi Nitsch, beloved husband of" (another pause) "Margarete Nitsch, and devoted father of" (a quick glance at the sheet) "Günter and Hubert."

The man whose praises he was singing was unrecognizable to me. During the entire time I lived with my parents after we were reunited with my father in 1950, my father had had nothing but contempt for the clergy, only coming to church for Hubert's and my confirmations and also, with great reluctance, once a year on Christmas.

Beloved husband? Devoted father? Was this the same man who had cheated on Mutti while we were living under the Russians? Who had abandoned the three of us in a refugee camp for almost two years from 1949 to 1950 and who, after we were finally reunited, often smacked my brother and me around and criticized Hubert unmercifully? Now that I thought about it, was it because of him that I was so averse to marriage for myself? I could imagine nothing worse than becoming an unfaithful husband as he had once been. Having grown up with him as an example, could I really trust myself to be true to one woman for the rest of my life?

Mutti was weeping in the chair beside me. Even Aunt Käte and Uncle Bruno, who, together with their mother, had shamed my father into taking us back in 1950, had broken down in tears. Only my brother Hubert sat, stony-faced, lost in his own thoughts. I didn't dare meet his eyes.

Later, after the coffin was lowered into the ground, and even more floral wreaths covered the grave, Charlotte drove me back to Mutti's apartment. "You know," she said as she headed down Neusser Strasse, "it would be nice if you could meet my son. I was thinking that we could get together on the morning of the 24th in the dining room of the Kaufhof Department Store, if that would work for you."

"Will your husband come, too?"

"No, of course not. He'd blow a fuse if he even knew you were here in Cologne. He gets so jealous I don't even dare mention your name. Listen, I know he'll be busy in his architecture office that morning. So I will just tell him I have to run an errand. You will meet Alexander and me, won't you? Say at 10 a.m. at the pay booth inside the underground parking garage?"

So, I thought, *Charlotte does still have feelings for me*. Knowing that, the idea of somehow meeting her behind her husband's back was really appealing.

"Thanks for the ride!" I said. "I'll be there!"

CHAPTER 71

Just like every other time when my parents' older relatives got together, when we got back to Mutti's apartment the conversation turned to the good old days in East Prussia before the war. The Russian invasion in late 1944 and early 1945 and the awful events that followed were never discussed. It was as if, for their generation, those events, which had robbed me of the best years of my childhood and of my education, simply hadn't happened.

Just when I was considering going out for a breath of fresh air, my Aunt Käte suddenly spoke to me. "So, Günter," she said, "when are you coming home for good?"

All eyes turned in my direction. "I'm not, Aunt Käte. I'm going to stay on in New York."

Uncle Bruno, whom I always thought of as an unrepentant Nazi, looked at me in stunned amazement. "I just don't get it," he said. "How can you live with all those different kinds of people? I know I couldn't stand it."

When I didn't reply, Aunt Käte spoke up again. "Now Bruno, dear, don't get yourself all worked up. Give the boy enough time and he'll realize he belongs here." Then she turned to me. "But there's another thing I'd like to clear up. If I'm not mistaken, you're now thirty-four years old. So, when do you plan on getting married and giving your mother some grandchildren?"

I shrugged my shoulders. "To be honest, I haven't the slightest interest in getting married. Why should I? I'm having too much fun."

Aunt Käte looked at Uncle Bruno and rolled her eyes. "Since we're on the subject, do you at least have a steady girlfriend?"

"Actually, I've got two right now. One's a teacher and the other's . . ."

By now Mutti had had enough. "Spare us the details please! And Käte, please stop cross-examining the poor boy if you don't mind!"

But Uncle Bruno insisted on getting in the last word. "Still, Günter should cut out the nonsense and come back home to Germany. An East Prussian like him has no business living in that godforsaken country."

There was so much I wanted to say in response to Uncle Bruno but, considering the occasion, I decided to change the subject instead. "Speaking of East Prussia," I said, "I've decided to take Mutti to Frankfurt for a few days to visit her East Prussian cousin, Helmut."

"You never told me anything about that," Mutti protested.

"I wanted to surprise you. Besides, it's already arranged. I made the phone call last night. Anyway, I won't take 'no' for an answer. It'll do you good to get away from here for a while, don't you think?"

"I'd really like to do that," Mutti said. It was the first time I'd seen her smile since I had arrived from New York.

The next morning after an early breakfast Mutti and I took the tramway to the main Cologne railroad station where I bought roundtrip first class tickets to Frankfurt for the two of us. "This is the life," Mutti exclaimed as she sat down on the cushioned seat in the first class compartment. "First class! Imagine that!" As the train rolled along past castles perched atop the hills overlooking the Rhine River, Mutti was glued to the window. "This was a wonderful idea," she finally remarked. "Do you realize that your father and I only took three vacations together over the past twenty years? Just three!" Then, after a pause, "Are you sure you can afford all this?"

I knew full well that there was no way I could ever repay my mother for the risks she took to provide for our family during the Russian years. "It's the least I can do. Don't worry about it," I assured her and I let it go at that.

Mutti's cousin, Helmut, who had once famously said, 'You don't have to buy the whole cow if you want to drink a glass of milk,' had gotten married. But I had to admit that he had made a good choice in his wife, Doris, who spent the next five days showing Mutti and me around Frankfurt while her husband was at work.

"Maybe you can convince Günter to settle down and get married," Mutti said to her cousin on our last evening together. "He sees nothing wrong with dating more than one woman at a time and not committing himself to either of them."

"Oh, Gretel," Helmut said, "don't you worry about that. Let him have his fun. Believe me, some young woman will catch him one of these days. How old is Günter now anyway? Thirty-four? Come on, I was already past forty when Doris and I got married. Give him time!"

****

Mutti and I got back to Cologne on December 23rd, and the next morning I met Charlotte and her baby son in the underground parking garage of the Kaufhof Department Store. From there we went upstairs to the cafeteria where Charlotte put hazel-eyed Alexander in my lap. Then she handed me thin slices of banana for him to nibble on. I was amazed how tightly he grasped my finger with his tiny hand. I had held

Walter and Tamara's son, Benjamin, many times, but this was the first time in my life that I wished with all my heart that the baby I held were mine.

"Isn't he sweet?" Charlotte asked as she reached for her son. "Here, let me hold him so you can enjoy your breakfast." I reluctantly handed the little boy back to her.

"Tell me," I said. "You mentioned that your husband is the jealous type. What exactly did you mean by that?"

"You're not going to believe this. You know he's nine years older than I am, right? He simply can't stand the thought that I knew anyone before I met him. So when we got married he made me turn over to him all of the photos I have from when you and I were together."

"He tore them up?"

"Worse than that. He put them into a small wooden box and nailed it shut. Get this! I don't have permission to open the box until he dies."

If I were ever foolish enough to get married, would my wife do the same with the large box brimming with pictures of everyone I had ever dated from Charlotte right down to Victoria and Amalia that I kept in my apartment? I couldn't imagine myself letting that happen.

"So I guess he doesn't trust you?"

I realized the minute I asked it, how foolish my question was. After all, this was now the second time in a week that she was sneaking around behind her husband's back to meet me.

"I don't know why he gets so jealous. But he's a good provider and a wonderful father to Alexander, so I'm willing to put up with that."

"So just to be clear, he doesn't know that I'm in Cologne?"

"Oh no. As far as he's concerned, you're still far away in New York. My life is much simpler if I let him continue to believe that."

An hour after we had met, I brought Charlotte and Alexander back down to the Kaufhof parking garage. I kissed Charlotte good-bye on both cheeks. Then, just for a fleeting moment, as I stood there watching them drive away, I actually felt sorry for Charlotte's clueless husband. But better him than me!

CHAPTER 72

I now was faced with another full week in Cologne and very little to do. Right after breakfast every day Mutti took me shopping. She assured me that the Turkish butcher and the Turkish vegetable storeowner in her neighborhood were much nicer and had cheaper and better quality products than their German counterparts. In the late mornings she and I sat together on the couch poring over old family photographs. For a change of scene, I treated Mutti to coffee and cake at Café Kranzler on Offenbachplatz near the Opera House or I took her out for ice cream to Café Reichard, directly across from the Cologne Cathedral. When Mutti was busy sorting through my father's things, I stopped in to the fast food shop on Hohe Strasse to say hello to Hubert, who was behind the counter making waffles. I also looked up Theo Schrick, one of my old business college classmates, just as he and his girlfriend were about to leave for a long-planned ski trip to Kitzbühl in Austria.

With the approach of New Year's Eve, I couldn't bear the thought of staying home with Mutti who, I knew, would spend the evening glued to her television set watching the traditional viewing of the British short film *Dinner for One* followed by the annual year-end variety show. A year had passed since the disastrous evening when I had thrown away my lucky tie after splattering Irene with gravy in a Greenwich Village restaurant. Now, unwilling to spend New Year's Eve cooped up with my mother in her apartment, I put on my best suit and headed for the Gürzenich, Cologne's most famous banquet hall, where I knew that festivities would be in full swing. As expected the event had long since been sold out, but a twenty Deutschmark bribe to the doorkeeper got me a seat at a long table in the midst of two large family groups. I scanned the neighboring tables, quickly rejecting the young couples who were clinging together or gazing lovingly into each other's eyes, before identifying my target at my own long table: an attractive blonde sitting next to an overweight young man. He was sweating profusely having just managed to trip all over the young woman's feet while they danced the waltz. The young man whipped out a handkerchief to wipe the sweat off his bloated red face and neck. From where I sat, I could almost imagine hearing his date's cry for help. The minute the young man excused himself to go to the restroom, I made my move.

When I strode over to her, bowed slightly, and asked, "May I have the next dance?" the pretty blonde eagerly accepted. I had sized up the situation correctly.

Sophie was a student at the University of Cologne with a double major in English and German. When she learned that I was living in New York, she was eager to practice her English with me. "I hope I'm not intruding. I wouldn't want to upset your boyfriend," I said, testing the waters still further.

"Xavier? No, don't worry about him. He's just a family friend. Those are his parents over there. Why do you ask?"

"Because I'd like to dance with you some more, that's why."

"I'd like that," Sophie replied. "Here comes Xavier now. Let me talk him into switching seats with you."

Sophie and I danced until 2 a.m. and, when she was about to drive home with her friends, I invited her to have dinner with me in the old part of town the following afternoon.

"As tempting as that sounds, I don't know if I can spare the time. I've got two term papers due next week." Xavier's father honked the horn of his car impatiently. "Listen, I've got to go. Here's my phone number. Call me tomorrow and I'll let you know."

****

Early the next morning, as Mutti and I sat together in the kitchen over a breakfast of fresh buttered rolls slathered in honey, I described my New Year's Eve adventure in the Gürzenich. "You're incorrigible," Mutti said. "How many women do you need in your life anyway? Besides, shouldn't you really stay home with me tonight? After all, it *is* your last evening in Cologne." Mutti reached over to refill my coffee cup. "You know what? And I don't think I'm being selfish. I really hope that girl, what's her name? Sophie? I hope when you call her, she tells you she is too busy to see you."

But, much to Mutti's disappointment, Sophie had found the time. We arranged to meet at 5 p.m. in an Argentinian restaurant not far from her studio apartment. "I'd really like to hear more about your life in the United States," Sophie explained as we enjoyed a quiet meal together. "My dream is to study and live there one day, but my boyfriend doesn't like the idea."

"You mean Xavier? From last night? I wouldn't let him stand in your way."

"Not him, silly. My actual boyfriend who's on vacation right now in the south of Spain."

"You know," I said when we had finished our meal, "I'd be interested to see where you live. How about if I come up to thaw out for a few minutes?"

"Well," she hesitated. "You really shouldn't."

"If it's your boyfriend you're worried about, do you really believe he hasn't met any girls while he's away?"

"Well, if you put it that way. Sure, why not? I guess it's okay," Sophie replied. "It would just be for a quick look around, right?"

It took longer to see the apartment than Sophie had expected so it wasn't until 4 a.m. that I got back to Mutti's place. The bottle of red Spanish wine Sophie and I had drunk together as we had listened to Spanish music on her stereo warmed me despite the bitter January cold. To celebrate the events of the evening, I was whistling 'Málaga' as I came around the corner of the building past Mutti's bedroom window only stopping when I reached the front door. Then, trying to be as quiet as possible, I crept inside, got undressed, set the alarm clock for 7 a.m., and crawled into bed.

****

Groggy after having gotten only three hours of sleep, I woke up to the alarm on the morning of January 2, 1972, quickly packed my suitcase, and then joined Mutti in the kitchen. "Did you really have to whistle like that? I'm sure you woke up half the neighbors," she chastised me.

"Sorry, Mutti. I was in a really good mood. I couldn't help it."

"Well, let's talk about that. Are you really proud of yourself, spending the night with a young woman nearly half your age?

Honestly, Günter, I'm concerned about your lifestyle. How long do you think you can keep this up? Why don't you just marry one of your girlfriends in New York and settle down?"

I shook my head. "Sorry again for whistling. And when it comes to marriage, I just haven't found the right one yet."

"Maybe you're looking in all the wrong places. Have you considered that?"

"Well, you know what they say. It's always in the last place you look."

Outside in the parking lot my taxi driver honked. I hugged Mutti, who was fighting back tears. Then I picked up my bag and rushed outside. My train would be leaving from the main railroad station in less than an hour.

****

I dozed on the ride between Cologne and Koblenz, where I had to change trains. Then, travelling on from Koblenz my thoughts drifted back to another New Year's Eve when some of my army buddies and I had driven to Luxembourg for the evening. It was then, thirteen long years earlier, that I had met Nathalie Bolieu, a beautiful young woman whose parents had wanted me to marry her. Since I had two hours before my flight left for New York, I decided on the spur of the moment to dial the Bolieu's telephone number. To my amazement, Nathalie answered the phone. For a moment I had no idea what to say.

"Hello? Hello?" Her voice sounded the same as it had all those years before.

"Nathalie, it's me, Günter. Do you remember me? We met back in 1958."

"When you were in the *Bundeswehr*, right? Of course I do. So much has happened in the meantime." She paused to take a breath. "Are you married?"

"No. You?"

"I was. I've got two children and I recently got divorced. That's why I'm staying with my parents right now. Tell me, do you come to Luxembourg from Cologne very often?"

"Actually I've been living in New York since 1964. I'll be flying home in two hours."

"Two hours? Then I have time to see you. I'll be there in about ten minutes."

"You needn't go to the trouble . . ." I began, but she had already hung up the phone.

A quarter of an hour later, Nathalie joined me. Her face lit up when she spotted me in the terminal. "You haven't changed a bit!" she exclaimed. I couldn't say the same. Nathalie looked care-worn and unquestionably older than her thirty-one years. The combination of an unhappy marriage and a bitter divorce had evidently taken its toll. I had to wonder whether my life would have turned out any better if I had been the one who married her, as her far-right-leaning father had once pressured me to do. For him, there would have been nothing better than having a 'real German' as a son-in-law. The thought had chilled me at the time; it still did.

With a start, I realized that Nathalie had asked me a question. "Come again?"

"What would you say if my little girls and I were to come live with you in New York? Wouldn't that be wonderful?"

Terrifying would be more like it, I thought. "I already have a girlfriend in New York," I rushed to reply. "I couldn't consider that."

"Well, at least give me your address," Nathalie persisted, "so I can look you up in case I get over there."

I looked at my watch. "Sorry, there's no time! I don't want to miss my flight." I gave her a quick hug and raced to the gate. The last glimpse I had of her, she was standing forlornly, waving good-bye.

Another narrow escape, I thought. *What ever possessed me to make that phone call anyhow? If only it were this easy to extricate myself from my relationships with Victoria and Amalia, would I find someone I'd actually want to marry?* I had my doubts, but maybe it was worth a try.

****

Sweating profusely in my father's sheepskin coat, I was waiting for my suitcase to arrive on the baggage carousel in the JFK airport when a young woman tapped me on the shoulder. "Hey!" she exclaimed. "Aren't you the dude from Hunter College who punched the guy who shoved Professor Rosenthal?"

I spun around. *Which side was she on? Is she friend or foe? She was smiling. All was well.* "Yes, that was me. Why do you ask? Were you there?"

She grasped my hand. "Of course I was there. I saw the whole thing. You're a real hero of mine for what you did that day. That took guts, facing down that guy the way you did." She waited for some response from me and, when none came, she tilted her head at a charming angle and reached over to touch the soft texture of my coat. "Say! You wouldn't have time to join me for a cup of coffee would you?"

The last thing I needed at that moment was to take on another girl. "There's my suitcase!" I exclaimed, as my battered brown leather bag came into view. "It's been nice chatting with you, but I've got to go now. So long!" and I was on my way to the bus stop before she had another chance to speak.

****

As I rode the airport bus back to Manhattan, I thought with more than a twinge of guilt about the strange events of the past two weeks. For one thing, how could I have run off to spend time, first with Charlotte and then with Sophie, when Mutti needed me to be at her side, especially after Mutti had confided in me about her difficult financial situation? For years my father had only paid the minimum contribution into the German Social Security System. Now, because of his lack of foresight, Mutti was left with a meager old age pension that was largely used up by the time she paid for her utilities and for the monthly maintenance on her apartment. To the extent that I could afford it, I had vowed to take up some of the slack.

And when it came to the subject of finances, I had to think again about Victoria, who always spent more than she earned, and about Amalia, who had so much money she sometimes made me feel like I was bought and paid for. As for Sophie, the university student, the problem with her had nothing to do with money. She just made me feel old. And I *was* old compared to her. While I was busy playing the field like I was still in my twenties, Walter Licht had gotten married. Jeanine had gotten married. Charlotte had gotten married. Even Mutti's cousin, Helmut, that old confirmed bachelor, had gotten married. *Perhaps Mutti was right. Perhaps I really was incorrigible*, I thought to myself as I collapsed into my bed on the Upper West Side just after 11 p.m. and instantly fell asleep.

CHAPTER 73

Two thick folders filled with marketing inquiry letters were stacked on my desk when I arrived at the Chamber early on Monday morning, January 3rd. I was skimming through the letters when Miss Block came in at a quarter to nine.

"My, aren't you in bright and early!" she said cheerfully.

"I guess I'm still on German time."

"Well, I hope you had a good trip. How's your father doing?"

"Thanks for asking, but unfortunately he passed away the day before I got to Cologne."

"Oh, I'm so sorry!"

"That's life I suppose. What's new around here?"

"Ruth Haab and I have kept busy answering requests for addresses. The more complicated requests that we couldn't dispose of ourselves are in those folders." She was quiet for a moment. "You look really tired, Mr. Nitsch. Maybe you should have taken a few more days off after what you've been through."

"Actually, I'm raring to go. Is there anything else I need to know before I attack these folders?"

"I almost forgot. Mr. Ledermann wants to talk to you about an item some German businessman would like to market here. He put the matter on hold until you got back. I'll let you know as soon as he gets in."

Mr. Ledermann arrived promptly at 9 a.m. and, a few minutes later, I joined him in his office. "Miss Block told me about your father. My condolences," he began. "It was cancer, right? He couldn't have been all that old. What a shame."

"He was just sixty-two."

"The same age as me. Sixty-two. Imagine that." He shook his head sadly and stared off into space.

I gave a polite little cough. "Was there some matter you particularly wanted to talk to me about, sir?" I asked in an effort to change the subject.

"Oh, yes, of course. The calendar! About two weeks ago, as a matter of fact it was just after you left for Cologne, the owner of a German printing company wound up in my office looking for a distributor for this." He handed me a twelve-month calendar each page of which was decorated with a charcoal portrait of a different famous African-American. "Tell me, who would want to buy a thing like that?"

I looked at the well-drawn likenesses some of which, such as the ones of Dr. Martin Luther King, Jr., Frederick Douglass, Harriet Tubman, and Louis Armstrong, were familiar to me. I could already think of one person who would like to own a calendar like that. For that matter, I wouldn't mind having one myself, if only because Louis Armstrong's single of "Mack the Knife" had been the very first record I had ever bought. I was just fifteen years old at the time and, when I brought it home, my father had acted as though the world were coming to an end.

"In my opinion," I replied to Mr. Ledermann, "provided the business owner is willing to pay for the necessary advertising then, yes, I'm pretty sure he would find a market for it. But judging from the poor quality of his business card, I'm not sure he's going to be willing to do that."

"But you really think there are people who would hang this thing on their wall?" Mr. Ledermann took back the calendar and flipped to the portrait of Harriet Tubman. "Just look at that ugly mug with her awful Negroid features. She's almost apelike." He shuddered and turned to another page. "Or take this Douglass guy. Have you ever seen anyone so primitive in your life?" I was stunned into silence. "Well, have you?" Mr. Ledermann persisted.

"Frankly, sir, I don't share your opinion. I think they're wonderfully accurate portraits of some really great Americans."

"You surprise me, Mr. Nitsch, but then again you've been up to Harlem more than once, if I remember correctly, so I'll have to take your word for it I suppose. Have Mrs. Haab send the man the addresses of some calendar distributors and contacts to a few trade publications he could advertise in and let's be done with it. That's all for today!"

It took me the better part of the morning to digest what had just happened. I had always had the highest regard for Mr. Ledermann and his hate filled outburst seemed totally out of character. Surely as someone with a Jewish father who somehow managed to survive in the Third Reich, he must have been aware of what ugly stereotypes actually looked like. I couldn't begin to imagine how much he must have been blinded by ignorance, fear and hate in order to view the twelve lovingly drawn portraits in the calendar in that same light.

****

I had expected to stay longer in the office on my first day back but towards 5 p.m. I was so jetlagged that I decided to go home and catch up on my sleep instead. It wasn't meant to be. I had just taken off my coat in my apartment when Victoria called. "Hi, welcome back! Will you be coming over tonight? If you're too exhausted I'd understand, but maybe you can at least tell me a little about your trip on the phone."

Suddenly I was no longer tired. "Give me ten minutes to pick up some pastrami sandwiches at the deli and then I'll be right over."

"So," Victoria said as we munched on our supper a little while later, "you felt good when you held Charlotte's little boy in your arms? You could have one of your own, you know. I'm more than ready to have a baby. What do you say?"

"For heaven's sake, Victoria. We've been over this a million times, but let me say it again. I have no intention of ever getting married and the last thing I need right now is to be tied down with a baby, yours or anyone else's."

"It's just that neither one of us is getting any younger, you know. I won't mention it again."

"Good, then let's talk about something else," and I told her the story about the calendar.

"Come on, Gunter. You should know by now that that's the way most white people in this country think about black people."

"I don't know about most, but I certainly didn't expect it from Ledermann of all people."

"Tell me this. How many employees does the Chamber have?"

"Thirty, give or take."

"And how many of the thirty are African-American? No, let me guess. None, right? So why should you be surprised?"

"You need to speak German to work there," I said lamely.

"And I suppose that's something only white people can do? While we're on the subject, why haven't you ever brought me along to any of your Chamber functions? It's because you must have known I wouldn't be welcome there."

"Well, as long as you bring it up, that's a topic I've been meaning to discuss with you. I've been asking myself why we're doing this to ourselves? Honestly, whenever we're together and people make racist remarks it really gets to me. Sometimes it's almost unbearable. And it can't be any different for you!"

"Hold it right there!" Victoria said. "I'd like to know why you're telling me this *now*? After all these years of our being together, why should our skin color suddenly matter to you?"

"It doesn't matter to *me*, "I said, suddenly unsure how to explain myself without sounding like a racist myself. "But apparently it *does* matter to just about everyone else."

"Well, let me ask you this," Victoria responded. "If you *were* the marrying kind, would you want to marry me or do you think it would it be too much trouble dealing with the consequences?"

I was tired and my guard was down. I decided to hold nothing back. "Since you put it that way, I have to be honest. 'Dealing with the consequences' as you put it would always be difficult for me, but I think I could learn to live with it. It's all the other things that would hold me back."

"Such as?"

"For starters, do you still have more than twenty credit cards?"

"Of course! I need them. Why?"

"Well, it's always bothered me that you buy things, especially books you don't read, and clothes and shoes you really don't need, and you often spend more money than you earn. While we're at it, when I met you, you weighed 120 pounds; now you're up to 150. Yet, whenever I try to persuade you to take up jogging or tennis you've laughed it off. And then there are all the university courses you drop.

When it comes to making positive changes in your life, you're the biggest procrastinator I've ever known!"

"Are you trying to get rid of me?"

"I'm just saying that maybe it's time we thought about going our separate ways."

"I don't know what's come over you, but this is the last time I'll ask you over the day after an overseas flight. Nothing you're telling me is new. So why should we end our relationship now? Race makes a difference to you? I'm not colorblind either. I've often worried that you'd end up marrying some white girl and moving to the suburbs, just because that's what's expected of you. But we both know you belong right here with me, regardless of what anyone thinks. So, no, I don't want us to go our separate ways. I want to be with you and if that bothers other people, that's just too bad. And as for those Chamber receptions you've told me about, with all those white guys cozying up to you just to get business leads, have I really missed anything? I don't think so. So what do you say to all that, Mr. World Traveler?"

Breaking up with Victoria wasn't going to be easy.

CHAPTER 74

*A*s part of my marketing responsibilities for the Chamber, I often attended as many as a dozen receptions a month and, despite what Victoria thought, I always found interesting and unusual people to talk to. Take, for example, the late afternoon gathering for several hundred people hosted by the Frankfurt Trade Fair at the St. Moritz Hotel on Central Park South at the end of February. It was my job to introduce myself to the executives of American subsidiaries of German firms, especially concentrating on those who were newcomers to the New York metropolitan area. Yet, in making the rounds, I also took the time to chat with executives from major firms like Mercedes Benz of North America, BMW, BASF and Siemens as well as with the many lawyers, headhunters, CPAs and consultants I already knew.

There was Dr. Otto Walter, the doyen of the German-speaking lawyers, who, after being disbarred in Nazi Germany because of his religion, immigrated to the United States. Starting over from scratch, he eventually founded his own enormously successful firm where many of the young German-speaking lawyers now working in Manhattan had gotten their start.

On the far side of the room, chatting with the German Consul, was Dr. Ernst Stiefel, who had the unique distinction of being admitted to the practice of law in four jurisdictions: New York, Düsseldorf, London and Paris. Dr. Stiefel was another refugee from Hitler's oppression. Despite his extraordinary educational background in Germany, he had started off in New York working as a lowly restaurant dishwasher, eventually becoming a brilliant writer and orator as well as one of the most prominent attorneys in both the United States and in his native Germany. His law firm represented some of the largest German corporations in the United States.

Sipping a glass of Blue Nun wine near the open bar was Fritz Weinschenk, an attorney who frequently traveled to the Federal Court in Düsseldorf to represent American Holocaust survivors at the trials of former SS officers and concentration camp commandants. At first very businesslike and reserved in his dealings with me, in recent months Mr. Weinschenk had become much friendlier after assuring himself that I had only been seven years old when World War II had ended.

Just the opposite was true of Peter Sichel, the German American wine merchant and a regular guest at Chamber functions, who had created the highly successful Blue Nun brand. As far as I could tell, Mr. Sichel, who at the moment was talking with an executive from BASF, never really warmed up to me or to anyone else at these affairs. It was rumored that after Peter Sichel had fled Nazi persecution and come to the United States at the beginning of World War II, he had worked for many years for the CIA in Germany after the war. That might have explained the invisible wall he cautiously put up between himself and whichever person he was talking to.

After saying hello to Mr. Weinschenk, I also spoke briefly to Hans Ullstein, an executive recruiter with one of the largest American executive search firms. He was a member of the family that founded the Ullstein Verlag back in 1877. At one time one of the largest publishing firms in Germany, the company had been temporarily 'aryanized' during the war years. Mr. Ullstein, a handsome man who looked younger than his age, had a talent for biting sarcasm. "So, Mr. Nitsch," he greeted me. "How are you? Aren't these receptions all the same? Too many predators and not enough prey!"

Just then someone off to my right called out, "Gunter, how are you?" It was Mrs. Sonnenburg's acquaintance, George Perau. He pulled me aside and looked around to make sure no one was listening. Then he put his arm around my shoulder before he spoke. "Amalia got back from her ski trip last night." He lowered his voice still further. "Say, you've been seeing each other for almost a year now, haven't you? So, not that it is any of my business, but do you two have any plans to tie the knot? She'd be quite a catch you know." Then he winked at me and wandered off. *What an idiot*, I thought, *I wonder if Amalia put him up to this.*

Suddenly I spotted Mr. Joseph Holzkopp, a marketing executive with an American Fortune 500 company. Standing a smidge under 5'5" and squinting through eyeglasses as thick as the bottom of a milk bottle, he had a full head of blond, stringy hair parted on the right side. Mr. Holzkopp had taken me to lunch in upscale restaurants a few times over the past two years to pick my brains about German business ventures and I had always found him to be a brilliant conversationalist albeit with decidedly conservative political views. Still, if all of what Rolf Klingenberg had told me was true, there was evidently more to Mr. Holzkopp than met the eye.

"Holzkopp?" Rolf had said when I first mentioned the name. "He's one of a kind. Or at least I hope he is. He was born in the U.S. to German parents and he speaks German like a native. Get this! After working in Argentina for a while, he spent twenty years working in

Franco's Spain. He's a great admirer of Franco by the way. But here's the really crazy part. Soon after Hitler came to power, he rushed over to Germany to join the Nazi special security force, the SS."

"He did WHAT?"

"You heard me right. Anyway, the irony is that the Nazis turned him down and he still bears a grudge about it."

I walked over to greet Mr. Holzkopp. "Oh, Mr. Nitsch, how nice to see you! Finally someone I can talk to. Doesn't it bother you that so many shysters come to these functions? Vermin, all of them! That's what they are! Vermin!"

"Pardon me, Mr. Holzkopp, but whom exactly do you mean?" I asked with pretended ignorance.

"Never mind that now. It's not so important. Here's what I really wanted to tell you. I've been meaning to invite you to my home every since we met. Would you be free to come visit me and meet my family? I was thinking of Saturday April first; that's the day before Easter Sunday. I could pick you up at the Staten Island ferry landing, say around two o'clock?" My curiosity having been long peaked about this strange little man, I was quick to accept his invitation.

A moment later all conversation stopped as Mr. Ledermann made a short presentation on behalf of the Trade Fair. When he was finished, the attendees rushed over to the two large buffet tables to help themselves to cold salmon and dill sauce, grilled chicken and tuna steaks, salads, bread and a variety of French cheeses. While piling food on my plate, I discussed the differences in corporate culture in Germany and the United States with Heidi Wagner, a junior executive from Siemens. The longer I talked with her, the more I liked her. "Say," I said, "since we have so much to talk about, would you like to continue our conversation on Saturday over dinner?"

"I'm going to have to turn you down," she said. "It's not that I don't like you, I do. But I just broke up with someone I have been seeing for the past two years and the last thing I need right now is to get involved with someone new. Besides, the transfer I requested back to Siemens headquarters in Germany just came through and I'll be leaving New York soon. But, listen! I'm heading home and since we both live on the Upper West Side, perhaps we can share a cab."

"Sure why not?"

We got our coats and waited together at the curb for a few minutes until we got into a taxi. The driver dropped Heidi off on Central Park West and 72nd Street, and I continued on in the cab, disappointed and alone, all the way up to West End and 104th.

****

Around 9 p.m. the following evening, my phone rang. It was Amalia who immediately gave me a stern tongue-lashing. Her voice was icy and shrill. "Now you listen to me, Gunter, because I'm not going to beat around the bush. Who was that young blond woman you went home with last night? How could you see someone else behind my back I'd like to know? And I thought I could trust you while I was away!"

My mind was racing. It could only have been George Perau! He must have seen Heidi and me get into the cab in front of the hotel after the reception. *What a sleazebag, tattling on me like that!* But then I caught myself. *Hold on a minute. Don't blame Perau, you idiot. Thank him instead. He's given you the opening you need.*

"Amalia, I'm really shocked that you have people spying on me. It was bad enough that you called me when I got home on Sunday nights

383

after we spent the weekend together. Let's face it. You've never trusted me. Every time you phoned, it was like I had a second mother."

"I just . . ."

"No, you have to hear me out! We are not married and I have no obligation to you. So, as far as I am concerned, I can date anyone I want, and that includes that 'young blonde' as you so crassly put it." Then, for good measure, I decided to rub it in. "She's beautiful and only twenty-five years old."

"Are you finished?" she asked. She was sobbing.

"I guess so, yes."

"I had no idea . . ." When she started to cry again, I hung up on her.

More phone calls followed over the next few days. Feigning righteous indignation, I slammed down the receiver each time. *Lucky for me*, I thought, *that Amalia never found out about Victoria. My long-term relationship with her would have been much harder to explain away.*

Then, a week later, I found a handwritten ten-page letter in my mailbox forgiving me for my alleged transgression (how I wished something had actually taken place!) and pleading with me to get back in touch. I ignored her letter as well.

Finally George Perau called me to try to get me to change my mind. But I stood my ground. "Listen to me, Gunter. Don't be so stubborn. Do you really know what you're giving up? I'm sure Amalia wouldn't want me to share this with you, but from what I've heard she's got at least $2,500,000 in the bank and she stands to inherit the house in Bedford and half of her mother's fortune when Mrs. Sonnenburg dies. Knowing all that, won't you consider changing your mind?"

How ironic. When I was sixteen years old, Mutti's cousin Helmut had shared another piece of wisdom with me. *"Never forget,"* he had advised, *"that you don't have to work for the money you marry!"* I had laughed about his remark at the time but now I knew better. "You're wasting your time, George. That argument doesn't cut it with me. You didn't have to tell me she was rich. Quite frankly, her wealth was one of the things that bothered me about our relationship."

When George Perau started to argue again, I hung up the phone and dialed Victoria's number to ask if I could come over.

****

"It's good that you called," Victoria said. "I've been trying to reach you. We've got to talk."

This didn't bode well. "Give me two minutes, okay?"

A stack of flattened corrugated boxes lay on the floor of Victoria's studio apartment near the window next to several rolls of masking tape. Other boxes, filled, labeled, and taped shut, stood against one wall in front of the empty bookcase. "What's this all about?" I asked, although the answer was self-evident.

Victoria moved a heap of her clothing to one side of the couch so that I could sit down. "Here's the thing," she said. She had rarely sounded so serious. "My sister, Eve, has been warning me from the minute she met you that you weren't going to marry me."

"We didn't exactly hit it off at that hospital picnic, did we, your sister and I?"

"Don't try to change the subject. The fact is that Eve was right. Listen, we've been together for nearly five years now and, in all that time, I haven't so much as looked at another man. But I'm tired of waiting for you to pop the question." Jeanine had once used almost the same words when she broke up with me. She just hadn't waited quite so long to do it. "It's never going to happen, is it? Well, is it?"

"Why bring this up now when we've already been over the same thing so many times? You knew I'd seen other women. I've told you I'm never getting married. Is it my fault that you chose not to believe me? You're not being fair."

"Well, if you really want to know, Eve has been hounding me for years to make a clean break of things. She's invited me to move in with her where she lives up near the hospital. And that's exactly what I've decided to do."

And, I guess people are right when they say, "Be careful what you wish for," because, just like that, I went from dating two women at once, to having no one at all.

CHAPTER 75

Most of the American visitors who came to see me at the German American Chamber of Commerce were down to earth, hardworking business people, but occasionally I was caught off guard. Every so often it was a case of mistaken identity.

"Hey, Mr. Nitsch," one man asked me. "Did you ever watch the TV show *Sea Hunt*?"

"Can't say I have, why?"

"'Cause you look just like that Lloyd Bridges fellow who starred in it. You're not related to him by any chance are you?"

Or there were those who were sure I had participated in World War II. After all, those visitors insisted, I was the spitting image of the German soldiers they had seen in the movies. So I must have been involved somehow, right? No matter that I was only a small child during the war.

But the oddest of them all was the businessman from Pensacola, Florida, who was convinced that he had met me when I was in a POW camp in North Africa in 1944.

"And why was I in that camp?" I deadpanned.

"Don't you remember? You were in the Luftwaffe and our boys shot you down. Gee, Mr. Nitsch," he added, when he saw my puzzled expression, "I wish I hadn't brought this up since you've evidently tried to block the whole thing out."

Then there was the banker from Jackson, Mississippi who hoped to entice German companies to relocate to his city. "You'd fit right in down there, Mr. Nitsch," he assured me. "New York is no place for someone like you. Find yourself a job with a nice German subsidiary down our way! Believe me, your quality of life would improve 100% overnight."

After everything I had heard from Victoria about the South, I decided to put the man to the test. "But do you really think a foreigner like me would be accepted in Jackson? Suppose, for instance, I wanted to join a country club down there. Would there be any objections?"

"Coming from Germany like you do, I guarantee you'd be accepted with open arms. It would be different, of course, if you were a Nigger or a Hebe. They wouldn't stand a chance of getting in, thank God." He leaned forward in his chair conspiratorially. "But I'm sure you wouldn't want to have people like that around either. Right?" I found an excuse to end our meeting shortly after that.

****

This is not to say that some of the West German businessmen I dealt with weren't just as challenging. Sometimes it was a matter of what they planned to do. One day it might be a letter requesting the Chamber's help in setting up a brothel in Alaska. Another day it was a firm claiming that its line of angora underwear would alleviate the pain of arthritis. Then there was the bikini bathing suit made of edible red licorice. And how could I forget the pink toothbrush with a handle shaped like a naked woman?

Even when businessmen had worthwhile products to market, I watched time after time as their jaws dropped when I mentioned the hourly rates charged by German-speaking attorneys and CPAs in New York City. And as soon as I mentioned that the fee would be 40 to 50% of the first year's annual salary, my suggestion that they use an executive recruiting firm to hire their top staff often fell on deaf ears. Then, half a year later, the same businessman, now greatly humbled, would return to my office.

"I wish we had followed your advice in the first place, Mr. Nitsch," instead of trying to do things the German way," would be the usual contrite refrain. "We published ads in *The New York Times*, *The Wall Street Journal* and two or three American trade publications for a fraction of the cost of an executive recruiting firm and got hundreds of replies. Not a single one met our specifications. May I have another copy of the list of executive recruiters please?"

Speaking of lists, there still was the occasional businessman who rejected the list of attorneys I offered him because the names "sounded too Jewish." For people like that, my response was always the same. They were unceremoniously shown the door. The ultimate visitor of this caliber was the owner of a textile mill from the Stuttgart area who began by softening me up with his life story.

"Would you believe we've had to set up our business three different times? My father founded the company in East Prussia. That's where you are from too, I understand. Am I right, Mr. Nitsch? Well, then I suppose you know first hand how all hell broke loose there when the Russians came in 1945? But long before all that happened, my father had the foresight to pack everything up and move the mill to Chemnitz. What a mistake that was! Who'd have thought the Soviets would end up controlling that area? And no one can make a success of things under a Communist regime. So we moved again. Now that we're in Stuttgart, business is going so well that I've already set up a sales office in New York City."

"That's pretty impressive," I said. "So how can I help you?"

He put down the pen he had been holding, leaned towards me, and cleared his throat. "I desperately need to hire an experienced sales rep for New England and I'm willing to pay a high salary plus a decent sales commission."

"Well in that case I can recommend some executive recruiters. With such generous terms it should be easy for them to find the right person for you."

"It's a bit more complicated than that," he said. "I want your advice about how to make sure I hire an Aryan for the position?"

"Come again?"

"Look, let me be frank. I didn't find out until after I hired the man to run my New York office that he was a Jew. I certainly don't want to make the same mistake twice. If I start out right away with an Aryan, I'll know things are in good hands. You do understand where I'm coming from, don't you Mr. Nitsch?"

I got out of my chair and folded my arms across my chest. "I understand exactly where you're coming from and I cannot say that I like it. How can anyone talk about wanting to hire an 'Aryan' in the year 1972? That obnoxious term has long since been relegated to the history books. In any case, I cannot help you and I'm asking you to leave. Good day!"

"Quite frankly, Mr. Nitsch, your attitude shocks me. I thought I could have an open and honest discussion with you as one East Prussian to another." The veins in the man's forehead throbbed with anger.

"I repeat. The subject is closed!" I said sternly as I towered over him. With great reluctance my elderly visitor rose from his chair, collected his hat and coat and, muttering angrily to himself, he left my office.

CHAPTER 76

*T*here wasn't a single black student in my Pace College MBA program and, as far as I could tell from the names, there were hardly any Jews. It was ironic, then, that one of my best professors, Dr. Jack Schiff, let us know about his German-Jewish background, and Dr. Tony Bonaparte, the Dean of the Graduate Business School, came from Trinidad. Both Dr. Bonaparte and Dr. Schiff constantly drummed into us the importance of public speaking. As Dr. Bonaparte put it, "Gentlemen, you should use every possible opportunity to give a presentation. Being smart and having ideas is not enough in a corporation these days. You have to be able to communicate in front of an audience."

To make us more comfortable speaking in public, Dr. Schiff regularly had each of us give a short oral presentation to the class on a subject of our choice. Naturally, most of us chose to talk about relevant topics such as product development, marketing strategies, and advertising campaigns. Not Joe Molitor. On that particular Thursday evening, Joe walked to the front of the room, glared out at us defiantly, and announced, "My topic tonight is 'Why I Hate Niggers.'"

One of my classmates shouted out, "Are you out of your mind?" Then we all waited in stunned silence for Dr. Schiff's reaction.

Dr. Schiff tapped his pencil on his desk for a moment or two, deep in thought. Then he said, "That's an interesting choice of topic, Mr. Molitor. I'm sure we'd all like to hear what you have to say. Please proceed."

For the next five long minutes Joe spewed forth every ugly stereotype you can imagine. Blacks are lazy; they keep having babies out of wedlock; they live off public assistance; they're all criminals, and on and on and on. When his time was up, Joe looked out at the class. "Any questions?" When no one spoke up, he stomped back to his seat.

Again we turned to Dr. Schiff. "How nice of you to share your opinions with us, Mr. Molitor. I see that you've made quite an impression on the class," he said with more than his usual touch of irony. Then, without further comment, he looked down at his class list. "Now, let me see, who's up next to speak." I was glad it wasn't me. Joe Molitor would be a hard act to follow.

****

Dr. Chan, who also taught marketing, had received both his bachelor's degree and his doctorate from Columbia University, after immigrating to the United States from his native China. He kept us entertained by comparing stories of remarkably successful product launches, such as the introduction of Doritos in 1966, with those that failed, such as the disastrous launch of the ill-fated Ford Edsel ten years earlier. Dr. Chan had gotten his own start in business during his sophomore year in college.

As he explained, "I soon noticed that many of my fellow students often needed to take as many as five expensive taxi rides to move from one apartment to another and, even then, they still had to hire the services of a moving company for their larger pieces of furniture. Figuring I could do a better job, I leased a Ryder truck and hired some big, strong guys from the wrestling team and the football team to do the heavy lifting. Then I put up flyers all over campus promising that I could do the job at a really competitive rate. Before long, we were busy moving students, not only from Columbia, but also from other New York City schools. After a few months, I'd made enough money to lease four more trucks. I don't mean to boast, but eventually my moving business was so successful that it took up way too much of my time. That's when I sold the whole operation for a good price to a couple of my classmates. And that, gentlemen, is how I learned how to make money!"

Suddenly Dr. Chan looked at his watch and said, "I see that our time is almost up and there's another story I'd like to share with some of you. If any of you have time, I hope you'll join me for a beer. As usual, the first round will be on me." Fifteen minutes later, the seven of us who didn't have to catch a train to the suburbs regrouped in Dr. Chan's favorite bar, not far from our classroom building.

"What I'm about to tell you is a little bit unorthodox," Dr. Chan said once we had all sat down. "But it shows what can happen when you use your noodle. While I was still working on my PhD, a manufacturer in Taiwan offered to sell me inexpensive shoes that I could then resell for double or triple the price in the United States. But the problem was that the import duty that would be imposed on each pair was so steep that there wouldn't be any profit in it. But, what's the American expression? There's more than one way to skin a cat? Well, I did my homework and I found out that there's no import duty on samples. So what did I do? I had the manufacturer in Taiwan ship 2,000 left shoes as samples to San Francisco and the matching 2,000 right shoes as samples to New York. Once the merchandise on both coasts cleared customs, I had the shoes from San Francisco trucked to a warehouse in Brooklyn. And after that it was simply a matter of paying minimum wage to a few recently arrived Chinese immigrants who put the pairs back together." He leaned back in his seat and finished off his glass of beer before continuing. "I won't tell you how much money I made on that deal, but I'm pretty sure I was the wealthiest doctoral candidate in all of Columbia University at that time."

"But didn't you take a risk?" one of my classmates asked.

"Of course I did. That's the only way to get ahead in this world. The bigger the risk, the bigger the reward, I always say."

Three of my classmates and I talked over Dr. Chan's story as we rode uptown together on the subway after leaving the bar. The man had guts. We agreed on that. But, we all concluded that for each of us, no matter what Dr. Chan had claimed, the reward would not have been worth the risk.

CHAPTER 77

O n Saturday, April 1, 1972, I was about to enter the 96th Street subway station on my way to visit Mr. Holzkopp's family when, by chance, I ran into Jeanine, whom I had not seen since her wedding. "Jeanine! How are you?" I asked. "It's been quite a while. How's married life treating you?"

"I guess you haven't heard," she said. "About a year ago Giorgo was teaching history in a high school in the South Bronx. That was his life dream, you know, to teach history." Her voice trailed off for a moment. "Anyway, there was this Negro girl in the class. Grossly overweight, lazy, foul-mouthed, nothing like the Haitian girls I knew growing up. She hadn't done her homework, and when Giorgio criticized her she broke off a chair leg and beat him to a pulp while the other students looked on and cheered."

"How awful!"

"When I saw him in the hospital, he looked so terrible I was sure he was going to die. They kept him there for six weeks! Six weeks, can you imagine? Once he recovered, he quit his teaching job. He couldn't face going back. Can you blame him? Anyway, right now he's studying accounting at Baruch College at night and working for an accounting firm during the day."

"I'm awfully sorry about what happened, but you must be relieved that Giorgio switched jobs."

She beamed. "Yes, and aside from not risking his neck every day, he is making a whole lot more money now than he ever did as a teacher."

"Well, it was good seeing you; give Giorgio my regards. Oh, I almost forgot to ask. How are your sisters doing?

"Martine just got back from Haiti, the first time she ever went back. She's still working at her old job. Teddy's in school and Jacqueline's also studying at Baruch College. Let's keep in touch!" She held my shoulders for a second and turned so I could give her a peck on the cheek. The aroma of her expensive perfume wafted over me as she said good-bye. "*Adieu, mon chéri! À bientôt!*"

****

Squinting through his thick lenses like the nearsighted Mr. Magoo, Mr. Holzkopp was waiting for me at the Staten Island ferry landing. It was only when I was standing directly in front of him that he recognized me. Smiling broadly, he reached over to shake my hand as vigorously as if my arm were the wooden handle on an old-fashioned pump. We walked out together to his car. Hunched forward over the steering wheel of his shiny black Mercedes, Mr. Holzkopp peered through the windshield as we crept along at a steady fifteen mph as other cars passed us on the left.

"I've been looking forward to your visit, Mr. Nitsch, and I especially want you to meet my daughter, Frieda. For someone with so much to offer, I can't understand why she has gotten herself

397

involved with a longhaired hippy. You must have run into people like that, dripping in beads and acting cool. I can't stand the guy and I sometimes think she's dating him just to irritate me. Frankly, and I don't mean to put you on the spot or anything, but I was hoping if she met someone with your good German upbringing, it would knock some sense into her pretty little head."

Since I hardly knew how to respond to Mr. Holzkopp's comments, I just listened politely. The visit was hardly off to a good start. It would only get worse, as I would soon discover.

The Holzkopp family's solid brick ranch house stood at the crest of a steep hill. The large bay windows in the living room provided an unobstructed view of lower Manhattan on the other side of New York Bay. Opposite the windows, hundreds of books on World War II in English, German and Spanish filled a massive mahogany bookcase.

"Ah!" Mr. Holzkopp exclaimed. "Here she is! Let me introduce you to the lady of the house."

A short, plump, morose, careworn little woman with untidy gray hair, Mrs. Holzkopp was wearing a black skirt, a white blouse and a food-stained apron. If she had been presented to me as Mr. Holzkopp's mother rather than his wife, I wouldn't have been the least surprised. "Nice to meet you Mr. Nitsch," she said in a voice so flat that she could hardly mean it.

"Frieda!" Mr. Holzkopp called out. "Come meet our guest!"

Except for her short stature (she couldn't have been more than 4'11"), Mr. Holzkopp's daughter was her mother's exact opposite. She was a vivacious, beautiful young woman with a radiant smile, a firm handshake, perfectly symmetrical features, and thick, chestnut brown braids twisted into an elegant chignon.

"I hope you'll excuse us, Mr. Nitsch," Frieda said. "My mother and I are getting things ready in the kitchen."

"While the gals are at work, there are some books I want to show you," Mr. Holzkopp said. "Wait here a minute if you don't mind and I'll be right back." A few minutes later he returned, carrying three books. "These are so valuable that I keep them locked up in the desk in my study," he explained. "*Mein Kampf* in German and in English are both first editions. And this is probably one of the only copies of *Der Lehrplan* you will ever see. It is more or less impossible to buy one anywhere." He handed me the booklet. "Are you familiar with it? It is the curriculum for the ideological education of the SS and the police."

"No sir, I can't say that I've ever heard of it."

"Should I lend it to you?"

I flipped through the roughly eighty pages, many of them decorated with the oversized thunderbolt insignia of the SS. "Thanks, Mr. Holzkopp, but I think I'll pass. I'm really not all that interested in the topic and, besides, I wouldn't want to take the responsibility of borrowing such a valuable item."

"I understand," he said with evident disappointment. "But just so you know, once I'm retired I plan to translate this little manual into English. That way Americans will be able to appreciate what it took to turn young men from all over Europe into the most effective fighting force the world has ever seen. *Meine Ehre heisst Treue.* My Honor is Loyalty. I love the sound of it, don't you? You can't have a better motto than that."

He would surely have gone on in the same vein if his wife had not called us both into the dining room. On an embroidered damask tablecloth, the table was set with elegant porcelain cups and saucers, cake plates with delicate, hand-painted floral designs, and small, sterling silver forks and spoons. In the center of the table next to a large silver coffee pot were two kinds of pie, a bowl of freshly whipped cream, and a container of Breyer's vanilla ice cream. "I see you're admiring the tablecloth," Mrs. Holzkopp said with sudden enthusiasm. "It's beautiful, isn't it? Years ago we bought half a dozen of them for practically nothing in Portugal, all with different handmade designs. And, in case you're wondering, our dishes are Rosenthal from prewar Germany. I love being surrounded by elegant things. But enough about that, please have a seat before the ice cream melts."

"You know, I suppose, that Rosenthal was founded by Jews?" Mr. Holzkopp asked me.

"Please don't get started on that," Mrs. Holzkopp begged.

"Don't interrupt me, dear. You know, Mr. Nitsch, when it comes to the Jews, I'm a tolerant man. Let me put it this way. If there were a big explosion and all of the Negroes in the world were to suddenly disappear, no one would miss them, but the same wouldn't be true of the Jews. It goes without saying that most of them are vermin, but I really hate to admit it, some Jews have actually made worthwhile contributions to society. Not many, mind you, but enough so that people would notice if they were gone."

Mrs. Holzkopp spoke up. "Come on Karl, do we have to talk about that? I know Frieda would want to hear about Mr. Nitsch's experience working fulltime and going to Pace at night. Wouldn't you, dear? Frieda is doing the same right now, teaching during the day and attending Wagner College in the evening."

"Yes, but I'm seriously considering quitting my job and going fulltime for a Master's or possibly for a PhD."

"That would make me proud," her father said. "With your brains you should be teaching at a college level and not wasting your time with those little brats in elementary school. Say, here's an idea. Since you two young people have so much to talk about, why don't you take Gunter on a long walk, while your mother and I clean up in the kitchen?"

Had I heard right? Had Mr. Holzkopp just called me by my first name? He must already see me as his future son-in-law. *Not so fast, Mr. Holzkopp,* I thought. *Not so fast.*

Once Frieda and I left the house and were out of earshot, she turned to me. "Gunter, first of all I want to apologize that my father has such wacky ideas about World War II, blacks and Jews. Just between you and me, there's no stopping him once he gets going. I have listened to this stuff all my life and I know he's not going to change. The other thing is a little harder to bring up. My father really likes you and has talked about you for quite some time. You see how he's trying to throw the two of us together, don't you? What he doesn't want to accept is that I have a boyfriend whom I dearly love."

"He's not too subtle about it, is he? But you needn't worry. I already have a girlfriend. You know, Frieda, you're very pretty and you have a great personality, but even if the two of us were unattached, and putting aside the fact that I'm twelve years older than you, the difference in our heights alone would make us a bad match."

She blushed. "Thanks, I'm glad we cleared that up. Let's take a walk!"

An hour later, while Frieda and her mother prepared supper, Mr. Holzkopp filled two steins with Beck's beer. Then he switched to German. "That dishwater the Americans call beer has nothing on this," he said. "I only drink imports. Prost!"

"Prost, Mr. Holzkopp!"

"You know, it breaks my heart that your generation only knows the distorted history of the Second World War that they get from scumbag Jewish writers. Do any of them ever bother to mention the unbearable conditions the Allies forced down the Germans' throats in 1918? Of course not. Mark my words, Gunter, one day the world will come to its senses and realize that Hitler's only goal was to protect Christian

Europe from the forces of Jewish-inspired communism." I had hoped he was finished but, unfortunately, he was just warming up.

"Thousands of books describe what the Germans allegedly did to the Jews, but who is willing to talk about the fact that the Jews had already taken over Germany by dominating the legal profession, the press, the left wing political parties, banking and retailing? Did you know that by the early nineteen-thirties, over eighty percent of all lawyers in the big German cities were Jews? And who's willing to write about the worldwide boycott of German goods that Jewish groups started in 1933? No one, that's who.

"Which brings me to the subject of the Holocaust. That six million figure is pure hogwash. And as to those who died in the camps, like I said, it's my opinion that they brought it on themselves. There's no two ways about it." He leaned towards me. "What most Americans have not yet recognized is that the Jews are doing the same thing to this country that the German Jews did to Germany. And, mark my words, it's only a matter of time before Americans wake up and say, 'Enough is enough!' Then all hell is going to break loose. But there will be one big difference. Unlike Germany where it took years to get rid of those parasites, we will do it here in a fraction of the time, since all God-fearing Americans are already armed to the teeth. God! I hope I live long enough to see it!"

I was speechless! I had had about as much of Mr. Holzkopp as I could take. *Perhaps*, I thought, *I could claim that I didn't feel well and had to go home.* But I missed my chance to escape. "Okay, the two of you," Mrs. Holzkopp announced from the entrance to the living room, "please join us. Supper is ready!" Reluctantly I followed Mr. Holzkopp into the dining room.

Normally I would have enjoyed the Hungarian goulash, red cabbage, and mashed potatoes that Frieda and her mother had prepared. But, all things considered, I was lucky I was able to force the food down. To my relief, there was no mention of a vast Jewish conspiracy during the meal. Instead, while we were eating dessert, Mr. Holzkopp found a roundabout way to return to the subject of graduate school.

"Just like they said in *The Godfather*, I'm about to make Frieda an offer she can't refuse." He turned to his daughter. "Listen, Frieda, if you quit your job and matriculate fulltime, I'm going to replace that piece of junk you've been driving around in with a brand new Porsche."

Frieda beamed "Do you really mean it? You've got a deal!"

"I don't have to tell you, Gunter, that the Porsche is the high-speed car driven by the German police on the Autobahn. You know, it's simply legendary what Germany made of itself after its cities and infrastructure were pulverized by senseless Allied carpet bombing."

By this time, I understood Mr. Holzkopp well enough to know that he was about to fire off another broadside. "Sorry to interrupt," I said, "but I have some studying to do so I really have to get back home. Thank you both so much for your hospitality." It came as no surprise when Frieda was asked to drive me to the ferry slip.

"He doesn't give up, does he?" she said when she dropped me off. "I hope you don't think any of the hateful stuff my father was spewing rubbed off on me."

"No, of course not. I really like you as a person and I wish you all the best."

"Same here," she said. "I also hope you don't think I sold out about the Porsche. I'll never get another chance like that. And, Gunter," she called after me as I turned to enter the ferry terminal, "thanks again for being so understanding."

CHAPTER 78

Right after the semester at Pace ended in June, I took a seaplane from Miami to the Island of Bimini where I boarded the *Yankee Clipper* for a ten day Windjammer cruise in the Bahamas. The sleek sailing ship, which had once been owned by the Vanderbilt family, had a highly skilled captain who had the thankless job of presiding over an inept thirty-man crew, many of whom were Vietnam veterans with little or no sailing experience. The food on board wasn't fancy, but it was hearty and plentiful.

Nearly all of my fifty-five fellow passengers were young married couples. And even when it came to the few single women on board, I had little chance of finding someone new. Because the air conditioning in our cabins didn't work, most of us slept on deck in sleeping bags, all lined up like sardines in a giant can. This arrangement, understandably, was hardly conducive to romance.

We usually sailed during the day, anchoring at night in some small port on one of the many Bahamian islands. In the morning before breakfast about a dozen of us would swim around the ship three to five times in the choppy salt water. Breakfast always tasted better after that.

Most days I spent many hours sitting alone in the crow's nest. From there, depending on the wind, I would either be leaning way out over the deep blue water of the Caribbean or snapping photos of the shapely girls in tiny colorful bikinis sunbathing directly below me on deck. It was from my vantage point on the crow's nest as we slowly drifted along on one hot nearly windless afternoon that I observed three waterspouts on the horizon. Far below me on deck, the captain was also nervously observing those twirling pipes of water through his binoculars. But, apart from this near brush with disaster at sea, the days passed in lazy relaxation and I returned to New York nicely tanned and as unattached as I had been when I left.

****

Victoria phoned me a few days later. "Guess what? I'm no longer living with my sister."

"Actually, I'm not surprised. You and Eve never did have much in common."

"It wasn't that so much as her smoking four packs of cigarettes a day. I had to get out of there before I choked to death. Anyway, I just wanted to let you know that I've moved into a hippy commune on West 85th Street near Riverside Drive."

"Really? Well, that's certainly a change. So tell me. What's life like in this hippy commune of yours?"

"I heard about the place from one of the other teachers at Head Start. There are twelve of us altogether, two to a room in an old brownstone building. It doesn't matter who your roommate is, although mine happens to be a girl. No one much cares either way. We all have jobs during the day and most of us also take courses at night. Everybody chips in for food and everyone take turns doing the cooking. We have the most interaction with each other over dinner."

"And you like it there?"

"Well, I'm willing to give it a try. But so far, so good. It beats living alone."

"I'm glad it's working out for you."

"But wait! I haven't told you about the best part of the house. There's a large sauna in the basement and, in the middle of the same room, there's a tiny, 8-foot deep rectangular pool filled with ice-cold water. There's just enough room on the low stone wall around the pool for all twelve of us to sit down."

"So I suppose everyone jumps in the pool after they've been in the sauna, like they do in Europe?"

"Yes, that's what most people do. Of course I never go in because it would ruin my hair."

"It all sounds pretty wild."

"It's not completely chaotic. There are some rules we have to follow. For instance, you have to take a shower before you can sit on the stone wall but that's only because everyone who comes down to the basement is naked as a jaybird."

"I assume Eve hasn't visited you there?"

"Of course not. She'd faint dead away if she saw the place. But listen, Gunter, I was wondering. Even though you and I aren't dating any more, we're still friends. Right? So would you like to come over and try the sauna some time?"

"Sure, why not! I'm game!"

"How about Friday evening? It would be nice if you could bring a bottle of Chianti to go with the spaghetti and meatballs we'll probably be having. But be sure to leave your swim trunks at home."

****

Victoria introduced me to the group as 'an old friend' and left it at that. As we sat, either on an assortment of mismatched chairs or cross-legged on the floor, eating our spaghetti dinner, I studied the other occupants of the house, all but two of whom were in their twenties or early thirties. Most of the young women had long flowing hair. Most of the men sported bushy, unkempt beards. I wondered what kind of day jobs they had, but didn't dare ask.

Once the dishes had been cleared, washed, and put away, Victoria brought me up to her room where her roommate, a curvy young woman wearing nothing but eyeglasses, stood bare-breasted with a towel slung over her hips.

"Hey! Thanks for the wine," she said before heading down to the sauna. "I hope you'll come more often."

A few minutes later, clad only in towels, Victoria and I joined nine others in the basement where, it was immediately apparent, the towels were for sitting on and not for covering up.

After spending ten minutes sweating in the sauna, everyone took turns jumping, one at a time, into the icy water. Everyone, that is, except Victoria, who didn't dare let a drop of water touch her neatly coiffed Afro.

As the evening wore on and, one by one, people headed back to their rooms, I found myself alone in the basement with a tall young woman. She had an hourglass figure and long curly hair. Standing there stark naked as I was, my attraction to her couldn't have been more obvious. But knowing that Victoria was right upstairs, I did what

I supposed was the gentlemanly thing to do under the circumstances. I jumped back into the pool and submerged myself in the frigid water to cool down in the truest sense of the word. By the time I climbed back out of the pool, both she and my chances were gone.

CHAPTER 79

"**I** really need to meet someone," I complained to Peter Vollmann as the two of us headed to the West End Bar for breakfast after our Saturday morning tennis match. It had been five long months since Victoria had broken up with me.

"I know just the thing," Peter said. "I heard that there's going to be a mixer for tall people at the Roosevelt Hotel next Friday evening. Give it a try!"

Figuring I had nothing to lose, I took Peter's advice. As usual at these events, there was a surplus of women, some of whom, despite heavy layers of makeup, still looked old enough to be my mother. At previous mixers I had always taken a few minutes to look everyone over before making my move. But, that night, among so many men and women who towered over me, I had to change my tactics. So, putting on my most charming smile, I waded into the crowd. All around me I could hear the same questions asked over and over.

"How tall are you?"

"6'9"."

"So you must play basketball, right?"

"How tall are you?"

409

"Nearly seven feet."

"And you never played basketball? Really? Are you sure?"

Just as the orchestra struck up a slow waltz I noticed a woman who was nearly my height. She had a narrow face, prominent cheekbones, and shoulder-length blond hair. I introduced myself and asked her for a dance.

She flashed me a smile and we stepped out onto the dance floor. "With a name like Gunter, I suppose you must be German," she said.

"Yes, I am. And you are?"

"Barbara Sattenstein. You know, I thought you were German even before you asked me for a dance because you're tall and blond."

"So are you."

"I helped a little; my hair is actually brown." After a moment's hesitation, she went on, "This may be an awkward question, but were you in the German Army during World War II?"

When will people stop asking me that? "No, because I was only seven when the war ended."

"Oh, then you're a little younger than I am. Forgive me for asking all these questions, but do you live with your mother?"

Now I had to laugh. "I beg your pardon? Of course not. My mother lives in Cologne, Germany! Why do you ask?"

She blushed. "Some time ago I dated someone your age who lived with his mother. It was nothing but a nightmare."

Spare me the details, I thought, and I quickly changed the subject. "I work for the German American Chamber of Commerce. You?"

"I'm a buyer in the garment district for a wholesaler who handles a line of Pierre Cardin suits."

"You know, it's funny that you thought I was German because when I saw you I wondered if you were French. Has anyone ever told you that you look a lot like the French pop singer Françoise Hardy?

Her hit 'Tous les garçons et les filles' was popular in Europe a year or so before I left Cologne."

"I've never even heard of her."

"Now I have a totally different question."

"You want to know how tall I am, right? I'm 5"11' in my stocking feet and, to be honest, I've always had a complex about my height, ever since I was in my teens. It beats me why some women wear high heels to look taller. I'd rather take off a few inches if I could."

When the mixer ended, Barbara invited me over to her place for a glass of wine. She lived in a one-bedroom apartment on East 28th Street, a six-minute taxi ride from the Roosevelt Hotel. Stepping into someone's living room could tell me a lot about a person. Just to take two examples, there had been Rose and her obsession with pyramids and Suki with her nude photos and neatly stacked Chianti bottle towers. Barbara's apartment, by contrast, could have come right out of *Better Homes and Gardens*. Brightly colored flowers filled crystal vases on each of the end tables alongside the couch. Under each vase a crocheted doily protected the polished surface of the wood. The latest edition of *The New York Post* and a copy of *TV Guide* had been neatly placed at exact right angles to the edge of the coffee table. There wasn't a speck of dust anywhere. Come to think of it, the place hardly looked lived in.

While Barbara went to the kitchen to get the wine, I went over to study the bookcase. The shelves were empty except for twenty-seven cookbooks clustered together in one row and neatly organized by subject. So that was it: *TV Guide*, *The New York Post* and cookbooks. Apparently Barbara's tastes in reading were similar to those of my old flame Charlotte in Cologne.

"You mentioned that you're going to Pace," Barbara said when she returned with a bottle of California white wine, a box of Triscuit crackers, and a thick slab of Vermont cheddar cheese on a rolling serving cart. "Did you happen to run into a student there named Milton Lubich? He must be a few years older than you."

"He was in my accounting class, why?"

"Milton is married to my best friend. Bernice. She and I have known each other since we started kindergarten together back in Brooklyn. It's a small world isn't it?"

"Say," I said when the last drop of wine was gone, "if you don't have any plans tomorrow, I wouldn't mind seeing you again."

"Or," she countered. "You could just stay over here and save yourself the trip."

****

Since she worked in the clothing industry, Barbara had an outstanding wardrobe. She looked stunning no matter what she wore, whether it was a dress, a pantsuit or just an old pair of jeans and a tee shirt. It made me feel good to be seen with her, whether we were attending a show or just taking long walks together in the park. One thing I did find strange though. Soon after we met, Barbara bought two large scrapbooks. In one she collected business cards from each of the restaurants where we ate as well as the ticket stubs from all of the events we attended. Photos of the two of us went into the second album. I had to wonder whether she had stacks of similar scrapbooks from previous relationships stashed away somewhere, just like the box of photos of my former girlfriends I kept in my apartment. But, all the same, I loved spending time with her.

Later that month, Barbara and I went out to dinner with her friends Bernice and Milton Lubich. In contrast to her husband, who had all the quiet reserve of a future CPA, Bernice was bubbly and had a good sense of humor. "You know, Gunter," she confessed to me, "when Barbara told me she had met a tall *goy* from Germany, my first reaction was, 'Oh . . . my . . . Gawd,' but you're every bit as nice as she described, even if you aren't Jewish."

"I'm glad you think so," I said, not sure whether or not I had just been complimented.

"Anyway, the three of us are only secular Jews, right Barbara? That means we go to *shul* once or twice a year on the High Holy Days to put in an appearance and we try not to eat pork when anyone's looking."

"Maybe you should tell Gunter about the Sandpiper?" Barbara suggested.

"Oh yeah. That's the restaurant I'm part owner of in Fire Island Pines. Hey, why don't you and Barbara come out and spend a weekend with us in our beach house right after Labor Day? How about September 8th? Waddaya say?"

"Isn't that the first night of Rosh Hashanah, dear?" Milton asked meekly.

"It's also one of the biggest weekends of the year at the Sandpiper. As far as I'm concerned, that takes priority."

"Well," I replied, "I've never been to Fire Island so that sounds like a great idea."

"You've never been? Boy! Are you in for a treat!"

"What's so special about Fire Island," I asked Barbara when I brought her home.

"It's a whole different world," she said. "Wait and see."

****

413

On the Friday after Labor Day, Barbara and I caught a Long Island Railroad train at Penn Station. En route to the Fire Island ferry slip, we had plenty to talk about. Only three days before, we had both been horrified by the massacre of eleven Israeli athletes and a German policeman at the Munich Olympics and it was hard to shake those images from our minds.

"Let's not talk about that any more," Barbara suggested.

"How about this? I've told you my father was a master pastry chef in Germany. But you've never told me what your father does."

"Did, not does. He retired a few years ago and moved with my mother to South Miami." She hesitated and then plunged ahead. "You're not going to believe this."

"Try me!"

"He owned a penny arcade shooting gallery near the Apollo Theater in Harlem. You know the kind of place I mean? Air rifles chained to the counter and customers pay to try to hit paper targets and win useless prizes like stuffed animals and oversized balloons? It wasn't exactly a moneymaker for the family and, besides, it could be dangerous when the customers got rowdy. My father is 6'4" and he could usually manage on his own, but he still had to call the cops some times when things got totally out of hand. As a madda of fack, I was glad when he finally gave it up. Anything else you want to know?"

"Since you ask, I was wondering what your high school classmates were like. I never got to go to high school myself."

"Most kids were easy to get along with but, no offense, the most conceited students were the German Jews. When they arrived from Europe they barely spoke English. And a year or two later those know-it-alls were on top of the class. Nearly all of them went on to college. To the top schools, no less. Again, no offense, but your accent reminds me of the way some of them tawked."

"I'm trying hard to lose my accent, but I guess it's a losing battle. Henry Kissinger came when he was seventeen and he couldn't get rid of his accent. So imagine how much harder it is for me. I was twenty-six."

Barbara had an accent, too, although, as a foreigner, I thought it best not to mention it. She said 'cuppa cawfee' instead of 'cup of coffee' and 'Lawn Guyland' when she meant Long Island and, when she was in doubt, she would ask, "Are you shuah?" Well, I was sure of one thing. If Barbara could put up with my accent, I could certainly put up with hers.

****

Nearly all of the other passengers on the ferry were deeply tanned young men, some bare-chested, others in tank tops. They wore shiny hot pants or tight-fitting jeans, and loafers without socks. Most of them had glistening biceps, bleached blond buzz cuts, and well trimmed beards. They wore several rings on each hand and multiple strands of gold chains around their necks and wrists. Their ultimate destination, like ours, was the Sandpiper Restaurant in Fire Island Pines. By 11 p.m. that evening, between five hundred and six hundred gay men were dancing there to the hard beat of throbbing disco music.

Until the dense cigarette smoke hovering around us like a blurry blue poisonous cloud forced us to beat a hasty retreat, Barbara and I joined the others on the dance floor. "Did you see how everyone was staring at us?" I asked Barbara as we walked back to Bernice and Milton's beach house.

"Well, now you know what it feels like to be in the minority," she replied. "I think it's nice that gay men can come to The Sandpiper to relax and feel safe. Not like it was a few years ago. Remember the Stonewall Inn? How the police raided the place? When was it, 1969?"

"Yeah, sure, I remember that night," I said but I didn't tell her how close I'd been to the action.

CHAPTER 80

*I*n November, exhausted after a three-week-long business trip to Chicago, San Francisco, Los Angeles, and Houston to collect information and prepare another market study about German imported food products, I treated myself to a two-week vacation at Club Med in Martinique. My main objective in going away had been to relax, swim, and play tennis. Instead, I ended up taking a crash course in scuba diving. After two hours of instruction in the safety of the swimming pool, we boarded a small boat and headed out to a nearby reef.

I had done some snorkeling during the Windjammer cruise to the Bahamas but that experience paled in comparison to the amazing underwater world of strangely shaped corals and colorful tropical fish in the crystal clear water. Free of worldly distractions, I suddenly had time to reflect a bit on my life. Now that my thirty-fifth birthday was fast approaching, did I really have all that much to show for myself? Of course I had come a long way from the newly arrived immigrant who stepped off the *France* in 1964 with hardly any education and barely $400 to his name. But when it came to things that truly mattered—a wife, a family, a home—there was no one in sight with whom I could be happy. Certainly not Barbara, even though she was fun to be with. *Well then*, I decided, *if I was going to be a life-long bachelor, I might as well enjoy myself.*

The ratio of men and women on the scuba diving boat was about four to one but on the tennis courts, during meals and at night at the disco the young women greatly outnumbered the men. So, without even trying, during that first week I spent my free time with a brunette from Philadelphia and during the second week I befriended a newly arrived French Canadian divorcée, neither of whom I especially cared about.

On the second to last day of my vacation, Cemao, our scuba instructor, brought us to a reef to show us an especially beautiful coral formation. We were down ninety feet, a new record for us, when I suddenly ran out of air. Remembering what I had been taught, I pulled the little hook on my tank to open the reserve. To my horror, nothing happened. No reserve. No air. As soon as he saw my frantic signals, Cemao swam over to me and grabbed on to my weight belt. Then he and I took turns sharing the air from his regulator as all five of us slowly rose to the surface together.

"Cemao," I said later that evening, "thanks again for saving my life. Should you ever come to New York, be sure to let me know and I'll take you out to lunch." Since my wallet with my business cards was locked away in the Club Med safe, I borrowed a pen so that I could write the address of the Chamber on a paper napkin.

He gave me a big grin and shook my hand. "*Merci beaucoup, mon ami.* I may very well take you up on that invitation one of these days."

CHAPTER *81*

*I*n March of 1973, a few months after my trip to Martinique, Mr. Ledermann called me into his office. After I had taken a seat he said, "I've enjoyed working with you, Mr. Nitsch, so I wanted to give you plenty of time to plan ahead for when I retire. I'm sure you've heard that I'll be turning sixty-five next year? When that happens, despite the rumors circulating around the office, my present deputy isn't going to be my successor. The higher ups in Bonn have selected a younger man around your age to replace me. Right now he's managing the German Chamber of Commerce and Industry in Tokyo and before that, he was at the Indo-German Chamber of Commerce in Bombay and the German-French Chamber of Commerce in Paris."

"Pretty impressive!"

"Not so fast," he warned me. "This is highly confidential. I don't think you'll be able to stay at the Chamber once he takes over. According to what I've heard, he might not be the easiest person to get along with."

"Well, he can't just come in and change everything. There are thirty of us and just one of him."

"My dear Mr. Nitsch, you're terribly mistaken. Please keep this under your hat for heaven's sake, but I'm told he's going to bring in a new deputy, a new finance manager, a new assistant, and even his own secretary from our headquarters in Bonn. What do you say now?"

"That certainly puts things in a different light. Thanks for the heads up. Of course I will keep all this confidential. One last question, if I may. When is your replacement expected to arrive in New York?"

Mr. Ledermann sighed. "I presume that he and his team will get here several months before I leave."

Apparently Mr. Ledermann had similar off-the-record conversations with some other members of the staff because, only a few days later, we were all having whispered conversations about our future at the Chamber. It was clear that there would be a major shakeup. It was only a question of who would stay and who would go.

****

Whenever an important issue like this came up, I would call my old friend Walter Licht in Queens for advice. Walter heard me out for a minute and then he said, "Look, rather than discuss this over the phone, come for dinner on Saturday and we can talk then. Besides, we'd like to meet your new girlfriend. So be sure to bring her along."

As Barbara and I rattled along on the #7 train to Queens Boulevard and 69th Street, it was much too loud for us to carry on a conversation. I had no idea what Barbara was thinking, but I was hoping she wouldn't notice how worried I was about what Walter's wife might say. When I had shown up with Victoria for the first time, the two of us had barely stepped inside when Tamara burst out with, "Ginter, you really have a thing for *schvartzes*, don't you?" Victoria, to her credit,

420

had understood the remark but had tactfully ignored it. I could only wonder what Tamara would come up with this time.

She didn't take long. "Barbara! So nice to meet you! My, are you tall! A regular giraffe! If you wore heels you'd be the same height as Ginter. He's a real German hunk, wouldn't you say?" Then she turned to me. "Ginter, why haven't you brought Barbara here before? After your two *schvartze* girlfriends, you go and hide a nice Jewish girl like this from us all this time? What's the matter with you?"

Walter rolled his eyes. "Come on Tamara, that's enough now. You don't want them to leave, do you?"

But Tamara wasn't finished. "Walter, don't kvetch. You know I'm just joking. Anyway I was about to ask Barbara to join me in the kitchen so we can get to know each other while I fix dinner." And off the two of them went.

Walter and I sat down in the living room and, while I folded paper airplanes for little Benjamin, I told Walter about the upcoming changes in the Chamber.

"Well, if you ask me, it sounds as if even more than four heads will roll. Maybe, you should start looking around now. That is really what Mr. Ledermann was hinting at, wasn't it? And, since we're on the subject, I've got some big news, too. I'm about to quit my job to set up my own business."

"Wow! That's a major step."

"The way I figure it, if I'm going to put in sixty to eighty hours a week, I'd rather get the benefit of it. Anyway, Tamara and I are planning to buy a house further out on Long Island, some place that has a good school system. I'm going to set up shop somewhere nearby."

"I heard that," Tamara said as the two ladies rejoined us. "Can you imagine? My Walter a businessman? Of course not a businessman like you, Ginter. You go to work with a fancy briefcase and wearing a nice suit. Walter, he has his tool kit. But it's a living, right?"

What chutzpah, I thought, *considering that Tamara was working as a lowly manicurist.*

As usual Tamara had prepared quite a spread: a tossed salad, borscht, pot roast, and apple pie for dessert. While we ate, Tamara peppered Barbara with questions about discount Pierre Cardin suits to which Barbara only reluctantly replied. When it came time for us to leave and Barbara and I were putting on our raincoats, Tamara suddenly turned to me. "So, Ginter, when are you and this nice Jewish girl getting married?"

"For goodness sake, leave the poor man alone," Walter pleaded. "It was nice meeting you, Barbara," he added. "And as for you, Gunter, be sure to keep me posted about developments at the Chamber."

As Barbara and I walked to the subway, I put my arm around her. "I noticed you were unusually quiet during dinner. Was it because of Tamara? She's always been like that, completely irrepressible. But you can't say I didn't warn you."

"Lemme put it this way. You've sometimes asked me what I mean when I say, 'He or she is so Jewish!' Well, no one could be more Jewish than Tamara. The *chutzpah* of that woman! Would you believe in the kitchen she says to me in her thick Israeli accent that I have a real Noo Yawk accent like Edith Bunka from *All in the Family* on TV? Shouldn't she know bedda than to say that? My Gawd, she can't even pronounce your name. You've heard her. How she says Ginta instead of Gunta?"

"So did you shoot back?"

"I sure did. 'That's gawbadge!' I said and she says 'No offense. I was just being funny.' Does that sound funny to you?"

Secretly I agreed with Tamara. Very often Barbara did sound a lot like Edith Bunker. Still it wasn't nice of Tamara to say so. "That's just the way she is," I said. "She can't help herself sometimes."

Barbara shrugged. "Whateva. Fuggedaboutit. I guess it's really not that impawtant."

CHAPTER 82

*E*arly one April morning in 1973, after Peter Vollmann had beaten me decisively in two straight sets of tennis, the two of us once again headed over to the West End Bar. As I ate a hamburger and Peter lingered over his second stein of 'liquid bread,' I poured my heart out about the changes in store for the staff at the German American Chamber of Commerce. In the past I could always rely on Peter for business advice, but today his mind was apparently elsewhere. I tried a different tack to get his attention. "Anyway, it's a good thing neither of us is married, right? Whatever happens with our jobs, at least we're not tied down."

"Well, since you brought up the subject," Peter said with a sly smile, "I guess it's time to confess that I've gotten engaged. You remember Analyn, don't you? The accountant from the Philippines with the long black hair? Once the arrangements are made we're going to Manila to get married. Funny, isn't it?" he added when I didn't reply right away. "I was always sure you'd be the first to cave in."

"All I can say is WOW."

"There's another thing. I'm in the process of buying an apartment on the third floor of a brownstone on East 38th Street, a real handyman's special. So our tennis is going to have to wait for a while until I can get the place fixed up."

"I'm really happy for you, Peter, but are you sure you're ready to settle down with just one woman?" I asked, remembering the adventure with the Cuban twins.

"I think so! At least it's worth a try." Then he raised his stein in a toast. "Good luck, old friend. It looks as though you're now the last man standing."

****

Now that Peter was temporarily unavailable, over spring break during my last semester at Pace, I signed up for a ten-day trip to Jamaica with the Love Set Tennis Club. It was there, during the second week of my stay, that Maureen Kelly, a twenty-one-year-old redhead from Queens, New York, talked me into trying a marijuana cigarette for the first (and last) time. "Watch how I do it," she admonished me. "If you don't inhale, it won't do anything for you."

What was I thinking? The only result of this adventure with a young woman fourteen years my junior was a hole burned into the front of my brand-new white dress shirt and a foolish promise to take Maureen to see *Jesus Christ Superstar* when we got back to New York. The tickets would be expensive, even though the show was coming to the end of its run. I figured that if Maureen were to back out, I could always take Barbara instead.

But Maureen didn't back out and, ten days later and many dollars poorer, I met her in front of the Mark Hellinger Theater on West 51st Street for what turned out, for me at least, to be two hours of complete misery. I hated every minute of it! Maureen, on the other hand, totally enthralled, watched the show in wide-eyed amazement. "It was better than a drug high!" was her enthusiastic review. I had to take her word for it.

"You know what would make this a perfect evening?" she went on. "A carriage ride in Central Park. I've dreamed about doing that since I was a little girl."

"At this hour?"

"C'mon, don't be such an old fogey. I'm sure we'll find a free carriage on Central Park South. Wouldn't that be cool?"

The burly young coachman with a long blond beard was hesitant at first. "I'd rather take you down Fifth Avenue, but if it's the park you want . . . ?"

Maureen pouted. "Pretty please!"

"Sure, why not?" I reluctantly agreed.

Soon Maureen was cuddling with me as we listened to the slow clip clop of the horses' hooves on the nearly empty pavement. "Isn't this romantic?" she whispered as she pulled me down for a kiss. Just then, two young black men, one on each side, jumped onto the running boards. In an effort to shake them off, the coachman shouted, "Giddy up! Giddy up" and we had to cling on tight to avoid being tossed around as the swaybacked horse strained to break into a gallop.

When one of the young men yelled, "Let's get these motherfuckers!" Maureen burst into tears. "Oh my God, they're going to kill us all!" she shrieked.

"The hell they will!" responded the driver who was relentlessly lashing our assailants with his whip. "Take that you damned Niggers! And that! And that!" he shouted until first one and then the other young man fell off the carriage, landing like overripe apples, with a loud thump on the asphalt.

Maureen, who was still shaking when I brought her up to my apartment, selected half a dozen different kinds of pills from a small plastic container in her purse and washed them down with two glasses of water. "What's all that for?" I asked, even though I had my suspicions.

She was evasive. "It's just my medication. Don't worry about it. C'mon, let's go to bed."

The two of us didn't get to sleep until after 3 a.m. so it came as a shock when, around five in the morning, Maureen turned on the radio, twirled the dial to a rock station, and turned the volume up full blast. It was still pitch dark outside.

She smiled. "Oh? Did I wake you up? I couldn't sleep any more."

"For heaven's sake. Let me turn that thing off so I can go back to sleep."

But Maureen was defiant. "No way. I'm your guest and I want it on!"

I was definitely too old for this kind of thing. Groggy as I was, I pulled on my jeans, got Maureen dressed and brought her down to the street, where I hailed a cab. Handing her twenty dollars to cover the fare, I helped her inside. "Go home to your mother, Maureen. You seriously need help!" I said as I shut the door behind her. "And please don't call me again!"

When the cab drove off, I went back upstairs, drank two bottles of Pabst Blue Ribbon beer and climbed back into bed. Just before I fell asleep I decided to be especially nice to Barbara when I saw her later that afternoon.

CHAPTER *83*

*J*ust before our graduation, Pace was given full university status by the New York State Board of Regents, making us the first group to receive our MBA degrees from Pace *University,* which, we all agreed, would sound a lot more impressive on our diplomas than plain old Pace *College.*

"Wadda you mean, you're not going to rent a cap and gown?" Barbara asked as the big day approached. "Afta all the years you spent in school, you bedda do this in style. Not renting a cap and gown? Gimme a break!"

And so it was that on June 2nd, 1973, almost half a year to the day before my thirty-sixth birthday, I was wearing that strange costume as I introduced Barbara to a few of my classmates, including Joe Molitor of 'Why I Hate Niggers' fame. Joe ogled Barbara from head to toe before nodding approvingly. And no wonder. She was wearing a beige business suit with a knee length skirt that she had specially purchased for the occasion. I was sure no one in that crowd would notice her Brooklyn accent since most of my fellow graduates were native 'Noo Yawkers' just like her.

When the time came for Dr. Bonaparte to hand out our diplomas, he read off the names of the MBA graduates in alphabetical order. Joe Molitor beamed when his name was called, returning a minute later clutching his diploma. "See this! It could be my meal ticket to a big promotion!"

At my age I had no such hope for my MBA. Job-wise, I had probably gone as far as I was going to go, at least if I stayed at the German American Chamber of Commerce. Still, I was pleasantly surprised when my turn came and Dr. Bonaparte announced, "Gunter Nitsch, With Distinction."

"No shit!" Joe Molitor muttered between his teeth as I walked up to the platform. He was still fuming when I returned to my place. "It ain't fair. How can you be so much bedda than me? No offense, Gunta, but you're a fucking foreigner. Just listen to how you tawk!"

"Sorry, Joe," I said, to be polite. The irony of his comment about my accent didn't escape me. "It wasn't up to me, you know."

****

After the ceremony ended, I returned my rented cap and gown. Then Barbara and I went for an Italian supper in Greenwich Village. We had only been in the restaurant for ten minutes when Barbara leaned towards me. "Gunta, now that you have your MBA, why doncha give up your studio apartment and move in with me?"

"You're not still thinking about what Tamara said, are you?"

"Don't worry. I'm not tawking about marriage, just living together. Everyone's doing it these days. Waddaya say?"

There it was again. Quincy's third rule: *'Never let her give you the key to her apartment . . .'*

"You should know by now that I really like living alone."

Barbara frowned. "You men are all alike. Always procrastinating." (I was stunned that she knew that word!) "Anyway, irregawdless of that, I have some big news. My parents are going to be in town next week and they're dying to meet you. I want you to come for supper on Sattaday. No excuses please, okay?"

"Of course I'll come. Should I wear a suit and tie?"

"No, don't. My parents are very laid back. Jeans and a sport shirt would be fine."

"Should I bring some wine?"

"No, as a madda of fack, my fodder only drinks beah. Why doncha bring alawng some of that Lowenbrow you always drink?"

****

Mrs. Sattenstein was as tall and slim as her daughter. Her husband was an unusually tall, broad shouldered, barrel chested, good-natured man. "Nice meeting you, Gunner," he said as he gave me a crushing handshake.

"Barbara tells me that retired life agrees with you," I said to make conversation before supper. "But don't you ever miss New York?"

"Like hell I do! Forty years I worked in Harlem! And every day it was the same scum. I won't even call them Niggers. That's too good a term for them. Jungle bunnies, that's what they were. Jungle bunnies, plain and simple."

Barbara, who knew all about Victoria, squirmed uncomfortably in her seat. "Maybe you could explain to Gunta exactly what the business was like," she said in an effort to tone down the rhetoric.

"I'm sure Gunner's seen that sort of thing. We had plenny of coin-operated devices: pinball machines, skee ball machines and the like. But the air rifles were always the main attraction. And not just for shooting, mind you. I don't know how many times one of them jungle bunnies would rip a rifle off the chain and run off with it. And as for the rest of them? Do you think they cared? Like hell they did. They acted like it was all one big joke." So far he had kept relatively calm, but now, as he raised his voice, the veins on his neck throbbed. "I'll tell you this, Gunner. After all those years I've had to conclude that, with maybe one or two exceptions, the only good Nigger is a dead Nigger!" He pulled out a handkerchief to wipe the beads of sweat from his forehead.

Mrs. Sattenstein headed her husband off before he could continue. "Irving, stop it right there. Don't get so worked up. Remember what the doctor said? Why don't you tell Gunner how our business picked up right after the war?"

"All right, all right. As a madda of fack, things did get betta around 1946, the same year Barbara graduated high school. That's when the GIs were all coming home and everyone had more money in his pocket. So, sure, we did betta financially. But don't fugget that the ones who came back to Harlem after the war no longer knew their place. Many of them actually thought they were our equals, rememba? I could never get used to that."

"Irving, you're at it again! Stop it and let's eat!"

While we were passing around the platters of cold cuts and four different kinds of cheese, I thought about Mr. Sattenstein's remarks. Three things were clear. First and foremost, Barbara's father, who had seemed so pleasant when I first walked in, was actually a hopelessly intolerant racist bigot. I could only imagine if he and Holzkopp were forced to spend an hour together. Which one of them would drip the most hate?

I also now knew from whom Barbara had gotten the expression 'as a madda of fack', which made me cringe every time she used it.

But those weren't the only things that bothered me. Unless Barbara was only twelve when she graduated from high school in 1946, which was highly unlikely, she must have lied to me about her age. No matter how I did the math, she couldn't have been born later than 1928, which would make her at least forty-five years old.

When I left to go home around eleven o'clock, Barbara rode down with me in the elevator. "They really liked you," she said. "I apologize for my father's racist remarks, though. You know I don't share his opinions."

"I know that."

She smiled weakly. "As a madda of fack, it could have been worse if my mother hadn't cut him awf!"

"Listen, Barbara, never mind all that for now. What's really bothering me is, why you didn't tell me the truth about your age when we met."

"I guess that was foolish of me. And I nearly gave myself away when I tawked about the German Jews who came into my classes. I was sure you'd figure it out then. Please don't be angry with me, Gunta, okay? I really want to see you next Friday after my parents leave for Florida."

"Don't worry. I'll call you later in the week," I said and I gave her a hug. But it was a promise I wasn't sure I would keep.

****

My phone rang early the next morning. It was my cousin Frank, whom I hadn't seen in almost a decade. He was calling from Luxembourg to let me know that he and his wife were on their way to New York. "Iki and I were hoping you could join us for dinner at the Sheraton Hotel on Thursday evening," Frank said. "Oh, and before I forget, when we called your mother in Cologne for your phone number, she told us that you've got yourself a very attractive girlfriend, judging from her photo. She was hoping this might be the real thing."

"Well, I wouldn't exactly go that far," I protested. "She certainly didn't get that idea from me."

"All the same, be sure to bring her along. At least that way someone in the family will have met one of the girls you've been dating."

"Thanks, Frank. What time would you like us to be there?"

"Let's meet in the lobby at 6 p.m., okay?"

I was sure that Barbara would be thrilled to join Frank and Iki for dinner, even though it would mean leaving her parents alone for the evening. There wouldn't be a language problem. My cousin was a German diplomat and his wife was a high school English teacher. Both of them spoke English fluently. But, wait a minute! What was I thinking? As soon as Barbara opened her mouth, Frank and Iki would notice her nasal Noo Yawk accent. With a sinking feeling, I realized I couldn't bring Barbara to dinner with Frank. I really couldn't bring her to my office either. Nor to a Chamber luncheon. Nor, come to think of it, anywhere I might run into someone I knew from work.

All of which is why, on Thursday evening, when I came to the Sheraton Hotel to meet my cousins for dinner, I came alone.

****

Sometimes when I lay awake late at night, or more often when I was out jogging on the Upper West Side, I was struck by the realization that I might very well end up like one of the lonely old men who sat all day long on the benches in the middle of Broadway. Let's face it. When it came right down to it, I didn't exactly have a great track record finding someone else after Charlotte. How many had there been? Six? Seven? *Maybe*, I thought, *I was being way too picky*. I had my own faults, after all, as Irene Cardinal had once so bluntly pointed out to me. And she wasn't the only one who had dumped me. Both Jeanine and Victoria had done the same. Irene because I wanted to get married; Jeanine and Victoria because I didn't.

Not that I hadn't met my share of fruitcakes along the way: Carmen from Ecuador who dyed her beautiful black hair platinum blond; Jackie Schmidt who was only good at one thing; and the histrionic Dr. Sonnenburg who watched over me like a mother hen.

I had really loved Victoria. Maybe I still did. Were my objections to her really based on her reckless spending? Or was I just a coward because she, like Barbara, was someone I couldn't show off at my office?

The only thing I was sure of was that I wanted something more, but I couldn't really define what. And, unless I found out what it was, I was willing to cling to Quincy's rules until I died of lonely old age.

CHAPTER 84

Fortunately, since I was, once again, without a steady girlfriend, I had more than enough to do at the Chamber to keep me from feeling sorry for myself. Whether I was staying in a fine hotel or charging my meals to my expense account, or relaxing by the bar in the evening, the people I met on my business trips to San Francisco, Los Angeles, Chicago, and Houston did not have to know that, back in New York, I was now living the lonely life of a confirmed bachelor in a small studio apartment on the Upper West Side.

And I was no longer just doing market studies. Now, I also was giving speeches to local trade associations. My career as a public speaker had an inauspicious start at the Tulsa World Trade Club. Mr. Ledermann sent me there at the very last minute. Standing at the podium in front of all those businessmen, my throat had tightened and I felt as close to drowning as I once had off the beach in Acapulco. I wished, with all my heart, that I could have changed into a tiny mouse and run away. By the time I had stammered and stuttered my way through my prepared text without once looking up, only a quarter of the two hundred attendees remained in their seats.

Still, without giving myself too much credit, after stumbling through that first disastrous presentation, I became a more effective speaker as time went on, much to the delight of Mr. Ledermann who suffered from terrible stage fright and was only too glad to turn the responsibility for public speaking over to me. As a result, my responsibilities expanded to include speaking tours in Germany, where, traveling from city to city together with an American attorney, a CPA, and an executive recruiter, I instructed eager German audiences on how to invest and to set up a subsidiary in the United States.

****

On a cold winter day in February 1974, I had just been taken to lunch at the Top of the Sixes by Sarah Rabinowitz, a representative of the State Development Agency of New York. After the meal, she put on her heavy winter coat and I accompanied her down to the lobby as she continued to urge me to get more German companies to settle in New York.

"Well, I will certainly do my best to help," I said, eager to end the conversation because I was shivering in my business suit.

"Excuse me, Gunter," Sarah suddenly said with a nervous glance toward the street. "There's a tall, skinny black man with a huge Afro who is staring at you." She tipped her head slightly to the right. "Over there. Do you know him?"

And there, grinning broadly, with a blonde hanging onto each arm, stood Cemao, my scuba diving instructor from Martinique. "You mean him? He's not just *any* guy. He's the man who saved my life. I'll tell you the whole story some other time. Anyway, Sarah, thanks again for lunch but I hope you'll excuse me," I said as I waved Cemao into the lobby passageway.

"*Allô, allô mon cher ami,*" he said. "We were on our way to lunch and I wanted to show my friends the building where you work. I hadn't expected to see you!"

Not wanting to waste any time with small talk, since both Cemao and I were both shivering in the cold, I invited him to be my guest for lunch at the Top of the Sixes the next day. We arranged to meet in the Chamber reception area at noon and then head upstairs together to the 41st floor.

The food in the Top of the Sixes was nothing special, but the views were sure to impress a visitor from out-of-town like Cemao. Since I had eaten there more often than in any other restaurant in Manhattan, it was always taken for granted that I would be given a window seat.

But there was no warm welcome when I walked in with Cemao, who was wearing dungarees and at least three thick sweaters, one on top of the other. The maitre d' gave Cemao a disapproving look. "Good afternoon, Mr. Nitsch. I assume you are waiting for someone?"

"No, we're both here. I called yesterday and made a reservation for a window table."

The maitre d' pretended to search through his appointment book. "Someone must have given you the wrong information, Mr. Nitsch. I do not have any record of it."

Don't give me that! I thought. "Sir," I said sternly, "I would like to have a word with the manager!" But before we got that far, a young woman who had been my server on dozens of previous occasions spoke up.

"Actually, Mr. Nitsch is correct. I took that reservation myself," she said. "Now if you and your guest will just follow me, Mr. Nitsch . . ." and she led us to a table directly overlooking Fifth Avenue.

"*Le problème c'est moi, n'est-ce pas?*" Cemao asked once we were seated.

"*Non, Cemao, tu n'es pas le problème. Le maître d'hôtel est le problème. Il est vraiment un idiot!*"

"So tell me, Cemao," I asked as my friend worked his way through most of the coarse rye bread by himself in addition to polishing off a bowl of soup and a hefty portion of beef stroganoff. "Is one of the blondes you were with yesterday your girlfriend?"

"No, I wish! They are just sisters I met at the Club, nothing more." He slathered some butter on the last slice of rye. "Forgive me, Gunter, but do you think we could ask for some more bread? I rarely eat it back home, but here it's the only way to keep warm."

I signaled the waitress. "Of course. You can have as much as you like! By the way, speaking of Club Med, thanks again for saving my life!"

"Oh, about that, I have some good news for you. Now all of our scuba tanks have gauges! It's much safer that way, *n'est-ce pas?*"

After I paid the bill, I brought Cemao down to the lobby passageway to say good-bye, but when I reached out to shake his hand he gave me an unexpected hug instead. Except for my father when I had last seen him in Cologne, Cemao was the only man who had ever done so. As I watched him walk away, I decided to take the second chance at life he had given me. Maybe, at long last, I should try something new and finally settle down.

CHAPTER 85

"Tell me, Mr. Nitsch," Mr. Ledermann asked me a few weeks later, "do you have a New York State drivers license?"

"No, sir. I only have one from Germany where I learned on a stick shift. In the ten years I've been here, I have never dared to drive an American car with automatic transmission."

"I didn't think so. Well, if you want an old man's advice, sign up for some lessons and get yourself a license. That way, should you find yourself looking for another job once my successor arrives, you will have a better chance of getting hired. There aren't that many thirty-six-year-old men out there who don't have a driver's license, you know."

Even though I had no intention of giving up my position at the Chamber if I could help it, the day might come when I moved out of the City and could not rely on public transportation. With that in mind, I took Mr. Ledermann's advice and, the following weekend, I found myself seated in a dual-control car for my first lesson with Mr. Mendoza, an elderly instructor from the Philippines. Over the next few weeks, as both my skill and my confidence improved, we went farther and farther afield until the big day came when I drove Mr. Mendoza across the George Washington Bridge, returning to Manhattan via the West Side Highway. "Let's get off at 96th Street, Mr. Nitsch," Mr. Mendoza said, "so that you get a little more practice driving on Broadway before I drop you off at home."

I had just stopped at a red light when I spotted Victoria in front of Zabar's, the specialty store where West Siders had been buying imported cheese, cold cuts, smoked salmon, all kinds of breads, and hundreds of other tasty treats since 1934. A quick glance at my watch told me my ninety minutes were almost up. "If you don't mind, Mr. Mendoza, I'm going to get out here. I just spotted a former girlfriend of mine whom I haven't seen in ages."

"Sure, sure, that's fine. Which one is she?"

"Over there, the lady in the light blue dress!"

"That black woman? *She* was your girlfriend?"

"Yes, she was. Actually for several years."

He shook his head. "That's hard to believe. A guy like you and a woman like that!"

I waited for my chance to step out into traffic so that Mr. Mendoza could slide over into the driver's seat. The light had changed. Horns were already honking. "See you next week," I said as I slammed the car door shut in a burst of anger.

Victoria had spotted me by then. "My oh my, you're taking driving lessons! Are you going to buy a car?"

"No, it just seemed like the thing to do." I took a few steps back and took a good look at her. "You're as pretty as ever. How've you been?"

"Couldn't be better! I've gotten engaged and in a couple of months we're going to get married!"

"Some one I know?"

"No, I don't think so. His name is Gary and he teaches art in a Brooklyn high school. I've met his parents and everything. They're absolutely thrilled for us."

"That's great news," I forced myself to say. "Really great."

"So what about you? Are you dating someone?"

"No, not me. I'm as unattached as ever."

I was about to take my leave but she held up her hand to stop me. "Don't be in such a hurry. If you wait a minute you can meet Gary. Oh look! Here he comes!"

Gary was half a foot shorter and considerably younger than I was. His blond hair was several shades lighter than the color of his eyebrows, his handshake surprisingly limp. "Gunter! I've heard so much about you!" he enthused in a rather high-pitched voice. "We must get together and talk about European art sometime!"

I wished them both luck. They were clearly going to need it.

CHAPTER 86

*T*en years had passed since I had walked down the gangway of the *France* to begin my new life in America. Ten years! Had my life improved since then? Granted, I had managed to get an education and a job, but when it came to my personal life, despite all the fun I had had, there was nothing left except for the handsewn dashiki gathering dust in my closet and a box brimming with photos of my former girlfriends. Deep down inside I knew it was time to find someone to whom I could finally make a commitment and settle down. The question was, how to go about it?

An ad in the Friday edition of *The New York Post* caught my eye a few days later. "Tired of the Manhattan singles scene?" it read. "Spend your weekends instead at the Chateau d'Vie, a country club for singles in beautiful Spring Valley, New York!" Figuring it was worth a try, I picked up the phone and dialed the number.

"Larry Finkelstein at your service," the friendly voice of the membership director greeted me. "Thank you for inquiring about the Club. We offer golf, tennis, swimming, dining, weekend entertainment, everything to put our members at ease while they look for that someone special. Please come up and see for yourself! You can take our private station wagon from the East Side or a special bus from the Port Authority that comes right to our door every Friday evening and Saturday morning. Just ask for me when you get here."

The following morning I stepped off the bus alongside the six Chateau d'Vie tennis courts and headed inside the huge clubhouse to meet Mr. Finkelstein, a bald, heavyset man in his early forties. "So glad you came, Mr. Nitsch. May I guess from your accent that you're from Germany?"

"Yes, sir, I am."

"You weren't one of those Nazi soldiers, were you? No offense intended, of course."

I shook my head. *Here I was, thirty-five miles away from midtown Manhattan, and I still couldn't escape questions like that. Maybe this wasn't the right place for me after all.*

"Is there any special reason why you asked?"

"It's just that . . . oh, never mind then. I hope you've liked what you've seen so far. Come, let me show you around."

The clubhouse was situated atop a steep hill. Stairs out back led down past a volleyball court to the largest swimming pool I had ever seen. Off in the distance, was an eighteen-hole golf course. "Golf is extra but otherwise it's an all-inclusive fee," Mr. Finkelstein assured me, "except, of course, for a nominal charge if you decide to stay overnight. Our members say our fee is the best investment they've ever made."

"I did have a question about the membership. Since I'm thirty-six, do you think I'd be too old for the crowd that comes here?"

"No, not at all. We have some as young as their early twenties all the way up to a few in their late forties. And there are many more women than men, I might add, in case you're wondering," he said with a wink. "Here's a membership application if you'd like to fill one out."

Against my better judgment, I forked over a substantial check for the first month's dues. In return, Mr. Finkelstein handed me my green plastic membership card. Then he smiled broadly and shook my hand. "Well done, Mr. Nitsch. I'm sure you'll fit right in here. Welcome to the Chateau d'Vie!"

****

But I hardly fit right in. Aside from Harry, the one other German who had bravely ventured out to Spring Valley, the Chateau d'Vie membership was largely made up of the same types who wore *chai* pendants and had avoided me back in the City. It wasn't just my imagination either.

"Hey! Cut that out!" one woman had screamed at me on the tennis court when I delivered an especially hard serve. "You know what? The way you play reflects your nationality!" But at least she had agreed to play with me, unlike the forty-five-year-old Polish-born man with stringy hair who wouldn't even step on the same court with me because he was a Holocaust survivor.

Aside from the question of my nationality and my religion, I could not ignore the high percentage of club members who were embittered by failed marriages and ugly divorces. They would show up on the weekends when they had custody of their children and poison their little minds against their absent parent.

Apparently, for the women, the goal was to land a new partner with a good income. Otherwise, why give up the alimony they were living on? I certainly didn't have much to offer on that score.

Nor, except for Harry, did I find any friends among the men who lounged around the pool in their baggy, thigh-length American swimsuits, bragging about how much money they had made (or lost) in

Las Vegas when they weren't spending hours in front of the television set over the bar in the main hall watching sports. To them I was "the big German guy" in the tiny Speedos whom they called Hans, or Wolfgang, or Karl, or Otto, but seldom Gunter.

Besides, although they would certainly not have qualified as 'congenial people' had they tried to register at Skytop in the Poconos, they did have one thing in common with those folks. During all the weekends I spent at the Chateau d'Vie, I never saw a person of color, not a single one.

****

On Sunday, June 30, 1974, I boarded the bus at the Port Authority and took the side-facing seat behind the driver next to a young mother with two small, squirming children. It was my seventh trip to the Chateau d'Vie and, as we headed north towards Spring Valley, I was seriously considering terminating my monthly membership that very afternoon. *Why was I doing this to myself?* Granted the tennis was fun, provided, that was, that I could find someone willing to play with me. Sometimes I wasn't even sure why I bothered to bring along my tennis racket. And I did enjoy the pool and the fresh air and the chance to escape from Manhattan for a few hours on weekends. But the whole idea had been to meet someone and that, I concluded, was hopeless.

The bus gradually emptied as it made several stops before continuing up the hill to the Club. By the time we reached the parking lot, there were only fifteen or so other passengers, almost all of them young women. I kept my seat and let them leave the bus first. From way in the back of the bus a petite young woman in tennis shorts approached me. She had a narrow face, oversized eyeglasses, intelligent dark eyes, long, straight dark brown hair and a serious, almost grave, expression.

"I saw that you brought your racket so, and I hope you don't mind my asking since I'm just a beginner," she began, "but would you like to play tennis with me?"

"Sure," I said as I stood up to follow her off the bus. "Thanks for asking. I'd be glad to."

"On second thought," she said when I rejoined her near the courts, "if you'd been standing up, I might not have dared to ask you. What are you, 6'5"?"

"I'm actually only 6'2"."

"Well, that still makes you 10" taller than I am. Anyway, I'm Mary," and she smiled for the first time.

"Gunter Nitsch," I said, offering her my hand. "Nice to meet you. You know, if we rush we could probably get a court now!"

"I'll go get my racket from my locker. Be right back!"

****

"Are you a new member because I haven't seen you on the bus before?" I asked Mary after our hour of tennis was up.

"I joined a few months after they opened last year, but I always took their station wagon and then, just like that they discontinued it. So this was the first time I had to go to the Port Authority. By the way, have you also heard the rumors that the Club's in financial trouble? People say they only opened this place because they thought gambling would be legalized in New York State and now, well, no one knows how long it's is going to last. I'll tell you one thing. The way things look, I sure wouldn't pay them any money in advance."

After tennis, Mary changed into a blue and white bikini that showed off her slim figure before joining me in the pool to cool off. Later on, as we feasted on Southern fried chicken and corn on the cob prepared on an outdoor grill, we chatted about our lives.

"Oh, you're German?" was her first comment to me. "I was kind of hoping with a name like Gunter that maybe you'd be Swedish or Swiss."

"Is it that much of a problem?"

"Not for me, it isn't. But my parents are secular Jews and, this is no exaggeration, my father probably owns every book that was ever written on World War II."

"Well then, if I ever meet him, we'll have something to talk about."

"I like the way you think!"

My first impression that Mary was barely out of her teens was way off. In fact she had gotten her undergraduate degree from George Washington University and then had gone on to Columbia Law School. By the time we met that day in 1974 she was thirty-one years old and had already been practicing trusts and estates law in her father's office for seven years. However, even more impressive to me than her education was the fact that, despite being born in Manhattan, she didn't have the slightest trace of a New York accent.

As the time to catch the bus back to the City approached, the two of us sat together on a large boulder at the entrance to the Club driveway and continued our conversation. "Hey, you two," a young woman walked over to us to say, "didn't you hear that there won't be any bus? If you're stranded, my friend and I can give you both a ride into Manhattan."

"What did I tell you?" Mary said as we climbed into the back of the station wagon. "This place is on its last legs. That's why I'm not leaving anything in my locker when I go home from now on."

"I hear it's the mob that runs this place," our driver said. "It wouldn't surprise me, either."

It was a hot, sticky night when we were dropped off at 8th Avenue and 38th Street in Manhattan. Even so, we decided to walk the nearly two miles up to Lincoln towers where Mary had her studio apartment. And, as we walked, we held hands and chatted away about books we'd read, trips we'd taken, everything under the sun. It was as if we had known each other all of our lives.

It was quite late when we reached the lobby of Mary's building and, since it was also a work night for both of us, I was about to say good-bye and head over to catch a bus or the subway to take me the rest of the way up to 104th Street.

"You must be thirsty," Mary said. "Would you like to come up for a minute and have a glass of water or some orange juice before you go?"

I didn't know it then, but the minute I said "yes," my bachelor days were over!

EPILOGUE

*I*t is strange to think, looking back nearly four decades later, what a small window of opportunity Mary and I had to meet. As it turned out, right after Labor Day in 1974, barely two months after she asked me for that game of tennis, the Chateau d'Vie clubhouse burned to the ground. Only the charred remains of the chimney survived the fire. But by then I already knew that Mary was someone special.

My mother clearly agreed. After Mary and I had been married for two years, we visited Mutti again in Cologne. On our last day there, Mutti turned to Mary and said, much to my chagrin, "Mary dear, why did you marry him? Don't get me wrong. I'm really glad you did. But in my opinion, you could have done better!" No wonder Mary has always said that she had the best mother-in-law in the world!

****

And what of all the women I knew along the way? What became of them?

Three of them, Jackie Schmidt, Amalia Sonnenburg, and Barbara Sattenstein, never got married.

The last I heard, my Haitian girlfriend, Jeanine Rondeau, and her husband, Giorgio, were still together.

Victoria Hoyt's marriage to Gary lasted only two years; her second marriage, to an African-American academic, lasted sixteen years before also ending in divorce.

Irene Cardinal, who didn't think I was good enough for her, became a famous artist and finally found the man of her dreams when she was in her late fifties. I assume he must have owned a car and didn't have a foreign accent.

And Charlotte, the girl I left behind when I left Germany in 1964? Now that her children are grown, she and her architect husband divide their time between their home in Cologne and their apartment in the south of France. As far as I know, the box containing our photos remains tightly nailed shut. Still, after half a century, Charlotte always remembers my birthday every year although, over time, her birthday cards have given way to e-mails and her e-mails have given way to Skype. When I turned seventy-five, Charlotte appeared on my computer screen wearing the amber necklace I had given to her all those years ago. "You know what this means, Günter?" she asked me as she pointed to the necklace and Mary listened nearby. "It means that you have always been the love of my life."

****

During my first ten years in New York City I learned many hard lessons and made my share of mistakes. The America I had imagined while I was still living in Germany, where people of all races and backgrounds lived in perfect harmony and everyone had an equal chance for advancement, was a far cry from the reality I confronted following my arrival. At every turn, I met with individuals who, for whatever superficial reason, treated members of other groups as underdogs. From the shock of seeing Americans dressed as Nazi Stormtroopers parading in Washington, D.C., to the slurs hurled at Victoria and me, to the many instances of virulent anti-Semitism, to all the times I was blamed for World War II just because I was German, I experienced shocking bigotry.

Not that I was a perfect angel myself. On occasion, I wasn't able to overcome my own prejudices and doubts. And, when it came to the women I dated, I was always on the lookout for something better, always ready to find fault with others while ignoring my own faults. No one would ever be good enough to justify giving up my carefree bachelor life, or so I thought.

But if everything that happened made me ready to finally settle down with Mary, then it was all worth every minute. The last time we visited my mother in Cologne, she said to my wife, "Mary dear, I hope with all my heart that you will be able to turn my son into a civilized person." Mary jokes that it's still a "work in progress." And she's right.

CPSIA information can be obtained at www.ICGtesting.com
Printed in the USA
BVOW07s0320021213

337870BV00001BB/26/P

9 781491 837009